E. F. Dost
Columbus
11 / 15 / 96

Now Dayton is
trying to reinvent
Downtown.

grand eccentrics

Mark Bernstein

grand eccentrics

Turning the Century:
Dayton and the Inventing of America

ORANGE FRAZER PRESS • WILMINGTON OHIO

The writing of this book was supported
by the generous assistance of the Mead Corporation,
in celebration of both the Bicentennial of the City of Dayton
and the 150th Anniversary of Mead.

CELEBRATION
DAYTON '96™

Book design by Dan Johnson
Cover design and script by Tim Hanrahan
Color tinting by Tim Thrasher
DAYTON OHIO, 1903, words and music by Randy Newman
© 1969 Unichappell Music, (BMI) All rights reserved. Used by permission.
Warner Bros. Publications US Inc. Miami,FL 33014
Library of Congress catalog card number: 96-68626
ISBN: 1-882203-12-7— cloth
ISBN: 1-882203-13-5

Published by Orange Frazer Press, Inc.
Main Street, Box 214
Wilmington, Ohio 45177

Acknowledgements

Over the past eight years, this book has been nudged into being by the encouragement and with the assistance of individuals it is here my pleasure to thank. The book grew from a series of articles published in *Smithsonian* and *OHIO* magazines, with Timothy Foote at the former and John Fleischman at the latter not only helping shape the material at hand but urging me to pursue its larger possibilities. That pursuit was made possible by support from the Mead Corporation; more particularly, by Dudley Kircher of Mead, for whose interest in the subject and initiative on its behalf I am grateful. I am also indebted to Fred Bartenstein, for his help in securing underwriting for this book and, subsequently, for sharing his voluminous understanding of all things Dayton.

Robert S. Fogarty, editor of *The Antioch Review*, provided direction to the author's initial research into the time period, and much useful subsequent advice. Additional advice and counsel came from Carl Becker, Suzanne Clauser, Mary Matthews, Patrick O'Conner, Darlene Olson and David Weaver.

For assistance with research and in tracking down photographs, I wish to thank Marvin Christian, Dawne Dewey, Nancy Horlacher, Vicki Morgan, Nina Myatt, Janne Palermo, Sarah Sessions and Bill West. My thanks to Tony Dallas for reviewing and commenting on portions of the manuscript, and to him and Migiwa Orimo for suggesting its title.

That research was enlivened by the interviews conducted, either for the magazine pieces or during work on the book itself, with associates and family members of the men whose stories are told here. Particularly helpful were Xarifa Bean, Dr. Algo Henderson, Homer Hacker, Virginia Kettering, Ernest Morgan, Timothy Patterson, Fred Robbins, Wilkinson Wright and Roz Young.

More broadly, this book represents a continuation of a fifteen-year association with John Baskin, a remarkable, even terse, editor, the bestower of unavoidable advice, and the wearer of many hats —including, now, that of co-publisher of this book. John's co-equal at Orange Frazer Press, Marcy Hawley, oversaw the truly appalling number of production and other tasks that remain once the writing is complete, and did so with unflappable clarity, competence and good humor. This book represents a second continuation, one with Dan Johnson, the designer with whom I have worked for years and who is primarily responsible for the grace of this book's presentation.

Finally, the author's largest debt is to Katharine Shirey, who reviewed and commented on the successive drafts of the manuscript with fine editorial skill, understanding and stubbornness and who, equally important, maintained continuing faith that the project would reach a successful completion.

Mark Bernstein
Yellow Springs, Ohio
June 1996

TO MY FATHER AND MOTHER

Contents

Let's sing a song of long ago
When things could grow
And days flowed quietly
The air was clean and you could see
And folks were nice to you.

"Would you like to come over for tea
With the missus and me?"
It's a real nice way
To spend the day
In Dayton, Ohio
On a lazy Sunday afternoon in 1903.

— *Randy Newman*

a juncture in time

In 1883, America adopted standard time zones. Up until that point, every city, town and crossroads in this most democratic of lands had its very own time — with noon reckoned from the highest point the sun reached above the town square or over the post office on the longest day of the year. Ohio had Bucyrus time, Blanchester time, Sandusky time, Upper Sandusky time and as many other times as there were places to figure it and people to set the clocks. Local time was characteristic of a local nation. There were hundreds of different "noons," but just about everyone you were likely to run across on the small stage on which your own life played out had the same "noon" as you did. Whatever these local stages lacked, they told their own entire story. American life up until the late nineteenth century has been described as "a society of island communities" — an archipelago of small towns, each with its minister, physician, editor, blacksmith and undertaker, dominated by the farmers who surrounded the town, traded therein and defined its needs and character.

The adoption of time zones meant the nation was getting itself organized. The foremost agency of this organization, and the foremost advocate of standardized time, was the railroads. For them, operating across a continent slivered into local times meant confusion and inefficiency. Each railway line had its own time, too; in general, it clocked its arrivals and departures to the time struck in the road's headquarter's city. But while towns stood where their founders had put them, railway trains moved. One observer noted that a traveler from Portland, Maine, upon reaching Buffalo, had four different "times" to choose from: the New York City time of the New York Central, the Columbus time posted by the Lake Shore and Michigan Southern, the Buffalo time that was local to the station and the Portland time on the traveler's own timepiece.

America's first major industry had been local. Early textile mills cramped and elbowed their way to the few rivers in New England whose falling water could turn the wheels that powered the work within the mill. The textile business was an exercise in the coordination of things seen — belts and bobbins and the workers who tended them. The railroads were an exercise in the coordination of things unseen — a switchman in Pennsylvania throws a switch so a traveler from New York will reach Toledo in time to catch a train that has not yet left Cincinnati. To coordinate things unseen, you must first agree on what time it is. With the railroads, the national gained ascendancy in the American economy and, subsequently, in American life. The adoption of time zones followed by a few years three inventions that with the railroads shattered the hold of the local world: Alexander Graham Bell's telephone, which overcame distance; Thomas Edison's light bulb, which overcame the rhythms of light and dark imposed by the sun; and Nikolaus Otto's four-cycle internal combustion engine — the power source for the automobile, which overcame everything else. These combined to lower the waters that had isolated America's small towns, exposing land bridges between them, bridges railroads could cross and people could use to leave.

Today, we take for granted that we are corporate persons: we move within large corporations, big government, mega-universities, or else we revolve as stray valence electrons in the gravitational hold of such largeness. It was not so for persons born in the mid-nineteenth century. They came into and were raised up in the world of "island communities" and from those islands set out onto a sea of enormous possibilities. In this new national world that was being made, John D. Rockefeller piled up $2 billion, richer than anybody had ever been before and richer, if you allow for inflation, than anyone has ever been since. This book concerns itself with a half dozen men who moved from small to larger worlds, the opportunities they seized, and the consequences of their acts. Charles Kettering and James Cox were Ohio farm boys, who grew up behind the horse-drawn plow. Arthur Morgan, born in Cincinnati, was raised in the then raw small town of St. Cloud, Minnesota. Wilbur Wright was born in a farmhouse in east central Indiana, several years before his family moved to Dayton, Ohio, where Orville was born. John H. Patterson, a generation older than the rest, was the only of this group with roots in a place of any size: he was born in Dayton when it was a county seat of 8,000. It was a spot with some draw: all these men made their adult homes in or near Dayton, which forms the physical setting for this book.

As a common note, they shared the belief that one may safely ignore the problem as inherited. The Wrights achieved flight less by building upon what had been learned by those who had gone before than by casting it aside. Charles

Kettering, America's great industrial research chief, characteristically assigned research tasks to people with no background in the problems involved. When he turned the problem of engine knock over to a mechanical engineer named Thomas Midgley, Midgley replied that he knew nothing about fuel chemistry. That's okay, Kettering said, neither does anyone else. John H. Patterson grew up desperately eager to be a businessman, and almost as desperately ignorant of what businessmen did. He decided to follow his own best advice, creating thereby most of the forms of American merchandising — the trained salesman, the sales territory, the quota and the annual convention.

They were eccentrics. There may today be captains of industry who, like John Patterson, take four baths a day, wear underwear made from pool table felt and sleep with their heads hanging off the side of the bed so they may avoid rebreathing their just exhaled breath, but if there are, they keep pretty damn quiet about it. The Wrights were precise: at Kitty Hawk, Orville numbered the eggs their chickens produced so that each could be eaten in the order laid. By one story, Morgan, who pronounced on all subjects, once airily informed theater critic Brooks Atkinson that the only play that merited production was Ibsen's turgid drama of social responsibility, *An Enemy of the People*. Atkinson, a man of principled tact, replied, "I hesitate to agree with you." Morgan once wrote a play himself. Actually, it was less a play that a parable on the vicissitudes of fine character. And Morgan was its hero.

They were eccentrics, but they were grand eccentrics, individuals of reach and daring, fortunate to live at a time when the world was fluid and small and there and theirs for the shaping. In 1900, Wilbur Wright wrote his father that he was tackling the question of flight because it was almost the only great question that had not already been investigated to the point that the individual could add but little to its advance. Flight, indeed, may have been the last great technical feat to be achieved by what Wilbur and Orville were, gentlemen amateurs. Lives begun in small worlds played out on a large stage. In 1920, James Cox gained the Democratic nomination for President; that same year, Charles Kettering accepted the most important research post in the nation's keystone industry and Arthur Morgan took control of Antioch College, with the intention of making of it a lever to move the world. By then, John H. Patterson, who always figured himself to be a world mover, had returned from Paris, where he attended the Versailles Conference. There, at his own instigation, he rewrote the League of Nations charter along the lines suggested by the success of his own firm, the National Cash Register Company. A then young wife of a local manufacturer recalls being shipboard in those years on the Atlantic. When, she says, her fellow passengers learned she was from Dayton, "They acted like they were meeting someone from a place where things were happening."

John H. Patterson was a man of impulse. By one account, he was traveling in Bulgaria in 1902 when he noticed two things: people ate a lot of paprika; people had good teeth. To Patterson, this was sufficiently a matter of cause and effect that he cabled his commissary to order 4,000 pounds of the spice. In 1905, Patterson dangled a willing-enough photographer to get a bird's eye view of his domain — shown on page 13.

four sketches

Around the First World War Orville Wright kept an airplane at South Field, outside Dayton, Ohio. The

craft was stored in a hangar that sat in a pasture; one night the caretaker neglected to secure the hangar doors. Cows wandered in. The cows spent the night in the hangar, their heavy bovine bodies jostling Orville's airplane, cracking its ribs and spars. They nibbled on the cloth stretched over its wings, apparently found to their liking the taste of the dope used to seal the fabric, and tugged it off, chewing and swallowing the cloth by section. When Orville arrived the following morning he, for once, blew his top. Still, he did so in character. An observer reported: "Orville's was one of these very nice blow ups."

Orville Wright was mild, mannered and impish. Returning once from a speech given by a candidate for lieutenant governor, he commented, "If he is an honest man, he ought to sue his face for slander." In politics, he talked Socialist, voted Republican and praised Franklin Roosevelt, just to scandalize his sister-in-law. He did not so much challenge authority as ignore it. Orville dropped out of kindergarten on the fourth day of class. He neglected to inform his mother that he had given up on formal education. He continued, as before, to leave home each morning, to return home each noon and to speak brightly of the day's activities. Actually, he was playing at the home of a friend, with an eye on the clock. Susan Wright did not learn of her son's truancy until several weeks had passed, when she went to school to see how he was faring. Orville, unabashed, returned to class.

Orville was kind, sweet in fact, and all but morbidly afraid of public appearances. When Franklin Roosevelt came to Dayton to campaign for re-election, Orville was invited to lunch with the President. It was an invitation he could hardly refuse. Later, however, Orville found himself in the back of the President's touring car, being driven through cheering and curious throngs. When the car stopped momentarily in Orville's own neighborhood, he hopped out, thanked the President for lunch, and walked home. He walked with a limp. In 1908, he crashed while demonstrating for the U.S. Army the flying machine he and his brother had created. His injuries left him with recurring sciatica, one leg shorter than the other and an extra heel in his left shoe.

He was the son of a bishop of the United Brethren church, but he was not himself particularly religious, only rarely a churchgoer, a fact his father appears to have taken in stride. Orville avoided passing judgment on others, a trait he shared with his brother Wilbur, though in Wilbur's case such restraint may have taken some effort. A younger relative said of the pair: "It's a funny thing. They could both stand anything but dishonesty. A person that they knew could fail in business and do a poor job and not apply themselves well, and do everything wrong, but if they were honest, they would forgive them everything." Honesty was the linchpin of Orville's moral universe, just as accuracy was the central virtue of his professional life. Dishonesty, inaccuracy — both simply got things off course for no good cause.

Orville was saving by nature. Around 1910, a job applicant at the Wrights' factory noticed that during his interview, Orville kept bending down to pick up brass screws and other small parts that shirtcuffs had brushed off workbenches during the day. This made an impression on the job seeker: "They had financed the world's first airplane by the very meager earnings from their bicycle shop and he [Orville] realized the intrinsic value of those things." When Orville and Wilbur set out to conquer flight, they had no very great expectation of success. Better men than they, as they at first reckoned things, from Leonardo to Alexander Graham Bell, had failed in the attempt. "They first started flying kites when they were grown men," one Dayton resident recalled. "People in Dayton thought they were a couple of nuts. Flying kites, you know." Likely, it did not help that they wore suits while flying those kites. The brothers almost always wore suits. In their shop — tinkering with engines, tightening bicycle chains — the Wrights dressed as though they had just stopped off on their way back from a wedding, in white shirt and starched collar. Invariably, they emerged immaculate.

Orville and Wilbur had only a rough division of labor between them. Orville was the more imaginative, the better mathematician and, when faced with discouragement, the more optimistic of ultimate success. Wilbur was the more organized thinker — he had to a remarkable degree the engineer's capacity to assess a task in its whole and its constituent parts, and to keep parts, whole and the relationship between continuously and clearly in mind. Wilbur had drive, the impulse to do something large. Without his brother's directedness, Orville might have spent his life as what he, after Wilbur's death, became, a kindly favorite uncle who turned up at his nieces' and nephews' house with some new and imaginative toy. In achieving flight, it was Wilbur who played the public role — he conducted the voluminous correspondence, he presented papers at scientific conferences. Orville did nothing similar. When in the 1920s Orville agreed to serve on the board of trustees of the public library half a dozen blocks from his home, he set two conditions — that he would never have to chair a meeting, and that nothing he ever said at a meeting would be quoted in the newspapers. Orville thought reporters were idiots.

Prior to Orville's library years, the experimental section of the United States Army Air Corps was located near Dayton at McCook Field. Aviation then glowed with promise, and of the pilots at McCook, some were future generals, others expected to be, and all — in their youthful razzing and bravado — considered aviation to be the corner of the universe given freshly to them for the making of things grand, themselves included. Sometimes, when an experiment was scheduled at the field, Orville Wright was invited out to watch. He would drive out in the car with the special suspension system to cushion his back and the OW-1 license plates he got every year, and climb out. As he walked, one leg shorter than the other, to where the others were assembled, the razzing and joking died down. One present recalled, "There was a little awe whenever Orville Wright would come around."

Faced with bovine rampage — cows feasting on the wings of his aircraft — Orville Wright threw "a nice sort of blowup," not, said the observer of Orville's outburst, who knew

both men, like "what you'd get from a Kettering." What you got from Charles Kettering was sustained and inventive profanity carrying the accusation that not only were you wrong about the matter at hand, but that you and all who rode with you were an identifiable obstacle to progress — human, technological, social and economic. Progress was a subject Kettering knew something about. At his death, he held patents to a greater number of significant inventions than any American but Edison. His achievements in automotive technology gave the American auto industry a lead so great it later took a quarter century to squander; in other fields, he directed development of modern refrigeration and air conditioning and led creation of the lightweight diesel locomotive.

Swearing came first. Kettering claimed he learned to swear when, as a college dropout, he worked on, then headed, a crew that dug telephone pole holes for a local Ohio phone company. Profanity was both lingua franca and the established procedure for drawing sluggards back to their digging. With one recalcitrant worker, Kettering tried a different approach: he persuaded him that the seemingly boring, unhappy task of pole digging should properly be viewed as a challenge. That challenge was to dig a hole perfectly round. Soon,

Kettering's crew was experimenting to determine which shovels, which techniques and what plans of attack yielded the best result. The idea of turning task to challenge is an old one. Worth noting is that Kettering's crew, rather a rough bunch, accepted the challenge from one young, gawky and nearsighted. As a schoolteacher, which briefly he had been; as a supervisor of hole digging; as an entrepreneur and as a director of research, Kettering had a fabulous capacity to engage and inspire those around him. When Kettering was employed in private industry, half his subordinates once sought and secured permission from management to work through the company's annual shutdown. To take time off, they said, would dissipate the momentum they had going on the job in hand. By age thirty, Kettering acquired the nickname "Boss Ket" — which, mingling affection with respect, was how he was best known for the rest of his life.

It was a name most strongly associated with the automobile. The automobile had Kettering's heart: at one point, he took out a $1.6 million life insurance policy naming "automotive research" as its beneficiary. It was an infatuation he shared with much of the nation, and which Kettering characterized with a tale about a man who, having fallen on hard times, laments: "I lost my job and went to my father's to live. My wife went to her family's. We sent the children to the orphan asylum. I shot my dog. If things get much worse, I'll have to give up my car." Kettering's own favorite was a bottom-of-the-line Chevy, a preference he clung to even while tooling around his winter home in a Florida enclave for the very rich. Asked why he drove the only car in the neighborhood that wasn't a Rolls or a Cadillac, Kettering replied, "I don't want to be conspicuous."

Kettering loved to be conspicuous. He loved an audience. He loved to talk. He had a raspy, reedy voice — in quality, something like the upper register of a clarinet, an instrument he briefly tackled in college when service in the marching band was the only going alternative to participation in military drill. Kettering was a storyteller. He could, one senior corporate attorney who knew him recalled, sit at lunch with a dozen or so successful, strong-willed men and absolutely hold sway, telling story after story and telling them so well that none present felt he was hogging the limelight. A Kettering story was not particularly true. He claimed he had once sat at a dinner beside a distinguished physicist, to whom he posed a question that had been on his mind since childhood: Why, Kettering asked, is it possible to see through glass? Because, the physicist responded amiably, glass is transparent. "I know glass is transparent," Kettering said. "What I want to know is why I can see through it." To Kettering's mind, the physicist has not offered an explanation, but a tautology: you can see through glass; things you can see through are called transparent; therefore, glass is transparent. "That doesn't get us anywhere," Kettering told one audience. "All

we've done is gone out the front door and sneaked back in through the kitchen."
It is a characteristic story — a dig at the experts, a dig suggesting we know less
than we think we do.

Kettering's voice was distinctive, his eyes were defining. They were weak,
several times failing him under the demands of study. Kettering's chosen field
was engineering — blueprints to study, tables to consult, all the small fine print
of specifications. He simply could not focus on such things for sustained periods. Poor eyesight informed Kettering's approach to his work. "I never read,"
he said, "so I thought a lot." It is almost too simple a statement to make, but
Kettering's inability to see detail encouraged his inclination to take the large
view.

The broad stroke was Kettering's signature. He viewed air conditioning not
simply as the means to creature comfort in an Ohio August, but as a step toward ending poverty in the tropics: give the people near the equator cool places
to work, he believed, and they will raise themselves to plenty. He financed a
half-century of research into the nature of photosynthesis, believing that if the
mechanism whereby green plants convert sunlight to carbohydrates could be
understood, then food and fuel could be produced in endless abundance. Late
in life — late in both their lives — Kettering was presented to Einstein. The
physicist recognized the name. "Oh, yes," he said, "the auto mechanic."
Kettering should have been pleased; Einstein had no very broad knowledge of
names and accomplishments. Instead, Kettering was crestfallen. He thought
he had done more than that.

In *Paul Prescott's Charge*, the poor but earnest title
character is strolling nineteenth century Manhattan
when a horse-drawn carriage suddenly bolts. "With
scarcely a moment's premeditation, he rushed out into the middle of the street,
full in the path of the furious horses, and with his cheeks pale, for he knew his
danger, but with determined air, he waved his arms aloft, and cried 'Whoa!' at
the top of his voice." The horses, needless to say, stop. The carriage's passenger, one Mrs. Danforth, is the wife of a wealthy man, who rewards Paul with
the employment that starts him up the ladder of life's success. That's how it is
in the success novels of Horatio Alger — any young man can make his way in
the world, provided he is honest, eager, upright and stands in front of the right
horse at the right time.

Alger's protagonists, to draw upon the titles of his books, were *Brave and Bold, Strong and Steady* and consequently, *Bound to Rise*. Alger's books were a catechism to legions of the upwardly hopeful. Rags to riches — and an affirming rise it was to watch. As Frank Whitney, a wealthy man in *Ragged Dick*, states, "It is always pleasant to see a young man fighting his way upward. In this free country there is every inducement for effort, however unpromising may be the early circumstances in which one is placed."

The early circumstances of James Middleton Cox were unpromising — the farm life of rural Butler County, Ohio, two dozen miles southwest of Dayton. Cox was of the mold of Horatio Alger's likely young men. Self-made. Self-named, as well. His given Christian names of James Madison included a middle name that perhaps struck Cox as too derivative, so he changed it. Like many Alger characters, Cox, when young, forsook the farm for the ambitions of the city; like several, his first rung on his upward climb was work as a newsboy. Typically, Alger's characters were befriended by an older man, an adoptive father who aided

Orville, wedged between the sitting President and a one-time presidential candidate, bided his respectful time, then made his escape.

their rise. In Cox's case, an older businessman financed his entry into business; later, one of Ohio's most prominent attorneys — thirty-seven years Cox's senior — charted his ascent in politics. Alger's were not the "golden boys," the most gifted, the most handsome, the most redolent with promise. Born on the low side of circumstance, their success was never attributable to anything so ephemeral as good looks or charm. While his life could have modeled for one of Alger's heroes, sketched he looked more like a character from Dickens — Mr. Pickwick, perhaps. As an adult, Cox was short; indeed, a bit fire pluggish, with little of the ebullience or good fellowship one associates with those who succeed in public life.

Alger's critics have claimed that character notwithstanding, what mattered most to getting ahead in the author's seemingly moral universe was luck: the runaway horses of Alger's tales invariably belonged to those both rich and grateful. The author's defenders responded that the lucky circumstance is always at hand, ready for the taking by those alert and bold. As a young reporter, Cox contributed stories to the *Cincinnati Enquirer* by wire. One such story recounted a train wreck near Middletown, Ohio. Learning of the mishap, Cox set out immediately, not for the site of the accident, but for the telegraph station nearest to it. There, he directed the operator to transmit the entire local phone directory over the wire to the *Enquirer*'s office. As competing reporters brought their stories to the telegraph station for transmission, they found the sole telegraph line to Cincinnati engaged: by policy, anyone using the line had sole claim until their transmission was completed. Meanwhile, Cox was at the train wreck, gathering details. He then returned with his story to the telegraph office, where he still held first claim on the wire. His account was the first to reach Cincinnati. Luck had nothing to do with it.

Cox did not believe in luck. He did believe in equity: a level plane upon which all could, as he had done, strive. For a time at least, he believed in progress. Taking office as Ohio's reform governor in 1913, he pushed through the legislature and signed into law more progressive legislation than any predecessor — school reform, tax reform, prison reform and a landmark workmen's compensation bill. When that record raised Cox to national attention, one leading magazine summarized his career as "that of an agile, energetic, intuitive, brilliant, and hard-hitting man who has forged his way from the bottom to the top by sheer force of indomitable will, who seeks the limelight, and who never hesitates to make enemies." In short, the self-made man. Alger believed that life's rewards were democratically available to all young men of steadfastness and pluck; that idea was linked in kindred spirit with the notion that in America anyone — or, at least, any boy — could grow up to be President. Many who read and were inspired by Alger became lawyers and stockbrokers and businessmen. James Cox nearly grew up to be President.

Orville Wright was born in Dayton two years after his family moved to the city; James Cox arrived at twenty-eight as editor and publisher of one of its smaller newspapers; Charles Kettering took employment in the city the summer following his graduation from college. John H. Patterson was Dayton by birth, heritage and belligerence.

Some later Pattersons were inclined to look askance at John H. A great-great nephew says that John H. Patterson was "never anybody I was taught to be proud of." Not until adolescence did this descendant realize that NCR — National Cash Register, for generations Dayton's prime employer — had been founded and built by his great-great uncle, or that Patterson Boulevard had been laid over the old path of the Miami-Erie Canal, just as John H. Patterson had always said should be done. The men in the Patterson family, perhaps, place less stress on worldly accomplishment than on behaving like gentlemen. Said one Patterson man of another — and the sequence may be important — "he would never cheat at golf, or cards, or on his wife."

The Patterson to whom most family members most strongly advert is Robert Patterson. Born in 1753, he headed west as a young man; helped found Lexington, Kentucky; fought the British and their native allies during the Revolution; knew Daniel Boone; and for these and other accomplishments was named a colonel in the Virginia Line by Patrick Henry, when that orator was governor of Virginia. Robert Patterson was prominent in post-Revolutionary Kentucky — sheriff, for a time, of one-third the state and leader of Kentucky's delegation to the founding of Cincinnati. What prompted his move in 1803 to the half-dozen-dwelling settlement of Dayton is not certain. One family story has it that he left Kentucky after losing half of Lexington in a poker game. In Dayton, Patterson acquired 2,417 acres of land a rough mile south of the center of settlement, and gave his farm the aggressively ambiguous name, "Rubicon." Robert Patterson's youngest child, Jefferson, passed to his own eleven children the uncompromising motto "Right is Right, and Wrong is Wrong." His own seventh child — John Henry Patterson, born in 1844 — never saw reason sufficient to moderate that view.

John H. Patterson was most in his element in front of a roomful of subordinates, red chalk in hand, flip chart — a Patterson invention — to one side, discoursing on the subject dearest to his heart: how to sell cash registers. On one occasion, Patterson stopped mid-sentence, crushed the chalk and smeared the resulting powder all over his face until he resembled, in the words of one present, "a tousled but well-tailored Comanche." Patterson then threw his arms to the heavens and shrieked, "Dramatize, verbalize." It was just another day at the National Cash Register Company.

Tirades aside, Patterson was a fussbudget — never at rest, rarely at ease, jittery in movement and irascible in expression. Physically he was slight, a gamecock, with a Guards-style moustache and flared and often agitated eyebrows set against a florid face, which he wiped with a handkerchief to signal determination or distress. Generally, it was his determination; their distress. Once, a rising executive decided to relax after a grueling day by lighting up a cigar in his office. Mid-puff, he heard Patterson approaching in the hallway. Cigars were near the top of Patterson's nearly bottomless list of forbidden fruits, a list his executives were expected to memorize and cherish. A window on the opposite side of the executive's office stood six inches open. Coolly — believing his career to be on the line — the executive flipped the offending cigar across the room and out the window. Patterson then entered the office to ask just who was polluting his building. The executive, deeming indiscretion the better part of valor, said the offending odor was probably the legacy of some salesman. Patterson accepted the explanation; his opinion of salesmen was no higher than his opinion of anybody else.

Though a notably successful businessman, Patterson did not greatly seek and did less to flaunt personal wealth. Even after he was Dayton's most prominent industrialist, Patterson usually reached his office upon his bicycle. In 1907, he briefly abandoned that practice, substituting for his cycle a carriage flanked by four mounted riflemen, but that was only because he believed he was being stalked by armed assassins. While the assassins never materialized, plenty of other antagonists did. Patterson regarded this as the natural consequence of being what he called an "upstreamer"; that is, one who moved against the easy currents upon which lesser men were inclined to float, as he was himself inclined to tell them. Being an upstreamer was a license to berate — his employees, on the food they ate; his competitors, on the silly ways they ran their businesses; and Dayton's city officials, on how they were the ruin of a city blessed with and benefited by his family ever since Col. Robert Patterson first set foot in the place in 1803.

National Cash Register, from the air — 1905.

About his own actions, Patterson tried to be clear. "What do we live for?" he often asked. The question was rhetorical, the answer his own: "To do good." Which, among other things, he did.

Visiting circus elephants cool off in the Miami-Erie Canal in the 1890s. By the time this bath was taken, the canal was itself something of a white elephant. In the 1830s, the canal was the route by which most trade reached the city. By 1904, it was described as "a nasty sewer and a menace to health."

the setting

Whatever prompted Col. Robert Patterson to set his farm on the low hills south of the main site of settlement, it proved fortunate. The rest of Dayton was built in the wrong place, on the flood plain. From the first, the city was an exercise in intention against circumstance. Key to circumstance was the Great Miami River, which wraps itself like a backward-facing question mark around the city's downtown. As the Miami flows through Dayton, it gathers in the waters of the Stillwater, the Mad and Wolf Creek. Curiously, as it does so, the river's channel narrows. The tributaries join, the flow increases, the channel constricts. At high flow, water arrived from the north and east faster than the river's narrowing channel could carry it safely away to the south; the excess backed up and over the river's banks and into the downtown. In March 1805 "an extraordinary rise in the river" spilled enough water over the banks so that a canoe could be floated at First and St. Clair. Four blocks west of that spot, Daniel Cooper's levee broke on January 2, 1847, and water ran through sixteen city blocks. By one report, local officials placed the blame on residents who had carted away levee dirt to fill potholes in their streets and low spots in their yards. In February 1883, Ludlow Street reported twenty-two inches of water, and flooding three years later created pools in town "deep enough to swim a horse."

The response to these periodic drenchings was to take the dirt back out of the potholes and from the hills to the south and east and pile it on top of the levees, then feel secure behind their dull thickness. There was nothing much to worry about. At celebrations marking Dayton's centennial in 1896, Mary Davies Steele spoke slightingly of the fears of early settlers: "Some of us can remember how certain aged pioneers used to upbraid the founders of the town for putting it down in a hollow, instead of on the hills to the southeast, and expatiate on the folly which the people were guilty of in voting against the removal, after the terrible freshet of 1805, to high ground." She recalled that early settlers had prophesied in almost Biblical language, "'Someday there will be a flood which will sweep Dayton out of existence.'" Miss Steele spoke with the confidence of the almost twentieth century; she recalled that warning only to dismiss it. Mary Davies Steele was talking through her hat. Those early floods — ten in the city's first century — were, from the vantage of the Great Miami River, just practice shots, like a lanky but unmuscled freshman trying to get the hang of a javelin. When the river got serious, in 1913, it would hit Dayton with the efficient low-angled brutality of a middle linebacker with nostrils full of quarterback.

In the city itself, Main Street was platted wide — perhaps with aspiration, perhaps only to make it easier for teamsters to circle their horsedrawn wagons at the street's north end where in early days it ran dead up against the river. City life centered a few blocks south, at Main and Third Street, a crossroads marked by the old courthouse. Designed by a local businessman with an interest in the classics, it is a fully presentable replica of an ancient Greek temple, no one temple in particular, actually, though the eastern portico has been said to resemble the Temple of Bacchus at Teos near Ephesus. In 1859, Abraham Lincoln, inching his way to the Presidency, spoke from the steps of the courthouse on the issue of slavery. *The Dayton Daily Empire* reported: "Mr. Lincoln is a very seductive reasoner, and his address, although a net work of fallacies and false assumptions throughout, was calculated to deceive almost any man who would not pay very close attention to the subject and keep continually on guard." *The Empire* favored Stephen Douglas, who the year before had defeated Lincoln in the race for the U.S. Senate in Illinois. Lincoln was dogging Douglas' tracks across Ohio; the "Little Giant" had spoken in Dayton eight days earlier, introduced on that occasion by Dayton's congressman, Clement Vallandigham. The following year, Lincoln defeated Douglas for the Presidency; three years later, Lincoln exiled Vallandigham for arguing too vociferously against the Civil War that followed upon his election. Post-war, Vallandigham returned to the area to practice law; once, attempting to demonstrate that the gun allegedly used by his client to commit murder could not have been fired, he inadvertently shot himself, and died of the wounds. The jury found his client guilty.

By then, the courthouse steps from which Lincoln spoke had become the venue of Al Shartle. Shartle, a lanky man with rumpled hat, buttoned vest and

at his post when the stock market crashed in 1929. During that time, Shartle blacked the shoes of four presidents — Hayes, Garfield, McKinley and Harding — all Republicans. Shartle himself remained a Democrat. In 1920, he traveled to his party's convention in San Francisco, where he bent the ear of William Jennings Bryan on behalf of Dayton's favorite son, James Cox.

From the courthouse, Dayton's main commercial buildings spread up and down Main and east and west on Third. The corner's tallest structure was the Callahan Bank Building — directly across Main Street from the courthouse, eight stone stories peaked with a pyramidal clock tower. In 1891, the Callahan's elevator operator spent the free minutes he had between calls reading Tennyson and Shakespeare. He was Paul Laurence Dunbar; he had graduated the year before from Dayton's Central High School, a member of the same class from which Orville Wright dropped out. For a brief time, Dunbar edited a slim newspaper, *The Tatler*, for the black community on Dayton's west side; the paper was printed by Orville and Wilbur Wright. "We kept it going as long as our resources held out," Orville later recalled, "which was not very long." *The Tatler* folded after three issues. As a high school graduate, Dunbar had hoped for office employment. When no one in Dayton would give a black applicant white collar work, he became an elevator boy at $4 a week. Dunbar was to conclude that society offered him but two possible employments: he could be a menial, or he could be a poet. He became the latter. His second volume of verse, *Lyrics of Lowly Life*, gained the attention of William Dean Howells, then America's reigning literary critic. Dunbar, Howells wrote, represented "the first instance of an American negro who had evinced innate distinction in literature. ... Paul Dunbar was the only man of pure African blood and of American civilization to tell the negro life aesthetically and express it lyrically." That review launched Dunbar on a meteoric career, during which he learned that America didn't much want him to be a poet, either. He died at thirty-four of tuberculosis, drink and disappointment.

The courthouse, the commercial buildings, the nearby homes of the affluent — these all lay in a mile-square basin bounded by the Great Miami River and by the low hills to the east and south. Downtown, literally, was down, a fact that lessened the claim its buildings made on the horizon. In most neighborhoods, Dayton from street level was a city of churches, whose spires provided the landmarks that set the physical horizons and whose cycle of baptism, confirmation, marriage and burial marked the compass points of life. Dayton was a center of religious publishing; among others, for the United Brethren Church, whose headquarters was a block south of the Callahan Building on Main. There, much editorial work was handled by Bishop Milton Wright. Bishop Wright

"Orville Wright is out of sight In the printing business. No other mind is half as bright As his'n is."

Attributed to Paul Laurence Dunbar.

much editorial work was handled by Bishop Milton Wright. Bishop Wright lived to the west of the river; he had five children, of whom only the youngest — Katharine, his only daughter, the only of his offspring to complete college — seemed to have any push.

On the downtown's eastern edge, the Miami-Erie Canal trenched its way through the city. Here, goods were unloaded at the city's open market. Below the market lived Dayton's German population, the city's most numerous immigrant group, without in fact being very numerous. Overwhelmingly, the city was native born, Protestant and white — in 1890, the African-American population was roughly three percent of the whole. Migrants came less from central or southern Europe than from southeastern Indiana and northern Kentucky. What drew them was work. Dayton began as a place where things were traded. Post-Civil War, it became a place where things were made. Hayrakes, harrows and heating stoves. Steam pumps, water wheels and gas machines. White lead, paints and varnishes. Strawboard and paper boxes. Patent medicines, ale and chewing gum. Proud of its growing productive base, Dayton called itself "the city of a thousand factories" — at a time when factories suggested a promising future, rather than a remnant of the past.

Dayton was, as noted, an exercise in intention against circumstance. Built along a river as likely to drown as to enrich it, the city had no countervailing natural asset: no coal, no iron ore, no fine building stone, no stretches of tall standing virgin timber. Nor did it early on gain any major trophy of civil life: no capitol, no state university. The city began as a place where things were traded. It grew to be a place where things were made. From that, it became a place where things were invented. In this, it was the most Midwestern of places. In its development, the Midwest by necessity confronted large opportunities and long distances with limited resources. The gap between resource and opportunity was patched over with improvisation and invention. When Dayton started to invent, it began with practical things — the safety ladder, farm implements — designed from what was available and set to tasks right at hand. Invention builds on itself: it develops a pool of local craftsmen, a pool of local capital and that freeing sense that a mind can make and shape a thing imagined and set it to perform a task. By 1870, Dayton — by U.S. Patent Office figures — ranked fifth in patents secured relative to population; in 1880, third; by 1900, first. By then, imagination was the city's leading industry and its most significant export. The first major invention to leave Dayton for America did something of which Americans are peculiarly fond: it counted money.

Cash registers sat front counter and center as the symbol of the day's boom in retailing. The first real machine of business, they tracked sales, totaled receipts, tabulated credit charges and sounded a bell whenever another customer was hooked and landed.

"Immoderate even when right, powerful even when wrong" — NCR founder John H. Patterson was the declared foe of "All old fogyism," "Bossism" and "All that is bad." He launched a jihad against the city of his birth, spooned out malted milk to his employees, defeated many, terrified most and died an honored philanthropist.

the businessman

John H. Patterson grew up at his family's Rubicon farm, completed high school, served briefly and without incident in the Union Army, and attended several colleges, including Dartmouth, where he acquired a bachelor's degree and a lifelong disdain for college men. He thought little of higher learning; he thought little of family life. His marriage — which may have been prompted by the view that a businessman ought to have a wife — came late, to the well-born Katharine Dudley Beck of Massachusetts. It ended with her death from typhoid fever five years later, leaving him with two children, whose upbringing he largely delegated. His disdain for higher education may have come when he returned to Dayton, diploma in hand, and found himself unemployable. His degree disqualified him for physical work; his lack of experience disqualified him for everything else. He eventually landed a berth as a toll collector on the Miami-Erie Canal, an undemanding task that soon exhausted his limited capacity for boredom. He hung a sign outside his tollkeeper's office announcing he had coal and wood to sell. Actually, he didn't. He simply took orders for coal, marked them up, then passed them along to a nearby coal yard. When the yard went up for sale, he and his older brother Stephen borrowed $250 and

The coal was black, bituminous and otherwise undistinguished, and Dayton had plenty who dealt in its delivery. Patterson, now twenty-five, acknowledged there was no particular reason why anyone should buy from him. Reasons lacking, he created them. Customers then often questioned whether suppliers were providing fair weight; Patterson told his customers they could weigh his deliveries on public scales, then charge the weighing fee to him. Customers and dealers often disputed the number of deliveries made; Patterson introduced a system of receipts, color-coded for his illiterate deliverymen. Other dealers delivered coal in broken-down carts pulled by broken-down horses; Patterson used brightly-colored delivery wagons boasting the name "Patterson & Co." If coal arrived dirty from the mine, the teamsters were ordered to clean it. Once, two tons of coal was hand-sorted to remove sixty pounds of slate. One company employee stated: "Mr. Patterson shipped coal as though each lump were an Oregon apple." Patterson was learning the value of merchandising, and his own skill at it. He acquired a franchise to sell "Brooks" coal, believed superior. When Brooks tried to back out of the arrangement, Patterson replied, "It is not your coal that is making the sales. It is the way we are selling it. If you take away this agency you will regret it only once — and that will be all your life."

Within a few years, Patterson held half the coal business in Dayton. He also had a new partner, his more docile brother Robert. To protect their supply, the Pattersons bought three coal mines in southern Ohio, near Coalton. At Coalton, they operated a miner's store which, unaccountably, lost money. By Patterson's account, "We were doing a business of $48,000 a year, with almost no competition, and our prices were high.... But at the end of three years we not only had not declared a dividend but we had lost $3,000 and were in debt over $16,000." Patterson offered the store for free to anyone who would assume its debts, but found no takers.

The store was losing money because Patterson's clerks were systematically shortchanging his till. Patterson, unknowingly, was encouraging them. He offered bonuses to the clerk who sold the most goods. Soon, his clerks were running a kind of negative auction: if the clerk on the left was asking fifteen cents for a dozen of Patterson's eggs, the clerk on the right would let them go for a dime. Patterson was not alone. Control of cash receipts — or, less elegantly, the tendency of clerks to steal — was the seemingly insoluble problem of retailing. Money taken in was kept in an open cash drawer, a sieve that leaked receipts through employee theft, honest error and scrambled bookkeeping. One store owner was asked how his clerk could afford the diamond ring he was wearing. The merchant replied that the employee had paid for the diamond by pilfering the till. Why did he not replace so dishonest a worker? Because, the merchant explained, it was better to keep a clerk who already owned a diamond than to hire another who would steal until he got one, too.

Necessity became the mother of a not very good invention. In 1878, a Dayton saloonkeeper, James Ritty, supposedly distraught over employee theft, took an ocean voyage to get away from his troubles. Visiting the engine room, he saw the mechanism that counted the rotations of the ship's propeller. Back in Dayton, he and his brother, a machinist, adapted its principle to the counting of receipts. In 1879, Ritty patented his invention, grandly calling it "Ritty's Incorruptible Cashier." Barely a dozen of Ritty's contraptions were in use when John H. Patterson spotted an advertisement for the machine. Sight unseen, he ordered two. He sacked his employees, hired new ones and started afresh with "Ritty's" assistance. In the next six months, his store produced a $5,000 profit.

Twin financial failure placed the cash register's future in Patterson's hands. First, neither Ritty nor those to whom he sold his patents could make it a commercial success. Second, Patterson's budding empire went belly-up. Characteristically, Patterson pushed on the margins to gain greater control. He owned a coal distributorship; he owned coal mines; he decided to own a railway to connect them. In that attempt, he either overreached himself or, as he himself always maintained, was betrayed by Eastern investors who held part interest. The Pattersons sold out everything, wrote off more than half of their $40,000 investment, and began to cast about for a new venture. John H. Patterson's eye fell upon the cash register. In 1884, he plunked down $6,500 for majority control of the National Manufacturing Company, which held the Ritty patents.

Patterson's debut was ludicrous. Announcing his purchase at the Dayton Club, he was roundly informed that the company he had acquired was a failure, its product defective, its credit a joke and its location a slum. To Patterson, all this was news: he had bought the company without bothering to visit it. He sought out the previous owner and offered him $100 to call off the deal. Then $500. Finally $2,000, nearly a third of the purchase price, to cancel the purchase with no questions asked. The reply made by the previous owner did nothing to reassure: "I would not have it back as a gift." In his later years, Patterson was variously regarded as an inflexible monopolist, as a champion of labor, and as a major innovator in business practice. That was all still to come. In 1884, the new owner of the cash register business was likely in something approaching panic.

"We teach through the eye" became one of John H. Patterson's favorite admonitions. The reason for this, he said, was that "eighty-seven percent of all we know is learned through the eye," a precept he sometimes stated as: "The optic nerve is twenty-five times stronger than the aural nerve." Where he got these figures is not known. No matter. We teach through the eye. We show. We gather the workers together and project a stereopticon slide showing a large ball named "the company." On one side, management is trying to push the ball to the left; on the other, workers are trying to push the ball to the right. The ball goes nowhere. Now, on the next slide, we show how readily the ball moves when everyone pushes together. Patterson liked striking headlines, simple ideas, short sentences. "No ad," he claimed, "is large enough to contain two ideas." He liked drawing large words on blank sheets of newsprint, then tossing the sheet away — one sheet, one idea — and grabbing another; he had an aide stitch some sheets together, mount them on an easel for better display, and that became the flip chart. People must see it.

The thing easiest to see when John H. Patterson took over his newly-purchased enterprise was that the cash register business was broke and going nowhere. On January 1, 1885, the company faced accounts payable of $11,701.48; cash on hand, plus a generous estimate of receivables, did not reach half that figure. Patterson renamed his unwanted stepchild the National Cash Register Company. It operated from rented facilities, where his thirteen inherited employees could produce thirty cash registers a month. All of America was not demanding that many. Patterson set out to create that demand. Retailers and shopkeepers would buy, he believed, if only they knew how marvelous a machine he was offering. Patterson couldn't afford to hire salesmen, so he worked through commission agents. From them, he secured the names of 5,000 prospective purchasers; next, he wrote and printed up eighteen pieces of advertising literature. These he mailed out to the prospects, six letters a week for three weeks — apparently, the first-ever practice of direct mail advertising. Then, as now, not all recipients were pleased. One letter came back bearing the scrawled message: "For Heaven's sake let up. What have we done to you?"

What the exasperated recipient had done, in Patterson's view, was simple: he had failed. He had failed in his responsibility to his clerks, leaving them vulnerable to the temptations of the open cash drawer. He had failed in his responsibility to his customers, wasting on record keeping attention that should properly have been given to them. He had failed in his responsibility to his family, who suffered the income lost due to uncharged sales. And he had failed in his responsibility to himself, losing through evenings spent remedying the books the leisure that his enterprise had rightly earned him. Patterson calculated that 600 million of the world's people were at hazard due to the open cash drawer. He would reach them, sell them his register, improve their lives, get rich. His faith must have been sorely tried: in May 1885, cash on hand bottomed out at ninety-one cents — eighty-eight cents in the bank; three cents in the office safe. His trial continued. The company that he could not unload as a gift the day he bought it, he could not have sold at a profit any time in its first decade.

Pending insolvency goaded Patterson to expand. He borrowed $30,000 from a local bank; when further credit was refused, Patterson explained the facts of life to his banker: "I don't want to see the bank lose its money, but unless [my] company gets another loan, it will go under and the bank will lose." An additional loan was forthcoming — which Patterson promptly spent to print and post more direct mail literature. Patterson's minority stockholders regarded as lunatic his effort to spend his way to wealth; they threatened to bring suit against his stewardship. By some means — perhaps he and his brother mortgaged the family farm — Patterson found the funds to buy them out. He now had full control. He had a product in which he placed unswerving belief. What he needed was customers. He found his answer, as desperate men sometimes do, in a bar.

A story has it that a man walks into a bar, asks for a shot of whiskey, snorts it down, lays a 50-cent piece on the bar counter and walks out. The bartender pockets the coin, then notices that the saloon owner has been watching. Maintaining his calm, the bartender says: "Imagine that guy? Leaves a 50-cent tip when he can't even afford to pay for a drink!" That saloonkeeper, and others like him, was Patterson's first market. Most of his early sales were to tavern owners who feared that the dollars and change of the less-than-sober were finding their way into the pockets of the less-than-honest. It was a hard sell. Saloon employees regarded the machine as a thiefcatcher that either impugned their honesty or narrowed their leeway for transgression. They took countermeasures:

when one of Patterson's first big buyers wanted to return the newly delivered registers as defective, Patterson hired private detectives to prove that employee tampering was the cause. Opposition was strong. Employees routinely destroyed the direct mail advertisements that arrived in National Cash Register envelopes. When Patterson shifted to blank envelopes, bartenders countered by destroying any mail postmarked in Dayton. Patterson outflanked them by sending mail in bulk to other cities and having it posted from there. Some NCR agents who turned up to demonstrate the cash register were given the bum's rush into the gutter. Patterson made up a small three-key model that, concealed in a box, could be brought in undetected. Finally, he told his agents to set up their display in a hotel room, then bring their prospect there, away from the suspicious eyes of employees.

Patterson's sales strategy was simple: direct mail to soften up the prospect, sales agents to tree the quarry. To prospects, he sent The Output — a compilation of testimonials and advertisements which by 1888 had a circulation of 135,000 and whose mailing consumed one-fourth of the two-cent stamps sold in Dayton. To sales agents, he sent a separate publication reporting on the successful tactics of their peers. One early field report stated, "We are now working on a new plan. We load a register in the wagon, send an agent out

Early cash registers had a clock face showing the receipts for the day.

with it, and tell him not to return until he sells it. It is working pretty well." Under the pressure of Patterson's evangelicalism, cash register sales perked up — from 359 the year he bought the company to 1,995 three years later. By March 1888, Patterson's factory could not keep pace with orders. He borrowed again and rushed to build a larger one: "Providing orders push," he wrote, "we will put up electric lights, and work two sets of builders, one in the day time and the other at night." The new two-story brick building went up on the high ground of the Patterson family farm south of the center of Dayton. By then, the company that had thirteen employees when Patterson bought it was boasting 123.

Patterson liked to claim he never had an original idea. Rather, he said, he scooped ideas up from others, shuffled them, then discarded those that failed to meet whatever standard he was applying at the time. This, indeed, was rather like how he later handled his executives, whom he hired, promoted and fired in a game of solitaire which perhaps not even he, and certainly not they, ever understood. But he was attentive to success, and curious as to its causes. In June 1887, Patterson queried his best salesmen, Joseph H. Crane, on the secret of his success. Crane was Patterson's brother-in-law; prior to joining NCR, he had been acknowledged the best wallpaper salesman in the state. In selling cash registers, however, he met with little initial success. Mulling this, Crane concluded that in each unsuccessful sales presentation he had failed to make one or more key points. To prevent this, Crane pinpointed the best arguments for the cash register, placed them in logical sequence, and repeated this presentation word for word to each potential customer. Patterson was intrigued. System he loved, successful system even more, and system that succeeded at sell-

ing cash registers he loved best of all. He had Crane's sales talk taken down verbatim. It was 450 words long — the first canned sales spiel — and Patterson ordered his salesmen to memorize it, use it and use nothing else.

His sales force resisted. Salesmen were then known as drummers, men who, at least in their own minds, lived by their wits and sold by their charm. The salesman was the man who walked in with brimming confidence and open palm. He was a harbinger; he'd been places, he'd seen things and he could tell you what people were thinking in St. Louis and Chicago. You weren't planning on going to Chicago, actually, but you felt worldly hearing that the Palmer House was first-rate. Selling was avuncular — "How's the wife? How's the family?" Selling was stroking, noticing, paying attention — "Seems to me, last time I was through here you talked about adding to that counter. Looks like you've made a good job of it." Selling was the striking of minor alliances — "If you ever need anything in Des Moines, that's home office, just let me know." Selling was a slap on the back, a fresh joke and a stale cigar when the deal was struck. It was this tradition — the exuberance of Professor Harold Hill, fleecing River City; the pathos of Willy Loman, fooling only himself — that John H. Patterson put to rest. It took him much of the next decade to do so, but Crane's sales talk set Patterson's path. In place of the gladhander, selling his smile, John Patterson invented the corporate representative — well-mannered, well-informed — selling cash registers.

He began by insisting that his salesmen look the part: "The man who is seldom turned down in an interview," one early NCR sales manual stated, "is the well-groomed, well-appearing salesman." Daily shaves and fresh collars were required. Later, he hired the head valet at the Waldorf-Astoria to give lessons on dress; he'd send promising younger salesmen to New York City to buy new suits at company expense "to get the hayseed off them." They'd get a taste for style, a taste it took money to support, money that in a just world came from the selling of cash registers.

He taught them suitable manners: "There is nothing that denotes the gentleman more than earnestness and politeness." The NCR salesman was not a repairman; indeed, he was forbidden even to carry a screwdriver. No backslapping. No jokes. No lounging. No cigars. When calling on customers, salesmen were instructed to know the name of the proprietor before entering the shop, to speak only when they were ensured of the owner's uninterrupted attention, and to state that "the object of your visit is to explain a method of conducting his business which will make him more money." The lure? "Give your [prospective purchaser] to understand that unless you can prove this assertion you do not expect him to buy."

He told them what to say. The point central to selling Patterson's machines was: "A National Cash Register is not an expense, because it pays for itself out of the losses it prevents." This theme was repeated with hundreds of variations in *Selling Points* and *The Book of Arguments,* which salesmen were expected to study, memorize and trot out to good effect. If, for example, a prospective purchaser flat out refused to look at the register, the salesman was to say: "Mr. Blank, when Mr. Westinghouse first took his air-brake to Mr. Vanderbilt, he stated that trains could be stopped by the use of it, and asked Mr. Vanderbilt to look at it, and the millionaire refused to waste time considering what he called a wild scheme. His action cost him millions of dollars. Any device that it is claimed would be an advantage to your business deserves at least an investigation." If a prospective purchaser "can't spare the money," the salesman was to ask: "Which money, the money you have or the money you lose? All we ask you to spare is the money you now lose."

There were appeals to equity: "When you pay your employees, the latter

Anyone who said "meet me at the Fair," was met as well by a glistening array of NCR cash registers. With an eye for promotion, Patterson shipped cash registers by the carload to the 1903 St. Louis World's Fair, along with photographs showing his machines being used everywhere from Pakistan to Alaska.

count the money to see if it is correct. Why shouldn't you count the money your employees take in for you?" There were appeals to suspicion: "Well, Mr. Blank, you seem to trust your employees, and it is far from my intention to shake your confidence in them. But tell me through which people a man loses money — the one whom he trusts or those whom he mistrusts?" There were appeals to vanity. The register's receipt, store owners were told, could be used to picture special sale items, "and can even carry a likeness of yourself." There was one central certainty. "Do not let [the prospect] sidetrack you by the statement that he knows all about cash registers. If he did, he would be using one."

Patterson's sales force fought a grudging rearguard action against such regimentation. He overwhelmed them — through hope of reward, fear of punishment and his vast capacity for sustained venom. In this, he was motivated by a fortunate choice of quirks. Patterson was a believer in the "cast-iron rule." This was an economic "law" propounded by an Ohio farmer named Benner, who argued that a general business downturn was always presaged by a drop in the scrap price of cast iron. Patterson traveled with two books: The Bible, and the latest edition of Benner's *Prophecies of Future Ups and Downs in Prices: What years to make money on pig-iron, hogs, corn and provisions*. When the 1892 edition of Benner's predicted doom, Patterson took to the road to batten down his sales force. He hit fifty cities in fifty-one days. He demanded that his salesmen, one by one, rattle off Crane's sales talk. He role played with them how they would handle a sale. He did not welcome resistance: in Denver, one frustrated salesman shook his finger in Patterson's face; the forty-nine-year old company president kicked in the side of the insubordinate's desk. They would do it his way. They would do it his way, because his way was best. They would do it his way, because hard times were coming and in hard times a cash register could not be sold as the emblem of a successful venture, but as the salvation of a shaky one. They would do it his way, ultimately, because he told them to.

The Panic of 1893 — the most severe economic contraction between the Civil War and the Great Depression — justified Benner's predictions and Patterson's precautions. Nationally, 600 banks failed, 15,000 businesses went under; meanwhile, National Cash Register set a new sales record. Patterson was about as unhappy as a man fully justified by events could be. Returning from his tour of the field, he reported:

> I have found nothing but excuses on this trip — excuses for not learning the primer, excuses for not committing the Book of Arguments,... excuses for not decorating the show windows and offices, excuses for not having the men come to the office early in the morning, excuses for not sending out advertising matter, excuses for smoking in the office, excuses for the state of the weather.

Patterson had had it with "born salesmen"; it was time to raise his own. In 1894, he opened the nation's first formal sales training program, housed in the Hall of Industrial Education at Fourth and Main streets in Dayton. He placed Joseph H. Crane in charge of the school. The former Ohio champion wallpaper salesmen soon had Patterson's recruits chanting that a National Cash Register was not an expense, because it pays for itself out of the losses it prevents. The school's graduates fit neatly into Patterson's marketing structure: they were assigned a territory, a quota and, if that quota was met, were rewarded with an invitation to the annual sales convention. Each of these innovations was Patterson's; each became all but standard in American business.

A storekeeper's pride and a thing of beauty and, to hear John H. Patterson, absolutely free: his registers, he claimed, paid for themselves from the losses they prevented. It was very likely true.

With all of this, business historian William Rodgers writes, "Patterson developed the dynamics and art form of salesmanship into a partially disciplined vocation, if not quite a bona fide profession: something requiring less demanding study, for example, than pharmacy, offering fewer opportunities for self-delusion and job advancement, but no less respectability, than journalism."

Under Patterson, all NCR sales personnel were male. He told them how to dress. He told them how to act. He told them what to say. He told them when to say it. After the turn of the century, he cut off their last line of retreat. He organized their wives. At a convention for the spouses of 500 salesmen, a banner listed the major points of instruction:

1. Serve simple well-cooked food.
2. Keep him cheerful.
3. Give him plenty of fresh air.
4. See that he gets enough sleep.
5. Lend encouragement at the right time.
6. See that he takes regular exercise.
7. Be economical and save for a rainy day.
8. Take a real interest in his sales record.
9. Read N.C.R. advertising matter.
10. Be cheerful yourself.

A salesman's lot was not a happy one.

Centrally, Patterson urged upon his sales force that with a proper attitude, and a proper faith in cash registers, nothing was impossible. At one year's convention for those salesmen who had met their quotas, attendees ate lunch in a small building that was just going out of service as the executives' dining room. Lunch adjourned, Patterson instructed an NCR superintendent to have the building leveled and the site cleared and green with grass by the following morning. Teams worked through the night, caving in the structure, carting off debris, shoveling topsoil over the depression in the ground and laying sod above the dirt. When salesmen arrived for lunch the following day, the building and all evidence of its existence was gone. The salesmen wandered over the site, tapping the fresh-laid sod with their toes, questioning their memories and each other. The episode became a piece of company lore. From Patterson's perspective, it was object lesson, forcefully delivered: anything could be accomplished. From another view, there was a second lesson: and anything can be got rid of. Including salesmen.

NCR claimed its registers were the solution to every proprietor's needs — and well-designed, well-executed sales materials gave the details.

"This honorable body," as one member called it, whose surviving members dined annually for half a century. The final statement in its minutes book reads, "and none of us has ever been ashamed of his fellows." Those fellows include three Wrights: Wilbur, center back; Lorin, front left; Reuchlin, front right.

the brothers

On October 23, 1886, Reuchlin and Lorin and Wilbur
Wright — the three eldest of Bishop Milton Wright's
four sons — attended the inaugural dinner of the
Annual Club of Ten Dayton Boys. It was a social club, its
members no one in particular, young men mostly from the same West Side
neighborhood as the Wrights. Their employments were modest: William
Andrews was a traveling salesman; Charles Alinger was a machinist at NCR;
Wilbur Landis was a printer; Edgar Ellis a soapmaker. The Wrights' liveli-
hoods were in keeping: Reuchlin, twenty-five, was a clerk; Lorin, twenty-three,
a bookkeeper; Wilbur — at nineteen, the baby of the group — listed his occupa-
tion as clerk at J. J. Hoffman's grocery.

The first dinner's menu was assertively male: raw oysters and fried oysters
and stewed oysters and iced Adams ale. The evening's recorded entertainment,
however, was rather more tame: member Joseph Boyd presented a copy of *The
Ohio Teachers Blue Book*, a volume he had compiled that gave the names and
salaries of all the school superintendents and teachers in the state. The dinner
became an annual event, with members gathering to dine and to compare notes
on life and circumstance, comments the club secretary inscribed in a large,
leather-bound minutes book. Thus, early on, W. E. Landis announced that he
has "been made painfully acquainted with the fact that I have arrived at the
advanced age of 26, from the scarcity of hair on the top of my head. Whether

tion in my mind, for it is a generally conceded point that the majority of printers are bald." Ed Ellis reported that he has become a register clerk in the Dayton Post Office. Frank J. Gilbert let it be known that he is "as successful as could reasonably be expected." Modest men, modest ambitions.

The Annual Club of Ten Dayton Boys was a small world, one of a series the various Wright brothers would inhabit. Their father — Bishop Wright — believed that trust could be placed in God, in family, and in not much else. Outside the circle of family, the Wrights stepped warily. Susan Wright, Bishop Wright's wife, was so preternaturally shy that once, asked by a grocer where she wished the groceries she had just ordered be delivered, she could summon to mind neither her name nor her address. Like the other club members — and like his brothers Reuchlin and Lorin — Wilbur Wright's early ambitions were local. Reuchlin and Lorin enrolled in Hartsville College, the tiny religious school in Indiana where Milton and Susan Wright had met, but after brief stays each returned home. Initially, his parents considered sending Wilbur to Yale, but circumstance and the decisions circumstance prompted kept him in Dayton: at eighteen, he was injured while ice skating, heart palpitations followed, and he concluded that he faced the life of an invalid. Wilbur became a devout reader; he was earnest, sober — when his father was traveling on church business, it was Wilbur who acted as head of household. Then Susan Wright contracted tuberculosis, and Wilbur appointed himself chief nurse, strong enough to carry her up and down the stairs of the family home at 7 Hawthorn Street.

Wilbur was earnest; Orville was entrepreneurial. As a child, he briefly collected old bones for sale to a fertilizer factory, then abandoned the undertaking when his first haul brought a return of only three cents. A few years later he entered the chewing gum business, attempting to sell a low cost substitute composed of small bits of sugar-coated tar, wrapped in tissue paper. Orville had an intermittent interest in school. Once, he leagued with several friends to force a dismissal of class by dropping a package of red pepper down the heating register. Their calculations miscarried. They had expected the classroom to be filled with an acrid cloud. No such cloud materialized. Several days later, when the pepper at last began to burn, the teacher apologized to the class, opened the windows and continued the lesson while all sat sneezing and wiping their eyes.

When Orville cared about school he did well. In seventh grade, he was named the best mathematics student in his grade in the city. Other matters tugged. With a neighborhood friend who owned a small printing press, Orville set up a printing business. Then, with Wilbur's assistance, he built a press from a damaged tombstone, metal scraps and buggy parts, and used the press to print woodcuts and the visiting cards then presented on social calls. On March 1, 1889, Orville distributed the first issue of a neighborhood weekly newspaper, *The West Side News*. His first edition — four small pages — carried an editorial pledge to publish whatever was in "the interests of the people and business institutions of the West Side. Whatever tends to their advancement, moral, mental and financial, will receive our closest attention." Contents were somewhat less grand than intentions. Early issues gave page one coverage to an anecdote on President Lincoln and General Sherman, to the eating habits of alligators and to toothpick production in Maine. Most reporting was local:

> Yesterday Eugene Staley and Wiley Decker went fishing at the Bridge Street bridge, and caught forty-eight goggle eyes.

> Dan High is building a new pigeon house on Broadway.

> An exciting ball game was played on the common back of the old pottery grounds. When our reporter arrived, the respective pitchers were trying to hold the total base hits of their opponents down below one hundred and fifty. There was some hope they would succeed.

Two months after Orville launched his newspaper, Wilbur signed on. They increased the size and number of its pages, and more aggressively sought to promote the newspaper and its neighborhood. Readers were urged to direct their purchasing power to local merchants: "Give them all the trade you can. Do not be afraid they will get too rich. If they are making money too fast, other merchants will come crowding in, and the West Side will receive the benefit of it all." For Wilbur, the paper provided a step outside his role as his mother's nurse, the chance to do something he could captain and promote. For Orville, the *News* turned printing from a hobby into a business, thus providing the excuse he needed for skipping out of his senior year of high school. For both it provided an exercise in precision: for all the ink stains it produces, printing from hand-selected lead type is a craft engagingly exact and clean. And an exercise in invention: their press had been designed not from any existing model, but from Orville's own sense of how a press might operate. Once, a visiting printer — Orville remembered him as being from Philadelphia — came to see the machine for himself. He crouched low, studied it from various perspectives, stood up and announced, "It works, but I don't see how the heck it works." And for both brothers, *The West Side News* was a reason to stay at home, where they remained even after Susan Wright's death, on July 4, 1889.

They published the weekly for a year, then converted their the newspaper to a four-page daily, *The Evening Item*. It was a well-written, well-edited production that sought to bring to Dayton's West Side all the world's news — one front page carried coverage of May Day demonstrations around the world and a round-by-round account of the bout between middleweights Pete McCoy and Johnny Reagan, won by McCoy, after Reagan, leading in the early rounds, tired. Inside pages presented local happenings and this report on life in Indiana: "Base ball is on the decline at Vincennes since the craze for chasing soaped pigs began." Editorially, the Wrights were Republican and high-minded: they argued for sound money, lectured labor on the self-defeating nature of strikes, urged the enfranchisement of Louisiana blacks and endorsed Prohibition and women's suffrage.

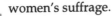

It was work — and insufficiently remunerative. *The Item* lasted only three months. On July 30, 1890, the Wrights published their valedictory: "The reasons can be stated in a few words: More money can be made with less work in other kinds of printing, such as job printing." One hears Wilbur's hardworking earnestness in the editorial's aggrieved tones: "If a man had the capital and was willing to work for very little money for the first year, a daily could be established which would pay a reasonable profit. As for us, we have only a small capital and do not care to wait a year before we begin to receive reasonable profits... It takes the people over here too long to make up their minds to support their institutions." The Wrights remained busy as job printers — earning $1.50 for 175 ribbons for the Miami Valley Poultry Association and $22.00 for 500 annual reports for the West Side Building & Loan Company — but with daily journalism they were through.

During their newspapering career, the Wrights gave regular coverage to the doings of members of the Annual Club of Ten Dayton Boys. A business trip to Pennsylvania by club member E. W. Ellis, Joseph Boyd's rescue of a pet squirrel from a menacing group of young boys, Boyd's fifth wedding anniversary and the marriage of club member Wilbur E. Landis were all reported in their pages. Like any organization of committed maledom, the Ten Dayton Boys club reacted with ostentatious lament whenever a member lapsed into matrimony, an act that became known within the group as "joining the majority." Thus, the minutes record the confession of William Andrews: " amid the cheers and groans of the various members he proceeded to confess that treasonable designs long cherished in his heart were advancing to their fulfillment and that before another year had begun he expected to flop over to the majority" Such announcements were greeted with a cacophonous dirge played on worn-out musical instruments kept for such occasions. Eventually, Wilbur was the group's lone remaining bachelor; his singleness drew running comment in the club's records. One year he reported "no wife at present." The next, minutes referred to " Wilbur Wright, who came as usual without his wife."

Before entering the bicycle trade, the Wright Brothers were demon cyclists. Of one trip, Wilbur wrote, "just as we came into Miamisburg we coasted a hill fully a half-mile long and steep — whew!... we came down a-flying." Medals shown were won by Orville in local competitions.

The club's other members were settling. At the dinner held in late 1893, William Andrews reported he was "still selling groceries for bread and butter for one of the best wives the town can produce." Wilbur Landis announced, "I am the happy father of a bouncing baby boy." They had found their niches: Landis was still a printer; Charles Alinger still an NCR machinist; Frank Gilbert still a photographer. They settled; Wilbur still bounced around. He had been a clerk in a neighborhood grocery, a mailing agent for a religious publication, a job printer and a newspaper publisher. Matrimonial prospects were bleak. At that same 1893 dinner, Wilbur reported to the club secretary, "There is so little prospect of an increase in my family that the fox horns, trombones, dingbats, etc., which the club formerly kept for case of emergency are rusted, covered with dust." Still, Wilbur had news on the business front. "About the beginning of April," he reported, "I embarked in the bicycle business and though times have been very hard and prices very unsteady, I have escaped bankruptcy."

A month prior to the 1893 dinner, Wilbur and Orville attended the Columbian Exposition in Chicago. Among its other attractions, the Exposition played host to a small but eager conference of those who believed that heavier-than-air human flight was possible. That conference ended before the Wrights arrived at Chicago, and there is no reason to believe they were aware of its existence.

Patterson laid out five tons of chicken, 400 bushels of celery, 2,000 pounds of halibut and "other provisions in the same proportion," then invited 10,000 NCR employees and Dayton citizens to what he termed "a little garden party." The meal polished off, the throng loosened its collective belt, sat back and puffed on the 22,000 cigars while the NCR president presented a 500-slide show of his recent trip around the world.

the philanthropist

One Saturday afternoon in 1897 a young girl fainted in a sewing class run by a church settlement worker in Dayton.

Visiting the girl's home, the church worker found that her father was in the workhouse, the larder was empty and the girl had fainted from simple hunger. The church worker, a young Antioch College graduate named Lena Harvey Tracy, supplied a basket of food, then took the mother, a Mrs. Morrow, to search for employment. They walked three miles to National Cash Register Company, where Tracy had heard work might be had in the company kitchen. They crossed the wide lawn outside the main NCR building, a sleek steel-framed structure surfaced largely with glass. Inside, they were directed to the employment office. There, an employment officer confirmed that work as a dishwasher was available, paying $5.50 a week.

Tracy later wrote: "Mrs. Morrow and I looked at each other. 'If that is all,'" Tracy told the employment officer, "'I'm afraid she will have to look elsewhere. She has a family to support.'" As the two women rose to leave, the officer stopped them, requested Tracy's card and excused himself. Some while later he returned to say, "Her wages will be $8.50 a week, and she may come tomorrow."

On departing, Tracy wrote, "We looked up with increased interest and admiration at the beautiful main building. The sunshine was pouring in at the windows and making the yellow painted steel between look like gold. The on the other side of the fence made this factory seem almost unbelievably inviting." Subsequently, Tracy learned the higher wage had been authorized by John H. Patterson, who the employment officer had left the room to consult.

That naive, idyllic image — the welcoming factory, the kindly owner — stood in staggering contrast to the conditions then prevailing in American industry. Industrialism had built the machine, then made machine-like those who tended it. Historian Daniel Rodgers writes, "From the children... dropping metal caps in place one per second on the cannery assembly lines, to the women shoe workers who each day fed upward of three thousand shoes through their stitching and eyeleting machines, to the tired and grimy men who stoked and fed and were maimed in appalling numbers by the iron and steel furnaces, such workers formed the core of the factory labor force." Pioneer social worker Jane Addams cited a larger woe. The factory worker, she wrote, "has a grievance beyond being overworked and disinherited, in that he does not know what it is all about," That is, not only was work drudgery, it was drudgery divorced from any apparent broader object. For those who toiled, the consequence was, in Randolph Bourne's phrase, "a smoldering apathy toward work."

Patterson's workers shared that apathy; by 1893 that smoldering turned into acts of arson. The following year, a $50,000 shipment of cash registers was returned from England as defective: acid — apparently poured into their gearing mechanisms by an aggrieved employee — was the cause. The ruined shipment represented several weeks' production. With characteristic directness, John H. Patterson moved his desk to the factory floor to learn what was behind the trouble.

It proved an epiphany. As Patterson later told a biographer, his workers "had no heart in their jobs; they did not care whether they turned out good or bad work. Then I looked further into conditions and I had frankly had to confess to myself that there was no particular reason why they should put heart into their work." He asked the workers for complaints, and got them. The place was too dirty, one said. Lockers were few and given only to workers favored by the foreman. The wash water was filthy by the time the night shift came on duty. Patterson claimed to have responded with this mathematical sense of equity: "All men should have the same kind of water to wash in; if one man has clean water, all men should have clean water; if one man has dirty water, all men should have dirty water. There is no reason why all should not have clean water. We will put in the wash-basins tonight." The basins were installed, with Patterson remaining to see the job done.

In the workplace, Patterson — always looking for new lands to influence — discovered an America right under his nose. In the ensuing months, a wage increase was granted, dirt and debris were removed, dangerous equipment shielded, fans installed to draw off the metal dust of grinding. Lockers were set up for all workers, free showers followed lockers, along with free brushes and combs — collected, washed and sterilized each day at company expense. Patterson proceeded with no particular plan. Once, he spotted a woman worker heating what Patterson took to be a gluepot on a radiator; it seemed, he told a subordinate, an awkward way to do things. It wasn't glue, he was told; she was heating her coffee. Patterson opened a company cafeteria, serving hot lunches for a nickel; a medical dispensary and a dental unit followed. As ever, Patterson was a bit compulsive. He had a study made of the work hours lost due to colds during the rainy season. Thenceforth, women workers heading home in rainstorms were handed company umbrellas, to be returned in the morning. To combat malnourishment, he had each employee weighed every six months; those found underweight were issued free malted milk each morning between nine and ten. In one year, 26,000 pounds of the powder was distributed.

Behind the era's appalling factory conditions was the knowledge that, with labor cheap and tasks routine, workers could easily be replaced from industrialism's "reserve army" of the unemployed. Rare in his own time — and still at issue today — Patterson proceeded in the belief that better working conditions returned more in raised productivity and higher quality than they cost to create. Initially piecemeal, his "welfare program" grew to encompass three broad objects: to engender self-respect, to broaden interest in the world beyond work, and to stimulate ambition.

Patterson, perhaps a bit sententiously, told a biographer, "The first step toward self-respect is decent living and working conditions. A man cannot come out of a hovel, have a dirty breakfast, go into a dark, noisome factory, and then do a good day's work." The shielded equipment, free showers and umbrellas contributed to better working conditions; so, too, did a new architecture. Patterson commissioned industrial architect Frank Andrews to design a series of "glass factories" — the first of which was the building admired by church worker Lena Harvey Tracy — which allowed most work to be done in natural light; then, he retained the landscaping firm headed by Frederick Law Olmsted, the designer of New York's Central Park, to lay out the factory grounds.

Factory conditions improved, Patterson proceeded on two further ideas: work would improve, he believed, when his workers took an interest in the world beyond the factory and when they had something to stimulate their ambition. To stimulate interest, NCR established a night school, a free lending library and built the 2,000-seat "Schoolhouse" auditorium, where lectures, movies, slide shows and concerts were presented each noon-hour. To stimulate ambition, Patterson turned to the lure in which he had the most faith: money. In 1895, he instituted one of the earliest of suggestion systems, with cash prizes to those who contributed ideas useful to the company. Thus, the following year, a $50 prize and a trip to Chicago were awarded to Rosa Stuckey, an employee of the indicator department. There, inks were hand-strained through bolting cloth, a process that led to enlarged joints on the hands of those who did the work. Stuckey sketched the design of a machine she thought could do the work instead. "I thought the thing out," she reported in a company publication. "I may have read about other things like it, but I cannot think that I ever saw a machine like this. But I have heard, or read, that wine is made by a machine, which holds the pulps, etc., of the grape and throws the juice out." For the company, Patterson said, the suggestion system prompted workers to take a proprietorial interest in their jobs. Perhaps as important, it gave workers an avenue out of the anonymity of mass production; as one winner put it, "I think the best thing about the Suggestion System is that it makes a man known."

Patterson's reforms were more popular with the day's reformers than with Patterson's fellow businessmen. Indeed, one visiting journalist sniffed, "I can't see that you people are any better off than kept women." Jane Addams, by contrast, saw NCR under Patterson as at least a partial realization of her belief that the disinherited worker could be brought within a shared factory "family." She attended an NCR event, where — with employee families on hand and free sandwiches and lemonade provided — suggestion system winners were honored, sales results announced, and a slide show presented on those countries recently brought within NCR's sales orbit. "At least for the moment," Addams wrote, "there is complete esprit de corps, and the youngest and least skilled employee sees himself in connection with the interests of the firm." National Cash Register, she added, was "the most noteworthy attempt to utilize democracy of commerce in relation to manufacturing." Patterson insisted that philanthrophy played no part in the program: it cut turnover, raised productivity and reduced shoddy work. Its motivation was proclaimed on placards posted through the premises, placards that read, "It pays."

If Patterson continued to push the margins, it was because the margins pushed back. His factory sat in a Dayton neighborhood known as Slidertown — a dreary expanse so named, supposedly, because all that failed in Dayton eventually slid there. The wide panes of glass that let his workers toil in sunlight were attracting the attention of rock throwing youths. To protect his turf, Patterson set out to improve the neighborhood. In 1897, he hired Lena Harvey Tracy, the church settlement worker, to direct welfare efforts at the factory; next, he extended her responsibilities to the neighborhood.

The local youths, a later company publication stated, were "Not bad boys. Just boys with nothing to do." This void Tracy filled. She captured the attention of the rock throwers by offering to let them use the "House of Usefulness" — the dreary name Patterson affixed to his neighborhood settlement center — as headquarters for a club. Informed that a club must have a purpose, the boys adopted the statement, "No boy can belong to the N.C.R. Boys' Club who smokes tobacco in any form." Broadening their scope, they proscribed beer as well. Organized, they were now redirected. An acre and a half of factory grounds were plowed up, divided into garden plots and offered to the boys; forty at first. Eventually, hundreds of children of both sexes took part. The gardeners were given seed, tools and instruction from an NCR gardener, who taught them to double-sow beets with onions and beans with peas. Some grew for sale; some grew for home; some grew for the cash prizes NCR offered to the best gardens, prizes distributed by President Patterson after the harvest. Two years as a gardener earned a boy a certificate and promotion to the Boys' Box Furniture Company, where discarded packing crates and other factory scrap were turned into bird houses, footstools and other objects for sale.

"I learned five valuable lessons in the boys' gardens:
1. The value of a dollar.
2. To work.
3. To be precise.
4. To overcome difficulties.
5. To co-operate."

— an ex-boy gardener.

The boys occupied, Patterson turned to the larger community. While in Dayton, John C. Olmsted had designed a few model yards for the neighborhood, showing Patterson how inexpensively a rundown property could be made attractive with landscaping and a coat of paint. Patterson set out to demonstrate this to Slidertown. He offered advice — residents were to pull down ugly fences, plant trees and flower beds and grow vines on woodsheds and fenceposts. He presented slide shows — the dreary before and the inviting after accomplished by landscaping. Advice failed, example helped, cash worked best: annual prizes for the best-kept premises, the best window boxes, the best vine planting, the best landscaping.

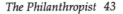

"There is really very little in the present industrial regimes," E. L. Godkin wrote, "to stimulate intelligence, excite the ambition, and sweeten the toil of ordinary mortals." John H. Patterson, a straw in the wind, created the very working conditions whose absence Godkin deplored.

The prizes were awarded according to three precepts a landscape gardener at Harvard had passed on to Patterson: plant in masses, leave open centers, avoid straight lines. Patterson told Tracy, "Upon those rules for a garden we will base the giving of our prizes." Soon, hundreds of Slidertown families, motivated by neighborly rivalry and Patterson's cash, were clearing away trash, reclaiming their yards and introducing massed plantings that left open centers while avoiding straight lines.

Patterson's programs expanded both within and without the factory. By 1899, NCR was operating Dayton's first kindergarten, a Sunday school, a savings bank for children, playgrounds, cooking and sewing classes for girls and women, girls' and boys' clubs, an Advance Club for women, a Progress Club for men and a Boy's Brigade. Over 4,000 employees, family members and neighboring residents were involved in these and dozens of other activities — including the dancing school, the autoharp society and the all-janitor glee club. The Sunday school offered nondenominational services and lectures on subjects close to Patterson's heart: health, travel and landscape gardening. As enrollment increased, the program was moved into the factory. Lena Harvey Tracy gives this description:

> It was an inspiring and really beautiful sight on a summer Sunday to see one hundred and fifty uniformed boys from the Brigade lined up in the factory yard, while thirty-four classes waited under their assigned shade trees to fall in line for march into the factory. When Mr. Patterson, with his children, Frederick and Dorothy, got off the streetcar, it was the signal for the procession to move, with Mr. Patterson, his children and the superintendent in the lead. The factory doors opened for us promptly at half past two. As we entered, each of us received a copy of the school paper, "Pleasant Sunday Afternoons at the National Cash Register Factory," and then our march continued to the third floor of the building where we were met by the Boys' Orchestra and a chorus of thirty from the Girls' Club. Half an hour was given over to a service of song, prayer and responsive reading, after which the classes separated to go to various offices and smaller rooms for their lessons.

At times, Patterson seemed less a businessman than a Protestant padrone, running some peculiar combination of welfare state and estancia, with himself at its mildly pietistic helm. Theoretically, a child born near the factory could attend the NCR kindergarten, deposit his or her life's first earnings in the company's Penny Bank, raise broccoli as a child gardener, build bird houses in the box furniture business and receive thereby the diploma that was a virtual

However much Patterson terrified his executives, he was viewed as benevolent by those on the assembly line, one of whom wrote: "Some time in his life he saw a picture of the working man and working woman, and he did what Lincoln did. He clenched his fist and set his jaw and said he will give industrial slavery a stoke that will wipe it off the earth," To many, Patterson was a champion of labor; when labor wanted its own champions, it formed unions.

guarantee of future employment with the "Cash." Once in NCR's employ, he or she had lectures, a lending library and a night school to stimulate the mind; a suggestion system and, later, a profitsharing plan to stimulate ambition; and a 300-acre employee park in which to stimulate the body, which, if undernourished, would be rejuvenated through daily doses of the company's malted milk.

By the close of the century, Patterson's employees were among the best treated in America: paid well, toiling in safe conditions and with an extensive list of benefits to choose from. Patterson regarded himself as a benefactor of labor; he expected labor to be friendly in return. Unions, he acknowledged, were often necessary things for workers whose employers were less enlightened than he. In 1901, an NCR foreman challenged any who wanted a union to step across a line. Seventeen did so — and were subsequently fired. Several hundred other workers walked off their jobs. Patterson's response was to lock out all 2,300 of his employees, and to keep them locked out until appropriate apologies were forthcoming.

Group exercises to start the day; mid-morning malted milk, lunch-time speakers, umbrellas on rainy days, "owl" classes in the evening — NCR took the precepts of "welfare capitalism" and pushed them to the hilt.

the farmboy

During the 1880s, half the townships in Ohio lost population. On the farm, mechanization was making for surplus hands, and those thus freed for a look around looked to go to town. The land was losing its hold, particularly on those young and ambitious. Too much was happening elsewhere, too much of which those who remained on the farm would not be a part.

From the fields of his father's farm two dozen miles southwest of Dayton, a young James Cox gauged his prospects in life and found them wanting: "In the middle of the forenoon, while I was following the plow, I would often see one of the neighborhood schoolteachers starting to work, and about four in the afternoon, while I still had long hours of toil ahead of me, I would see the teacher coming home." Teachers' hours looked better than farmers', so Cox took and passed the examination that landed him a teacher's post in a rural school. Teaching brought him near Middletown, where his brother-in-law edited *The Middletown Weekly Signal*. Cox took a side job as a newspaper delivery boy. Soon, he abandoned chalk dust for printer's ink; when the *Signal* went daily, Cox signed on as its local reporter.

The Middletown Signal was a sorry sheet — not nearly so well written or edited as the Wrights' newspaper. *The Signal's* front page was largely taken up by "boilerplate" — stale, formulaic accounts delivered to the newspaper on ready-to-print cast forms — and by such items as a report on an experiment that "will probably add to the medical literature the fact that the skin of a col-

turning white." James Cox's province was page three, local news. This he covered with energy, verve and no small wish to antagonize his elders. His account of one city council meeting began: "The first thing council should have done last night but did not, was to make some provision for a janitor.... The council should take turns, and with mop and broom attempt to find the linoleum that was laid down on the floor of the Mayor's office some years ago."

One longer piece of reporting shows Cox's style. He opens his story by telling the reader that several weeks previously his attention had been drawn to a party of three — one young woman, two men — staying at Middletown's Central Hotel. Curious, Cox had inquired who they were, but "the landlord's stating that he knew the parties prevented any further investigation." That visit, Cox now reports, was for the purpose of performing what proved to be an illegal and fatal abortion: "Mrs. Laura Kelly, a bride of but a few weeks, died from the effects of a criminal abortion performed at the Central Hotel in this city by Dr. W. P. Webb, of Eaton. The city is greatly excited. It is quite a place for lynching, and Webb may get justice meted out at the hands of a vigilance committee."

Cox recounts the courtship between Laura Jones, the "bright, vivacious and handsome" daughter of Eaton's postmaster, and Charles Kelly, "a well known, popular and highly respected young man of the same city." Kelly, Cox reports, "evidently was not a Platonic lover and the girl soon became enciente from the result of undue relations." To prevent disclosure, the couple decided upon the abortion; they then returned home, were wed "and received the congratulations of their many devoted and unsuspecting friends." Three weeks later the bride died "in extreme agony." Cox supplies the denouement:

> The cause of her death was the topic of conversation, and when the truth became known, the indignation of the citizens knew no bounds, the young husband in despair and grief endeavored to suicide, the girl's father on hearing the news swooned away and remained unconscious for several hours, while [Dr.] Webb skipped for parts unknown ...and had the people of Eaton gotten their hands on him, Judge Lynch [i.e., a lynch mob] would have presided at a solemn meeting.

The Wrights entered journalism to maintain a smaller world; James Cox did so to enter a larger one. Entree came in 1894, when, after his work covering the news in Middletown, he landed a berth as railway reporter for *The Cincinnati Enquirer*. There, Cox learned that in his new pond, he was a small fish. A business leader took exception to something Cox had written and pulled strings to have him bounced from the paper. The discharge left Cox dangling: he had recently married, and now had no assured income. In Horatio Alger's world, the hero in crisis is often aided by a surrogate father. Such aid was now forthcoming for Cox. His benefactor was Paul Sorg, the leading manufacturer in Middletown, who had sized Cox up as a likely lad when Cox was writing for *The Signal*. A special election was sending Sorg to Washington as Middletown's congressman; Sorg offered — and Cox accepted — the post of aide in the congressman's Washington office.

In his account of the fatal abortion, Cox nowhere attempted to justify his or his newspaper's intrusion into the misfortune. Indeed, he was by his own account a bit laggard. Had he not accepted the hotelkeeper's assurances that all was all right, he wrote, "a death may have been averted." In this intrusiveness, Cox was at ease with the emerging spirit of American journalism.

America was settled, Arthur Schlesinger, Sr. wrote, by church, school and press — the church linked men to God, the schoolhouse to a common culture, the newspaper to currency with the events of the day. From this description one takes the image of the country editor, begrimed with ink and random vituperation, culling the dispatches for items to bring to the attention of his readers. Post-Civil War, urban newspapers boomed — along with the cities whose rising populations they served. The urban press was personal, flamboyant, melodramatic. In 1872, James Gordon Bennett, Jr. of *The New York Herald* dispatched Henry Morten Stanley, who wasn't an explorer, to find Dr. David Livingston, who wasn't lost, then held his readers breathless with the unfolding of this non-event. Over at the *Sun*, editor Charles Dana dismissed Winfield Hancock, the 1880 Democratic nominee, as "a good man, weighing 240 pounds." While at Joseph Pulitzer's *World*, city editor Charles Chapin — confronted by a reporter who had been beaten up and bounced out by an intended interview subject — exclaimed, "You go back and tell that son-of-a-bitch he can't intimidate me."

The newspaper boom was fed by technology — the Mergenthaler Linotype and high-speed presses. The biggest change was the work of a Civil War general named Tilghman and a German chemist named Dahl, who developed inexpensive ways to turn wood pulp into paper. Cheap newsprint and big audiences produced big, cheap newspapers. As one New York City reporter summarized it, "The fundamental principle of metropolitan journalism is to buy white paper at three cents a pound and sell it at ten cents a pound." Increasingly, that paper was covered with scandal and sensation. Flamboyant journalism built large circulations; large circulations built big businesses: James Cox would ride the former trend to prominence and the latter to wealth.

Cox left for Washington an unfrocked reporter; after several broadening years in the nation's capital, he returned to Ohio as a newspaper editor. That jump in station was the handiwork of Paul Sorg. After finishing out the term to which he was elected and serving another, Sorg decided to step down from Congress; still, he looked to his protege's future. In 1898, Sorg put up $6,000 of the $26,000 Cox needed to buy *The Daily News*, then helped line up local investors to bankroll the remainder. Cox had wanted sole ownership, but Sorg's view prevailed: the surest way to interest prominent men in your success, he argued, was to borrow their money. The newspaper Cox acquired was a weak entry in a weak field. The previous ownership claimed 7,500 subscribers; once the sale was made, however, only 2,600 could be found. The staff was small. Finances were shaky. Cox later wrote, "The bookkeeper was once asked how much business we would have to carry to break even. His figures seemed to confuse him, but he finally said that if we had no news and every column was filled with advertising we would lose $500 a week."

Sorg had wanted backers; Cox, twenty-eight, wanted a target. Soon, he found one: Dr. Joseph E. Lowes. Lowes headed the local Republican organization, through which he dominated Dayton politics. His rule had a mercenary edge: Lowes used his hold over the city council to steer charters for utility operations and interurban lines to companies he controlled. His position was secured through an electoral fluke: the National Soldiers' Home. There, the 5,000 disabled Union veterans in residence voted for the party of Lincoln and Grant by margins so wide that even in lean years Lowes' candidates were generally returned to office.

Cox started spreading charges across his front page. He alleged that a utility Lowes controlled was gouging the public on street lighting. That Lowes coerced local firms into bringing business to him under threat of retaliation from officeholders under his sway. That Lowes had illegally gained a tax refund. That he tried to extort $50,000 from a private investor. The ins and outs of the alleged financial skullduggery were murky, but no reader could miss the import of the editorial cartoons Cox ran four columns wide every day on page one. Lowes was a presentable, plumpish man of middle years. In Cox's four-column wide front page cartoons, he was presented as dissolute, stubble on cheek and whip in hand, planting his foot on the head of a Republican elephant. Then, he was a swine, snout-deep in swill buckets labeled "political favoritism." Next, a coward, hurdling a picket fence to escape a bulldog labeled "public wrath." Then, a frightened old woman, bracing herself against closet doors from which political skeletons emerged. When a Republican paper took to Lowes' defense, Cox denounced it as "the bootlicking organ of the vulgar boss" and his cartoonist added a new figure, that of a jackass labeled "The Evening Apologist."

While the attack on Lowes went forward, Cox revamped the rest of his newspaper. He banned the stale, ready-to-print boilerplate from his pages, then filled his columns with fresher, fuller news accounts. *The News* expanded wire

I AM THE DOCTOR

You didn't have to
read the news
stories to follow
the plot; the
cartoon's message
was clear:
Dr. J. E. Lowes was
a public menace —
a coward, a tyrant,
a swine and, best
of all, a great
circulation builder.

*Cartoon originally
appeared
October 14, 1898.*

G.O.P.

"Dr. J. E. Lowes Is a Leader, Not a Boss." (The Evening Apologist.)

service coverage, printed more timely stock market quotations and hired Dayton's first women's page editor. Cox's editorship took on the frenetic, insular quality of a political campaign, in which he was both candidate and campaign manager. He later recalled: "I read all the copy, looked after make-up, answered the business correspondence and kept an eye on details, writing my editorials after dinner at night." In those editorials, Cox unblushingly claimed the high ground, raining denunciations down on Lowes: "It is the rights of the people that we advocate, the cause of justice which we champion, and being conscious of the rectitude of our intentions,... we will continue to portray [Lowes'] real character until his baneful influence is destroyed." Almost as an afterthought, Cox added: "There has been no personal abuse of any man in these columns."

Lowes thought otherwise. After weeks of seeing himself gracing Cox's front page as a swine, a bore, a tyrant, a manipulator and a coward, the Republican boss filed suit for libel. Specifically, he claimed the allegations of extortion and of illegal tax refunds were untrue and libelous. Lowes' suit was filed four days before the November election; Cox — terming his adversary "a thirsty leech" — urged county voters to return a verdict of their own at the polling place. The day before the election, the editor pulled out all the stops, with a front page filled with Lincoln, God and Cox's own most purple prose. In a quarter-page drawing, the Great Emancipator beseeched local voters not to let "government of... by... and for the people, perish from the earth." An adjacent headline announced: "Ministers Admonish Their Hearers to Act as God-Fearing Citizens; and wipe out all corruption in official life." And Cox, in a large-type editorial, told voters it was their "solemn duty" to correct "the abuses imposed on our fair city by a boss." He added that only those who would entrust local government to a man devoid of heart, conscience, shame, honesty or patriotism could vote for Lowes' candidates.

Which they did. Despite Cox's charges and fulminations, all seven Lowes-backed candidates won office.

Two months later, James Cox pleaded guilty to libeling Dr. J. E. Lowes. The editor paid a fine of one dollar. It was a dollar well spent. The attack on Lowes had helped make the *Daily News* the local newspaper to read. Circulation, and even advertising, were rising. A month after the election, Cox was on to other matters. *The News*, "following its constant policy of doing all within its power to assist the people," invited readers unhappy with their trash collection to write the newspaper with their complaints; the paper would take them to the attention of the authorities.

For Cox, challenging authority was good business and risky enough to be interesting. Soon after the assault on Lowes, *The News* charged that the owner of a local interurban line was attempting to use political influence to gain a more favorable right-of-way. By filing criminal libel charges against the newspaper and posting bond, the accused owner was able to have the county sheriff close and padlock the *News* office. The city's afternoon papers rushed out editions announcing the *News* had been shut down. Unbeknownst to the sheriff's deputies on guard outside the front door, Cox's staff was still inside, working on that afternoon's paper. Meanwhile, Cox secured from a supporter funds sufficient to post a redelivery bond and have the padlocks removed. Thirty minutes after his rivals announced the shutdown, Cox's paper was on the streets, proof positive the *News* was still in business.

It was great *Front Page* journalism — combative and arrogant and plenty legal enough. By 1900, the journal that had been nearly insolvent when Cox took control was Dayton's leading paper. That only added to Cox's self-confidence. Locally, he became known as "Coxsure" — as one critic explained, "for hair-trigger certain he is each day, though his next day's certainty may belie all that went before." He could afford to be certain. When Cox took over the newspaper, he had not wanted backers; now, in 1900, he dispensed with them — negotiating a series of personal notes, he bought the original investors out. *The Daily News* was now his. At thirty, Cox no longer needed to answer to anyone.

Build a better cash register, and the world will beat a path to your door. NCR was forerunner to the modern transnational corporation, doing business around the clock and around the globe. What else but cash registers could have brought delegations from France, Germany and elsewhere to this 1898 sales conference, held in Dayton's Victoria Theatre.

the businessman abroad

Answering to no one was something John H. Patterson had been doing for years. His view of things was essentially simple: he believed people could be moved to conformance by hope of reward or fear of punishment; he also believed that, whoever they were, they were at hazard to the open cash drawer. It was a flat view, but it traveled. In 1902, the NCR president boarded the *S. S. St. Paul* and sailed for Europe. His itinerary included England — there to witness the coronation of Edward VII — thence to Berlin, to preside at his company's European sales conference. He sailed with a larger purpose. Patterson was a convinced Anglophile: Boston he held was by rights the proper model for all America, but England was the mold from which Boston had been sprung. In England, he wrote, he intended to learn "how this great business enterprise — the British nation — is managed. I have often wondered how a little island out in the sea, with many disadvantages, grew to be the centre of so great an empire."

In England, Patterson saw much to praise, in no small measure because he saw much that reminded him of his own efforts. Visiting a country home, he noted approvingly, "the principles of open spaces, the massing of trees and shrubbery, and the avoidance of straight lines, are all observed," just as Olmsted had taught in Dayton. Attending a review of the British fleet, he concluded, "I believe that a business ought to be like a battleship in many respects — in cleanliness, in order, in the perfect discipline of the men.... I believe that our factory ought to be as orderly, as neat, and as clean as our men-of-war." Descending upon an NCR branch office on London's Oxford Street, Patterson found his hope realized: "I entered the building. Our office throughout, from garret to cellar, reminded me of the battleship in its order, its cleanliness, in the freshness and whiteness of the paint."

Patterson reached the wholly satisfying conclusion that England's glory, like his own, was a consequence of moral grandeur. England, he wrote, "has been for centuries, and still remains, the great civilizer of the world. I believe that her prestige rests on the good that she is doing to the world, and I believe that our strength lies in the good we are doing in the world." Good, of course, required the judicious use of force. Here, Patterson found a further parallel. After attending a military review at Aldershot, he concluded that the British army and the NCR sales force had much in common: "The chief duty they have is to fight; ours, to get orders."

NCR had been getting orders from overseas since 1886, when the company retained its first foreign sales agent, an Englishman. Soon, NCR agents were working their ways from grocer to beer garden throughout Europe and South America. In 1897, Patterson spent two months in Europe, where he descended upon fifty cities in fifteen countries to put some spine into his overseas operations. In Moscow, he inquired why hundreds of cannon barrels were stacked inside the walls of the Kremlin. The barrels, he was told, had been abandoned by Napoleon during his retreat; their display stood as warning to others of the folly of invasion. Patterson thought this a grand idea. Back in Dayton, he matched the Kremlin's display with one of his own. In a dimly-lit company hall — generally known as "the gloom room" — he piled up cash registers made by companies gone bankrupt challenging NCR. There, with nameplates rusting and springs twisted and popped, the ruined equipment stood, Patterson wrote, as "a warning to other people of what they may expect under the circumstances." Patterson did the Russians one better. Potential adversaries of the Czar had to find their way to the Kremlin to view the detritus of Napoleon's defeat; Patterson, on the other hand, paid mileage. He sent competitors free rail tickets so that, at no out-of-pocket cost, they could come and view the fate to which God and a just Patterson had consigned them.

At the Kremlin Patterson had found something to learn; more generally, he went abroad to instruct. Along with cash registers, NCR exported in wholesale lots the business methods that built and sold its machines. While currency denominations were adapted to local standards — Patterson's registers rang up sales in marks, lira, pounds, kronen, francs, gulden and, in British India, rupees — the machines and the methods for selling them were the same in Dusseldorf as in Dayton. To Patterson's thinking, since the temptations posed by the open cash drawer knew no boundary, NCR must be internationalist in response. In his letter from London, he admonished his American employees: "Let us not forget that our interests are closely identified with the interests of other civilized countries, and our prosperity is dependent upon their prosperity. Everything that helps them helps us, and all that hurts them hurts the prosperity of our Company. Half our orders will soon be coming from countries other than the United States."

Under Patterson, NCR became not an American company operating abroad, but an international organization. He respected local sensibilities. NCR operated under local names — thus, in Belgium, it was incorporated as La Nationale Caisse Enregistreuse. In each country, NCR all but entirely employed local nationals to manage, sell and repair. When potential European customers objected that the cash register was a "foreign" product, Patterson flanked their concern by opening a full-scale production facility on the Alte Jacobstrasse in Berlin. Patterson respected nationality because nationality didn't matter. The distinction between what it meant to be an Englishman and what it meant to be an Italian was largely dissolved in the new inclusion Patterson offered: what it meant to be an NCR salesman. Thus, in Norway, a sales agent was unloading a cash register from a small boat docked at a town where he was scheduled to meet a prospect. His grip slipped and the register plunged into the water. The salesman called to mind not some pungent Scandinavian oath, but instead the lines he had learned at NCR training school:

If you strike a thorn or rose,
Keep a-goin'.

Buoyed by this bit of American success litany, the salesman hoisted the register out of the water, dried and oiled its mechanisms, replaced its soggy paper labels, met his prospective purchaser — and made the sale.

Such intrepidness would have brought applause at the Berlin sales conference Patterson attended after leaving England. There, his precepts for success were spoken as a second language. Near the close of the conference, Patterson handed out prizes to the winners in a sales contest. Each recipient briefly cited the reasons for his achievement. The first-place winner attributed his victory to "love for the business, and faith in it." The second-place finisher cited "the merit of our machines; hard work and self denial." A runner-up touched all bases; his success, he said, was the result of:

1. Following N. C. R. instructions.
2. Industry.
3. Never giving up.
4. Always trying again.

These three salesmen were, respectively, a Russian, an Italian and a German. The evening ended with a song, lyrics composed for the occasion and sung to the tune of the American standard whose chorus begins, "Daisy, Daisy."

En masse, NCR's European salesmen stood and sang: "Quota, Quota."

In his letter home from Berlin, Patterson wrote: "The character of the singing made us realize how general musical cultivation is here in Germany."

"The human bird shall take his first flight, filling the world with amazement, all writings with his fame, and bringing eternal glory to the nest whence he sprang."

— *Leonardo da Vinci*

the miracle

Wilbur Wright was a writer of exceptional clarity and grace. By family accounts, he wrote easily, producing long, clear letters in a single draft. On May 13, 1900, Wilbur wrote to Octave Chanute a letter beginning: "For some years I have been afflicted with the belief that flight is possible to man." With that letter Wilbur announced he was entering the flight game. Chanute was a goateed sixty-six year old and a notable engineer — the first to span the Missouri River by bridge and the designer of the Chicago Stockyards. More to the point, he was a glider experimenter whose 1894 book, *Progress in Aviation*, was the best available summary of man's attempts to fly, attempts Chanute tracked through an international correspondence. Along with Samuel Pierpont Langley, the head of the Smithsonian Institution, Chanute gave the idea that heavier-than-air flight was possible the only fig-leaf of reputability it enjoyed in the United States.

Wilbur was entering the flight game just as that game appeared played out. At the turn of the century, British aviation writer Charles Gibbs-Smith writes those few trying to fly could be grouped into "chauffeurs" and "birds." The former imagined the flying machine "as a winged extension of the automobile, to be driven off the ground and chauffeured in churning progression through the air." As an advocate of this approach, inventor Sir Hiram Maxim spent $100,000 on a four-ton steam-powered machine: in its principal test, the craft managed to lift itself — or bounce — several inches off the ground. In contrast to Maxim's leviathan, the "birds" argued that flight must be a thing of grace and ease. Their principal practitioner was a German engineer, Otto Lilienthal, who beginning in 1891 launched himself on 2,000 glides of a dozen seconds or less in canopy-like structures of his own design.

The idea that flight was motoring died hard. As late as 1907, *Flying Ma-*

chines: Past Present and Future offered the judgment that Maxim could have taken to the air in his machine, but "as he had not solved the question of maintaining equilibrium and steering," chose not to do so. To the chauffeurs, the prime challenge was simply to get off the ground; that accomplished, airborne navigation — "the question of maintaining equilibrium and steering" — would, they believed, prove easy. By contrast, the birds regarded in-air control as the first, not the final, problem of flight. Strapped into his canopy, Lilienthal attempted to exercise control by counteracting the play of the winds with rapid shifts of his lower body, which hung free below his glider. It was daring, awkward and fatal. On a glide in 1896, he lost control and crashed, snapping his spine. Three years later, Percy Pilcher, a British experimenter, died in similar circumstances. By Gibbs-Smith's reckoning, by 1900 only one serious experimenter in heavier-than-air aviation remained active in Europe.

Reputable opinion held that experiment failed because flight was impossible. In 1896, Lord Kelvin, the eminent British naturalist, declined an invitation to join the Aeronautical Society, saying: "I have not the smallest molecule of faith in aerial navigation other than ballooning, or of expectation of good results from any of the trials we hear of." Not even a writer so enthusiastic for technology as H. G. Wells held out great hope. In a series of predictions published in the *North American Review* in 1900, Wells said an aircraft would fly and return its operator safely to earth "probably before 1950."

Skepticism was well-founded, given the simple difficulty of the task. Compare the airplane to the automobile. For an automobile to operate, it must have a power source linked to wheels that can be turned for direction and stopped for safety. This it needn't do very well: early models were underpowered and top-heavy. Still, an underpowered, top-heavy automobile will run; an underpowered, top-heavy aircraft will not leave the ground. Aviation offers no halfway houses: the thing either flies, or it doesn't. For an aircraft to fly, all the requirements of flight must be simultaneously present and in proper relation to each other — a wing surface to create lift, a propulsion system to create thrust, a control system to permit command and, not least, a pilot competent in the use of those controls. Consider, too, the hazard of experiment. An automobile runs on solid ground; if it fails, it fails. Push it to the side of the road and wait for a tow. An airplane rides on thin air; if it fails, it falls. And the air currents are no easy ride. If, one student of the subject observed, a piece of paper is held parallel to the floor and released:

> It will not settle steadily down as a staid, sensible piece of paper ought to do, but it insists on contravening every recognized rule of decorum, turning over and darting hither and thither in the most erratic manner, much after the style of an untrained horse. Yet this is the style of

steed that men must learn to manage before flying can become an everyday sport.

That observation comes from Wilbur Wright. In 1903, most automobiles were underpowered and top heavy — sluggish on straightaways and unsettling on curves. And in 1903, Wilbur and Orville Wright flew. They did so with a rough, unforgiving machine that had neither cockpit nor carburetor, but it flew. All aviation to the present is based on the work of the Wrights. Flight was one of man's longest-standing fascinations. In the words of the Psalmist, "Oh, that I had wings like a dove; for then would I fly away and be at rest."

Orville and Wilbur created those wings. They did it in fifty-five months, working part-time.

How the Wrights achieved flight is one story; the question that precedes it is why they bothered to try. As children, they had been fascinated by a rubber-band-powered helicopter their father brought home as a toy; as young men, they had followed the gliding exploits of Lilienthal. Still, many play with toy helicopters or track the efforts of a famed sportsman without themselves ever seriously attempting to fly. In writing Chanute, Wilbur described himself as "afflicted." This he was, both in his belief that flight was possible and by his personal circumstance. Wilbur was not greatly fitted for neighborhood journalism — James Cox might loose a greased pig at a city council meeting just to write up the reactions; Wilbur Wright, the bishop's son, would more likely be appalled at the suggestion. Nor was he fitted to be a small-time bicycle maker and retail businessman. He was intellectually gifted, energetic, disciplined, broad of view. Something was lacking. Acknowledging this, Wilbur once wrote a relative: "I entirely agree that the boys of the Wright family are lacking in determination and push."

What pushed Wilbur into flight may have been this: he was thirty-three when he wrote Chanute; he may simply have been aware that he was running out of youth. Flight, as Wilbur wrote in a letter to his father, was "almost the only great problem which has not been pursued by a multitude of investigators, and therefore carried to a point where further progress is very difficult." Flight was an open field, one in which he might still do something of note. In his letter to Chanute, Wilbur shared his own thoughts on flight and sketched out the lines of investigation he planned to pursue. His close was modest:

> I make no secret of my plans for the reason that I believe no financial profit will accrue to the inventor of the first flying machine, and that only those who are willing to give as well as to receive suggestions can hope to link their names with the honor of discovery. The problem is

too great for one man alone and unaided to solve in secret.

Wilbur was right. No one man could do it. It also took Orville.

To the task of flight, Wilbur and Orville brought an array of abilities and, as events were to prove, the necessary ones. They were craftsmen. Their first flying machine — the one flown at Kitty Hawk in 1903 — may be viewed today in Washington from the floor of the Air and Space museum. Considered with more than a glance, it shows a fine meshing of innumerable parts, a simple excellence of detail. Years in printing and cycling trades gave the Wrights exacting eyes, precise hands and minds experienced in the properties of materials. Key to the success of their craft is that they built it themselves and could therefore be assured that it existed in fact as they imagined it. Their sister Katharine describes in a letter her brothers working in the family parlor on the covering for the wings: Orville on the floor marking the fabric for cutting; Wilbur at the sewing machine joining the pieces together — cut and sewn to fit over the wings on the bias, and therefore less likely to rip.

Craftsmanship aside, flight posed a considerable intellectual challenge. When designing the propellers for their first powered aircraft, the Wrights reached the following point in their reasoning:

> The thrust depends upon the speed and the angle at which the blade strikes the air; the angle at which the blade strikes the air depends upon the speed at which the propeller is turning, the speed the machine is traveling forward, and the speed at which the air is slipping backward; the slip of the air backwards depends upon the thrust exerted by the propeller, and the amount of air acted upon.

To the mastery of such questions, each brother brought a fine intelligence. More important, they brought each other. Each was a crisp, logical thinker; to this, each aided the other as a sparring partner. Powered flight presented a bramble of intricate problems. A solo researcher might easily become lost; Wilbur and Orville had each other as, by turns, stimulus, soundingboard and support, to argue through the problem each step of the way. "I like Orville," Wilbur told other family members. "Orville likes a good scrap."

Those family members constituted another asset. During the years they worked on flight, the brothers lived at home with their father Bishop Wright and their sister Katharine. No other family member contributed to the technical task of flight; still, the family's calm certitude that Orville and Wilbur would achieve what they had set out to achieve buoyed them through setback and confusion. Finally — and in good measure as an extension of their home and upbringing — the Wrights succeeded in flight because they were of good character. The letters written by either convey a sense of innate decency, integrity, modesty. It took character to put up with the mosquitoes and short rations at their camp at Kitty Hawk. It took character to sustain the sheer drudgery of invention — to do, for example, the thousands of mathematical equations their wind tunnel work required. It took character, as well, to maintain their personal equilibrium under the cascadings of fame that were theirs in 1908, when, five years after the fact, the world finally believed they could fly.

The abiding quality of the Wrights' conquest of flight was their fidelity to their task. Orville and Wilbur did not stray. They set themselves the task of creating a heavier-than-air craft, controllable by its operator and capable of carrying that operator forward through the air to a safe landing point at least as high as that from which the craft had been launched. Wilbur began by assessing the status of the problem. The year before he wrote Chanute announcing his entry to the field, Wilbur wrote to the Smithsonian Institution; describing himself as "an enthusiast, but not a crank," he requested a reading list on aviation. From this list, he systemically reviewed the literature in the field: what had been tried, why it had failed. This reading settled one thing: in the division between birds and chauffeurs, the Wrights always nested firmly with the former. Of their contemporaries in experiment, the Wrights held in the highest esteem the German glider experimenter Otto Lilienthal. That esteem was not shaken by Wilbur's conclusion that Lilienthal was fundamentally wrong in his approach, a conclusion he put forward in his first letter to Chanute.

Lilienthal was mistaken, Wilbur wrote, first, because his approach did not give him nearly enough in-air practice: in five years of gliding, the German had aggregated only five hours of actual flight time. Wilbur observed: "Even the simplest intellectual or acrobatic feats could never be learned with so short practice, and even Methuselah could never have become an expert stenographer with one hour per year for practice." Lilienthal was mistaken, second, because swinging his hips and legs was a woefully inadequate means of maintaining balance. The winds, playing upon the whole span of Lilienthal's wings, had far greater "leverage" in upsetting his craft than Lilienthal, however agile, had in righting it. Lilienthal's experiments were more than courageous; they were extraordinarily risky, as his death demonstrated. Safe experiment was, however, a requirement, Wilbur wrote: otherwise, the sheer hazard of the undertaking would preclude the accumulation of the knowledge needed for final success.

Wilbur and Orville Wright are often referred to as a pair of bicycle makers from Dayton, Ohio. West Third Street, to be exact. By the time Wilbur wrote Chanute, he and Orville had indeed been making and selling bicycles for half a dozen years. Identifying the Wrights as bicycle makers a bit patronizingly suggests a cleverness with mechanical things, as though all the conquest of flight required was a dollop of Midwestern ingenuity and, perhaps, some luck. Still, no background was as likely to prove useful to the question of flight, once properly understood, as that of bicycle making, once properly appreciated. Prior to the Wrights, experimenters had attempted to design craft that were "inherently stable" — that is, built so that their wings and other fixed parts acted automatically to keep the aircraft on course. They failed. As bicycle makers, the Wrights knew inherent stability was not a prerequisite to safe travel. A bicycle is not inherently stable: left to itself, it will topple over on the grass or pile into a shrub. Yet a bicycle may be ridden safely because the cyclist is able to correct its course and keep it balanced. The key to flight, Orville concluded, was to provide the aviator with the means of maintaining balance.

This, Lilienthal fatally lacked. But Wilbur offered Chanute more than a critique; he believed he had a remedy: "My observation of the flight of buzzards leads me to believe that they regain their lateral balance, when partly overturned by a gust of wind, by the torsion of the tips of their wings." This was the single most important observation the Wrights were to make: that a bird in flight rights itself by recourse to wingtip adjustments. Gusted from its line of flight so that its right wing is turned up, a bird twists its right wingtip down and its left wingtip up, then maintains that twist until level flight is restored. Appropriately, Wilbur was in the Wrights' bicycle shop when he hit upon a means of applying this "torsioning," which bore nature's seal of approval, to the question of airborne control. Talking with a customer, he idly twisted a long, thin cardboard box in his hands. He noticed that the sides of the box maintained their strength even when the box was twisted. He imagined two sides of the box to be the upper and lower wings of a biplane: the twisting torsioned the ends of these "wings," changing the angle at which the wingtips hit the wind. This, in theory, provided a means for control in flight. As Wilbur explained to Chanute: "Lateral equilibrium [control across the wingspan] is gained by moving one end more than the other or by moving them in opposite directions."

To test the idea, Wilbur and Orville built and Wilbur flew a biplane kite of five-foot wingspan. The kite had a double set of strings secured to its wingtips; with these, Wilbur attempted to maintain the kite's lateral equilibrium by adjusting the relationship between the wings. It worked. The Wrights called it "wing warping." This principle, that balance across the wingspan can be maintained by purposefully adjusting the angle of the wing, is, in the form of ailerons, used by all aircraft to this day.

For Wilbur, the eleven months between his letter to the Smithsonian and his letter to Chanute were extraordinarily productive: he reviewed the literature in the field, assessed how Lilienthal had gone wrong, identified equilibrium as the problem to be addressed and identified torsioning as a prospective solution. Not least, he gained Orville's enthusiastic collaboration on the work ahead. That work now focused on two requirements: first, to test "wing warping" on a glider large enough to carry a pilot; second, to create a test circumstance that permitted not the few rushing seconds Lilienthal experienced in gliding, but hour upon hour of riding the winds to give that pilot proficiency in flight.

In *Visions of a Flying Machine*, Peter Jakab stresses that the Wrights proceeded in the conquest of flight by creating a series of prototypes; each, when built, represented all they knew about aeronautics; each, when tested, became the means for learning more. The first of these, built in 1900, was a biplane glider with an eighteen-foot wingspan. Wing warping was achieved by wires that ran from the tips of the lower wing to a cradle at the wing's center; the pilot lay in that cradle, warping the wings by sliding the cradle side-to-side. The craft also had a small forward elevator, or movable wing, which the pilot could angle up or down in the wind. Also known as a canard wing, this was a feature of all the Wrights' experimental designs. Its inclusion showed both the Wrights' understanding of air navigation and regard for their own safety. The brothers judged that Lilienthal had been killed when his glider was turned abruptly upward by a gust of wind. They had no name for this phenomenon; today, pilots know it as "stall." Any aircraft has a minimum airspeed required to produce the lift needed to remain airborne; when a craft falls below this speed, it stalls. In effect, it ceases to fly; the pilot, at least temporarily, loses control. The Wrights' canard wing was a guard against this. The wing was deliberately set so it would strike the wind at an angle different than the main wing. The Wrights, believed, correctly, that in an incipient stall state, the canard wing would stall first. This would cause it to drop, thus pulling the main wing into a safer, more level, orientation. With their wings made, they sought a place to ride them.

The Wrights were drawn to Kitty Hawk, North Carolina by its combination of wind for lift, sand for soft landing and the boostering of William Tate. Tate was

Kitty Hawk's leading citizen — postmaster, notary public and county commissioner; he learned of the Wrights' interest in the area when Wilbur wrote the government weather station at Kitty Hawk to ask about wind and weather. Kitty Hawkers, Tate later wrote, believed "in a good God, a bad Devil, a hot Hell, and more than anything else... that the same good God did not intend that man should ever fly." Tate, however, believed in promoting the home turf. He wrote the Wrights that Kitty Hawk offered excellent conditions for their experiments, such as "a stretch of sandy land one mile by five with a bare hill in the center 80 feet high, not a tree or bush anywhere to break the evenness of the wind current." To these attractions, he added the promise of his own hospitality. Fortunately so; the Tates provided Wilbur with emergency food and lodging when he arrived at Kitty Hawk in early September, famished and bedraggled after days in travel, lugging with him all the pieces of the unassembled glider.

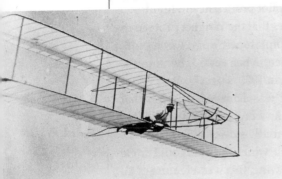

Orville arrived two weeks later; in the meanwhile, Wilbur pitched their tent, set up camp and began assembling the glider. It was smaller than intended. To ease travel, Wilbur had planned to purchase the eighteen-foot lengths of spruce to be used for the wing spars en route in Norfolk. No such wood was obtainable. Wilbur had to settle for sixteen-foot white pine, thus reducing the lifting area of the glider. At Kitty Hawk, he borrowed Mrs. Tate's sewing machine to alter the wing coverings to fit the smaller size. When the Wrights broke camp that year, Bill Tate requested and received salvage rights to the glider. His wife took the fabric back off the wings and, with the same sewing machine, sewed the wing coverings into dresses for the Tates' two daughters.

"I do not expect to rise many feet from the ground," Wilbur wrote his father before the first trip to Kitty Hawk, "and in case I am upset there is nothing but soft sand to strike on. I do not intend to take dangerous chances, both because I have no wish to get hurt and because a fall would stop my experimenting."

The Wrights' first visit to Kitty Hawk was not much more than a hobbyist's jaunt. Her brothers, Katharine noted, had not had a real vacation since they went to the Columbian Exposition in 1893; before departing — and perhaps expecting no great results — Wilbur wrote his father that at least they would get to see a new part of the country. They spent three weeks at Kitty Hawk, tenting out under a night sky so bright Orville could read his watch by starlight. Orville did the cooking — bacon and biscuits and coffee cooked and brewed on a gasoline stove, with hot meals ceasing whenever gasoline ran out. Wilbur washed the dishes — an inaccurate statement, as what he in fact did was scour them in the sand, which was endless. Orville wrote home:

> The sand is the greatest thing in Kitty Hawk, and soon will be the only thing. The site of our tent was formerly a fertile valley, cultivated by some ancient Kitty Hawker. Now only a few rotten limbs, the topmost branches of trees that then grew in this valley, protrude from the sand. The sea has washed and the wind blown millions and millions of loads of sand up in heaps along the coast, completely covering houses and

forest. Mr. Tate is now tearing down the nearest house to our camp to save it from the sand.

In their gliding efforts, the Wrights were knee-deep in Tates: Bill and his half-brother Dan helped with experiments; Dan's nine-year-old son Tom assisted as he could, occasionally serving as ballast. Assistance was needed because the glider simply did not perform as the Wrights had expected. Their plan was to build a derrick, rope the glider to it, then fly the glider as a tethered kite with Wilbur aboard. By doing so, they could test the efficacy of wing warping and, in relatively safe conditions, gain in a few weeks the airborne practice it had taken Lilienthal years to accumulate. Their calculations showed that an eighteen-mile an hour wind would lift the glider and Wilbur as its pilot. This, the glider flat out refused to do. In practice, it would lift only fifty pounds of metal chains, or nine-year old Tom Tate. Of one frustrating day on the sands, Orville wrote home: "We tried it with tail in front, behind and every other way. When we got through, Will was so mixed up he couldn't even theorize."

The Wrights' first visit to Kitty Hawk was all but unremarked. In Dayton, the only formal notice came in the minutes of the Ten Dayton Boys club, where the secretary wrote: "A motion was made that the report of Treasurer Wilbur Wright be deferred until another meeting be called by the secretary. Treasurer Wright being in North Carolina." Despite the frustrations of their three-week stay, treasurer Wright returned to Dayton in a sanguine mood. When the glider wouldn't carry him, he and Orville flew it from the ground as a kite, using wires to operate and test the wing warping mechanism. This, at least, brought success: their system proved a far superior means for maintaining horizontal equilibrium than any previously tried. In a summary report he prepared for the year, Wilbur wrote: "Setting out as we did, with almost revolutionary theories on many points, and an entirely untried form of machine, we considered it quite a point to be able to return without having our pet theories completely knocked in the head by the hard logic of experience, and our brains dashed out in the bargain." Their glider's most obvious failing was its deficient lift; this, they would puzzle through over the winter, then return to Kitty Hawk with an improved glider the following year.

George Spratt was a young physician with an interest in aviation; recommended by Octave Chanute, he arrived at the Wrights' camp mid-afternoon on

July 25, 1901. A few hours after Spratt's arrival, mosquitoes descended by the horde. In a letter home, Orville described the ensuing and unequal contest:

> They chewed us clear through our underwear and socks. Lumps began swelling up all over my body like hen's eggs. We attempted to escape by going to bed, which we did at a little after five o'clock. We put our cots out under the awnings and wrapped up in our blankets with only our noses protruding from the folds, thus exposing the least possible surface to attack. Alas! Here nature's complicity in the conspiracy against us became evident. The wind, which until now had been blowing over twenty miles an hour, dropped out entirely. Our blankets then became unbearable. The perspiration would roll off of us in torrents. We would partly uncover and the mosquitoes would swoop down upon us in vast multitudes. We would make a few desperate and vain slaps, and again retire behind our blankets. Misery! Misery!

In 1901, the Wrights were camping a few miles south of Kitty Hawk at Kill Devil Hills, a cluster of sand dunes, the highest of which reaches 100 feet. The dunes offered excellent inclines for gliding; the mosquitoes came with the territory.

Insects were not the only problem. Over the winter, the Wrights had puzzled out why their 1900 glider produced so little lift. Perhaps, they speculated, the fabric stretched over the wings "leaked" — they had done nothing to seal its surface. Perhaps the tables on lift, developed by Lilienthal and used as the basis of the Wrights' calculations, were in error. Perhaps their glider's wings were too flat — Lilienthal and Chanute favored wings with an upward curvature of one in twelve; their own had been one in twenty. The Wrights tested sealed versus unsealed fabric, but found no difference in performance. As they had no way to test the accuracy of Lilienthal's tables, they settled on the third possibility, opting in their 1901 glider for the more highly curved wings Lilienthal and Chanute recommended.

Appearance might have told them it was a mistake. All of the Wrights' work — the newspapers they printed, the bicycles they built — was marked by an elegance and grace of line. In contrast, their 1901 glider was a homely thing with stubby and unconvincing wings. In practice, it glided heavily and was difficult to control; worse, it produced only one-third the lift the brothers expected, well below the inadequate performance of the previous year. Once again, the Wrights canceled plans to fly the glider as a kite with Wilbur aboard;

instead, the best they could manage was brief glides of a dozen seconds or less down the dunes. Wilbur wrote, "Five minutes practice in free flight is a good day's record."

It was a slow way to accumulate the information needed for a better understanding of flight. The Wrights were meticulous. On each glide, they measured the angle of descent, wind speed and time aloft. They paced off the distance covered over the sand. Often, an assistant holding an anemometer ran along the gliding craft so its speed relative to the ground and relative to the wind could both be determined. Spratt helped with such measurements. He was the only contemporary interested in flight to whom the Wrights became close: in subsequent years, they urged his return to Kitty Hawk. Uncharacteristically, Wilbur confided in Spratt. The pair corresponded — Wilbur tried to chide Spratt out of the "blues" to which the latter was prone, as Wilbur had himself been prior to taking up aviation. When the pair debated aeronautical points, Spratt's confession that he was not Wilbur's analytical equal brought this reply:

> You make a great mistake in envying me any of my qualities. Very often what you take for some special quality of mind is merely facility arising from constant practice. It is a characteristic of all our family to be able to see the weak points of anything, but this is not always a desirable quality as it makes us too conservative for successful business men, and limits our friendships to a very limited circle.

Joining camp for 1901, George Spratt was present for the low point of the Wrights' fortunes: failure by day, mosquitoes by night. The brothers came through it with the good-humored resilience shown in Orville's account of the mosquito onslaught and through the capacity for analytical inquiry which Wilbur somewhat ambivalently acknowledged to Spratt. They did what they did best — gather information, then reason things out.

The brothers began by separating the two wings of the biplane and flying each, independently, as a kite. Neither handled remotely as existing aeronautical theory suggested it would. Previous experimenters had established that curved wings produce greater lift than flat ones. In their own experiments, the Wrights had inadvertently run past the limits of that rule. When a curved surface is turned nearly horizontal to the wind, the wind begins to strike the surface's leading edge from above, rather than below. This pushes the front edge down, greatly reducing lift. The more highly curved wings of the Wrights' 1901 glider presented more of their upper surfaces to the wind, increasing this downward pressure. The 1901 model flew worse because it was inadvertently designed to fly worse. Wilbur and Orville reassembled their glider. In doing so, they altered its wing curvature to match the flatter profile of the previous year. Immediately, control improved.

Almost as soon, other problems surfaced — with the aspect of the design the Wrights had regarded as their chief success: wing warping. On occasion, when Wilbur warped the wings to the left, the glider stopped midway through its expected turn and inexplicably began turning back in the opposite direction. It was as though an automobile driver turned the steering wheel to the left and the car hesitated, then made a right turn. Reaching camp in 1901, the Wrights believed their glider to be the "state of the art." In fact, it was — and the glider's dreary performance showed just how crude that art was. In his summary for the year, Wilbur wrote: "When we looked at the time and money we had expended, and considered the progress made and the distance yet to go, we considered our experiments a failure. At this time I made the prediction that men would sometime fly, but that it would not be within our lifetime." Years later, Orville claimed to a biographer that the comment had been his own: leaving Kitty Hawk, he told Wilbur that if the Lilienthal tables on lift were correct, "Not within a thousand years would man ever fly."

In mid-December 1901, Octave Chanute wrote, concerned the Wrights might be giving up their investigations of flight. Did they need financial assistance? "If... some rich man should give you $10,000 a year to go on, to connect his name with progress, would you do so? I happen to know Carnegie. Would you like for me to write to him?" Two days before Christmas, Wilbur good naturedly said no to Santa Claus: "As to your suggestion in regard to Mr. Carnegie... I think it possible that Andrew is too hard-headed a Scotchman to become interested in such a visionary pursuit as flying."

Chanute's concern was misplaced. The Wrights were not giving up on the problem of flight. They had it solved. Not in final form, but in essentials. Within three months of their dejected departure from Kitty Hawk, they had in hand the scientific data upon which flight would be realized. Their 1901 experiments convinced them that the Lilienthal tables on lift were seriously in error. For the Wrights, it was a declaration of independence, one that showed their self-confidence. Wilbur wrote: "Having set out with absolute faith in the existing scientific data, we were driven to doubt one thing after another, till finally, after two years of experiment, we cast it all aside, and decided to rely upon our own investigations."

Chanute had been variously helpful to the Wrights; he was their chief confidant and professional soundingboard. But in the final three months of 1901, the Wrights moved past Chanute so rapidly he did not realize the importance of what they were doing or that only they — operating on the furthest forward edge of the curve — could bring themselves safely home to landing. The Wrights leapfrogged the field with a clunkish-looking wooden box, six feet long, sixteen inches on a side, with a window on its top to allow its interior to be viewed. It was the first wind tunnel built specifically for aeronautical research. The wind current within the box was produced by a fan mounted in one end. As ever, the Wrights were meticulous. To have confidence in their results, they needed a steady, uneddied flow of wind within the tunnel. Wilbur later wrote, "We spent nearly a month getting a straight wind." Once test conditions were established, actual testing went rapidly. From bicycle spokes and hacksaw blades, they fashioned dozens of miniature wings, varying by curvature, by thickness, by the ratio of length to width and by the placement of the high point of curvature in the profile of the wing. Each was tested for the lift it produced at a dozen or more different angles to the wind. For the brothers, it was a high point. Orville later recalled, "Wilbur and I could hardly wait for the morning to come to get at something that interested us. That's happiness."

By writing off Lilienthal's work, the Wrights declared their intellectual independence. By rejecting Chanute's offered assistance with a benefactor, they asserted their practical independence. To be freed by a benefactor to work full-time on flight, Wilbur wrote Chanute, would only encourage them to neglect their business. Indeed, the requirements of that business, Wilbur added, provided a healthy restraint on their experiments — since they had neither time nor funds to follow every line of their curiosity, they were compelled to focus on the likeliest ones and compelled, as well, to keep solvent the business that paid their bills. In late 1901, Katharine Wright wrote to her father, who was traveling on church business, "The boys have finished their tables of the action of the wind on various surfaces, or rather they have finished their experiments. As soon as the results are put in tables, they will begin work for next season's bicycles."

With the wind tunnel experiments in the back room of their bicycle shop, the Wrights laid down an empirical basis for wing design. Wilbur later stated, "I believe we possessed in 1902 more data…, a hundred times over, than all of our predecessors put together." Their wind tunnel work told them how much lift a wing of a given shape or size would produce. It told them that at the speeds at which they would operate, longer, more slender wings would fly best; that flatter wings were more efficient than heavily curved ones; that efficiency was further improved if the high point of the curve was placed near the wing's front. In 1902, they used this information to design a near-solution to flight — a glider whose wing surface was only slightly larger than that of their 1901 design, but with wings that were longer, narrower and flatter.

The 1902 glider incorporated one new feature: a fixed rear rudder. This was in response to Wilbur's disconcerting experience the previous year, when banking the glider to the left produced a turn to the right. Each of their gliders used wing warping to maintain balance across its wingspan; in addition, each had a canard wing to maintain balance fore to aft. An aircraft, however, can lose balance on a third axis as well: like an automobile on ice, it can skid, with the craft pointed in one direction but flying in another. This skid is what Wilbur had experienced, and its sideways slippage was what the fixed rear rudder was designed to prevent.

The Wrights left Dayton for Kitty Hawk on August 25, 1902. As Kitty Hawk's all-purpose public official, Dan Tate had obtained permission for the Wrights to build a cabin and hangar without having to pay ground rent. Experiment began once the buildings were erected and the glider assembled. From the first, the new craft glided like a bird — skimming over the sand dunes in piloted glides of 500 feet or more. Dan Tate was impressed: "All she needs is a coat of feathers to make her light," he said, "and she will stay in the air indefinitely."

She stayed up there — almost always. Several disconcerting times, one glider wing rose, the craft began to drift in the opposite direction and that drift turned into a spiraling plummet. Nonchalantly, the Wrights called the problem "well digging," in reference to the holes dug in the sand when the lower wing hit the ground. In sorting through the mechanics of flight, the Wrights were stumbling upon its hazards: the spiraling plummet they termed well digging is today known as tailspin — a corkscrewing descent which, if occurring at heights higher than that at which the Wrights glided, can easily prove fatal. Orville's account of the problem's solution begins with an evening of too much coffee; with caffeine murdering sleep, he lay in his cot and pondered the matter. He concluded that the fixed rear rudder added to increase control could, at times, eliminate it. When the glider, banked for a turn with the right wing high, began to skid to the left, that skid increased pressure on the low side of the rear rudder. Such higher pressure slowed the forward travel of the left wing. As the left wing slowed, the right wing began to fly circles around it. The result was tailspin. As a solution, Orville proposed substituting a movable tail for the fixed one; the movable tail would act like a ship's rudder, allowing the pressure on the higher and lower wings to be equalized. In the morning, Orville presented his idea to Wilbur. Wilbur considered it, then suggested it would simplify the pilot's task to link the rudder's movements and the wing warping

Wrights flew their gliders as manned kites to learn how the craft handled the air currents — and how they must handle the craft. Such work was the basis of their second great invention: they didn't just create the aircraft, they also created piloting.

system to one control: a single motion, then, would bank the wings and turn the rudder. The system of flight control invented by the Wrights — the key to their claim as the inventors of flight — was now complete.

Wilbur was confident. He wrote home: "Everything is so much more satisfactory that we now believe that the flying problem is really nearing its solution."

At each step in the Wrights' pursuit of flight, their task grew larger.

Of the requirements for flight — a wing surface to create lift, a propulsion system to create thrust and a control system to permit command — they had from the first focused on the last, on control. Wing design and propulsion were, they believed, matters adequately understood; underscoring this point, Wilbur in 1899 declared, "The question of equilibrium is the question of flight." He was wrong. Even as the brothers created a control system that combined wing warping and canard wing, they realized that Lilienthal's tables on lift were seriously in error. To create reliable tables, they built the first wind tunnel designed for aeronautical research, then used the information thus gathered to design wings fitted for flight. Once the glider experiments of 1902 affirmed the correctness of their wing design, the Wrights considered themselves to be home free: they had control, they had lift; all they needed to convert their glider to a powered craft was an engine and propellers. Engines and propellers were established things — surely, adapting such existing technology to the needs of a glider would not be difficult. And they were wrong again.

Wishing to read up on the subject, the Wrights with an almost naive charm went to the Dayton Public Library to check out books on propellers. They found none. Disconcertingly, they found that no theory for propeller design existed; all the ship's propellers in the world were the result of simple trial and error. Further, they realized that a ship's propeller could not model for an aircraft propeller. A seagoing vessel moves forward when its propellers push back against water, which is essentially non-compressible; a flying vessel moves forward when its propellers push against the readily compressed air. With no theory of propellers to draw upon, they set out to create one. Once again, they were at square one. For a time, they were stuck there. Wilbur later recalled: "What at first seemed a simple problem became more complex the longer we studied it. With the machine moving forward, the air flying backward, the propeller turning sidewise, and nothing standing still, it seemed impossible to find a starting point from which to trace the various simultaneous reactions."

The Wrights filled notebook after notebook with calculations. As was their habit, they took opposing sides on each questions, then argued them through. Charlie Taylor, the Wrights' mechanic, recalled, "Both boys had tempers. They would shout at one another something terrible. I don't think they really got mad, but they sure got awfully hot." On several occasions, Wilbur and Orville argued opposing sides of a question so effectively that each abandoned his original position to agree with the view the other no longer held. Their key realization, as stated by Wilbur, was: "It was apparent that a propeller was simply an aeroplane [wing] traveling in a spiral course. As we could calculate the effect of [a wing] traveling in a straight course, why should we not be able to calculate the effect of one traveling in a spiral course?"

By June 1903, their propellers were complete. Each was eight and a half feet long, made of three layers of one-and-one-eighth-inch spruce, laminated together and then shaped with hand tools. An unusually exultant Orville wrote to George Spratt: " We worked out a theory of our own on the subject, and soon discovered, as we usually do, that all the propellers built heretofore are all wrong, and then we built a pair of propellers..., based on our theory, which are all right!" One student of the Wrights' work notes, "As with so many aspects of their aeronautical work, before the Wright propeller there were none like it, and after it there were none that were different."

By then, they also had an engine. It was the work, largely, of Charlie Taylor, the Wrights' mechanic. In the small world that was turn-of-the-century any-

In 1902, Wilbur tried to lure George Spratt to camp with these enticements: "we have not seen a dozen mosqui-toes in two weeks ...[the cabin] is more waterproof than before, and more sandproof ...and we now have good water." Tourist brochures make pretty much the same claims today.

where, Taylor may have met up with Wilbur and Orville because his wife's uncle owned the West Third Street building where the Wrights' cycle shop was located. The Wrights jobbed a few tasks to Taylor and were pleased with the dexterity and dispatch with which he handled them. In 1901, they hired him to do the repairs and mind the shop while the brothers went off to their mosquito-ridden disap-pointments at Kill Devil Hills. The Wrights paid Taylor

$16.50 a week. He proved invaluable. Taylor was resourceful and industrious, though his constant cigar-smoking and occasional profanity kept Katharine Wright out of the bike shop.

The Wrights gave Taylor the task; they did not give him much to do it with. Milling machines and boring machines and surface grinders would have made precise work easier and allowed tighter fittings of pressure parts. All the Wrights had to offer were the drill press and the lathe in the shed behind the bike shop. The tools available dictated the engine's design: Taylor had to build a lay-down engine — one in which the pistons move back and forth instead of up and down — because that was the only kind of engine that could be worked on the lathe. That work was tedious: Taylor, for example, had to take a piece of steel, drill out an outline with the drill press, cold chisel the outlined material free and then turn it on the lathe until a crankshaft emerged. Neither Taylor nor the Wrights made engineering drawings of the engine. Taylor later stated, "One of us would sketch out the part we were talking about on a piece of scratch paper and I'd tack the sketch over my bench."

The completed four-cylinder engine was a thing of simplicity. It had neither carburetor nor fuel pump: gasoline dripped from an ordinary tin can onto a reservoir on the side the engine, where it was vaporized by the engine's heat and pulled inside by the suction of the pistons. There were no spark plugs and no distributor: ignition came from a magneto that sent a current down a copper strip that ran along the pistons; when a rotating cam opened the strip, the current sparked, igniting the fuel. The engine had no way to cool its valves, which became red hot after a few minutes of operation. And it had two speeds, one of which was "off." During testing, Taylor's first engine seized up when gasoline dribbled down onto the camshaft; Taylor constructed a second. The Wrights had calculated it would take eight to nine horsepower to get their craft off the ground; when they cranked up Taylor's engine, it produced thirteen.

On September 23, the Wrights and all the pieces of their unassembled aircraft left for Kitty Hawk, where they reached the cabin and hangar constructed the previous year and heard Dan Tate's laments as to the foulness of the season. According to Tate, Orville wrote Katharine," the rain has descended in such torrents as to make a lake for miles about our camp; the mosquitoes were so thick that they turned day into night, and the lightning so terrible that it turned night into day." The Wrights spent three weeks assembling their craft, then got a taste of what Tate had been describing. A storm blew through in the middle of the night, forcing Orville from his bed to the roof to keep it from blowing away. Wilbur wrote home: "4 a.m. effort to repair roof of cabin in 75 mph wind — The wind and rain continued through the night, but we took the advice of the Oberlin coach, 'Cheer up, boys, there is no hope.'" When weather improved, the Wrights flew their craft as a glider to gain a feel for how it handled. It flew magnificently, at times remaining airborne for over a full minute. They were learning how to play the winds: on one occasion, Wilbur remained aloft twenty-six seconds, then landed only fifty-two feet from his point of launch.

The Wrights' mastery of the winds over Kitty Hawk was not, however, aviation's leading news that autumn. That came October 7, with the long-awaited launching of the Aerodrome, the creation of Samuel Langley, head of the Smithsonian Institution. Langley had pursued aviation for twenty years, without, however, gaining any great understanding of the subject. He believed — and codified as Langley's Law — that the faster an aircraft flew the less power it would require; he assumed that anything a model could do a full-sized craft could do as well, even though doubling dimensions increases mass by a factor of eight. Langley's Aerodrome was launched from the edge of the Potomac: it slipped down its launching rail and collapsed into the river, leaving the pilot to scramble free to escape drowning.

For many, the failure of so eminent an experimenter as Langley closed the door on reasonable hope for heavier-than-air travel. An even more eminent figure took that door and slammed it: astronomer Simon Newcomb — the first American since Benjamin Franklin to be invited to join the Royal Society — took Langley's failure as definitive. Newcomb was quoted in *The Independent* of October 22, 1903, asking, among other things: "How can he [an aviator] reach the ground without destroying his machinery? I do not think the most imaginative inventor has yet even put on paper a demonstrative, successful way of meeting this difficulty." Nine days after Newcomb's comment was published, the Wrights began mounting their landing skids under the craft; working methodically, they three days later began to install the engine.

Their troop, however, was thinning, grumbling as it went. On October 28, Dan Tate — retained by the Wrights as their $7-a-week man-of-all-work — announced he was going on strike. The work was too hard; the Wrights were too cheap: they expected him to chop wood when they could just as easily buy it at $3 a cord. George Spratt remained in camp until November 5. That was a bad day: a propeller shaft was damaged and the engine's magneto was not producing spark sufficient to ignite the fuel. With that news, Spratt departed, apparently deeply doubtful of the Wrights' chances, but taking the damaged propeller shaft along for shipment to Charlie Taylor in Dayton for repair. Chanute arrived the following day with the unwelcome news that transmission losses would reduce the power the engine delivered to the propellers by twenty percent. If this was correct, the aircraft would not leave the ground; the Wrights' machine did not have so great a margin of error. Chanute remained until November 12, trying to interest the Wrights in two laughably unflyable craft in which he had taken in interest; he departed, apparently unaware that for all his involvement in flight, he was ducking out just before its grand moment. Hope, however, was held out at a distance; the minutes of that fall's gathering of the Annual Club of Ten Dayton Boys record: "As to absent Will Wright, he seems to be bound to be only a little lower than the angels, and who knows but some morning the angels, looking over the battlements of heaven, may see our beloved member coming."

With Wilbur and Orville alone in camp, the weather turned. By November the outer banks no longer invite, the winds are blustery and cold and the ocean that in summer months welcomes becomes gray and leaden. On November 19, Orville recorded in his diary, "On arising found ponds around camp frozen, also water in basin." A few days later, he wrote to Katharine:

> In addition to the classification of last year, to wit, 1, 2, 3 and 4 blanket nights, we now have 5 blanket nights, & 5 blankets & 2 quilts. Next comes 5 blankets, 2 quilts & fire; then 5, 2, fire & hot-water jug. This is as far as we have gone so far. Next comes the addition of sleeping without undressing, then shoes & hats, and finally overcoats. We intend to be comfortable while we are here.

The propeller shaft sent to Dayton for repair arrived, but engine vibration kept working it loose from its sprocket. The brothers tried all manner of ways to torque it on tightly, without success. Bicycle men do what bicycle men must. The brothers heated the shaft and sprocket, poured Arnstein's Hard Cement into the threads, and screwed down tight. It held. They began test running the engine linked to the propellers. On November 28, Orville recorded in his diary: "After six or seven runs of from two to 3 minutes, we discovered something wrong, which turned out to be a cracked propeller shaft." This time, Orville took the failed shaft to Dayton for repair. Wilbur remained in Kitty Hawk, practicing his German and French. "An article from a German paper, giving some account of our machine," he wrote home, "has kept me guessing." On December 11, Orville returned with new propeller shafts, this time of solid sprung-steel. He brought word of Langley's second launch attempt, which like the first had ended nose down in the Potomac.

On December 12, the brothers mounted the shafts and made ready to fly, but the winds were insufficient. They could not fly on the 13th; it was a Sunday. Monday, they summoned five men from the government lifesaving station at Kitty Hawk to help move the craft into launch position. They laid out their runway, sixty feet of wooden rail down which the craft would slide. They flipped a coin. Wilbur won the toss. The aircraft slid into motion, Wilbur pulled up on the controls too suddenly, the craft slowed — stalled, really — and settled to the sand. Wilbur sent his father Bishop Wright a short telegram that included the words: "success assured."

It took two days to repair the damage the craft sustained on Wilbur's hop. Their next attempt came December 17. The Wrights hung out a cloth that was visible to the lifesaving station, announcing their intention to fly. Believing it was too windy for flying, Bill Tate — whose hospitality the Wrights had enjoyed through their visits to Kitty Hawk — neglected to check to see if the Wrights' signal flag was up, and missed the show. The Wrights had a camera with them. They directed one of the lifesavers, John T. Daniels, to snap the shutter of the camera just as the aircraft reached the end of its launch rail. He did as he was told, taking the most famous amateur photograph ever, the moment at which Orville — whose turn it now was — left the ground on man's first powered and controlled flight. He covered about 120 feet. Three more flights were made that, the longest being Wilbur's fifty-nine second flight of 852 feet. They were getting the hang of it. It was barely lunch time, and the Wrights began toying with the notion of flying to the telegraph station at Kitty Hawk. Then a sudden gust of wind flipped their aircraft over. It never flew again.

The Wrights telegrammed their success home, urging that the newspapers be contacted. Much is made of the absence of a furor in the press over the Wrights' accomplishment. In fairness, James Cox's *Dayton Daily News* did give the event brief, though front page, treatment, under a headline that read: "Dayton Boys Emulate Great Santos-Dumont." Alberto Santos-Dumont was a Brazilian who pursued aviation in France; in 1901, he had dazzled the French public by rigging an engine to a hot-air balloon which, in no particularly modest way, he then sailed around the Eiffel Tower. *The News'* editor — indeed, people generally — could manage no distinction between a hot air balloon ride and heavier-than-air powered flight. They could not report what the Wrights had done because, simply, they could not imagine it. When one curious reporter contacted the Wright home for details, Bishop Wright provided an account that closed:

> P.S. Wilbur is 36, Orville 32, and they are as inseparable as twins. For several years they had read up on aeronautics as a physician would read his books, and they have studied, discussed, and experimented together. Natural workmen, they have invented, constructed, and operated their gliders, and finally their 'Wright Flyer,' jointly, all at their own personal expense. About equal credit is due each.

The appeal of the automobile was simple; said one early car maker, "Everybody wanted to go from A to B sitting down." One early driver added: "After a day of hard mental effort in study or office, it is better than any medicine to push forward the lever and fly away with the ever faithful and obedient automobile."

Flight was the dream of centuries, but to Americans in 1903 the dream coming true was not flight, but the motorcar. That year, a young businessman offered to swap $1,500 worth of the roller bearings his company produced for a new maroon-colored Conrad made by one of his customers. The offer was accepted. The Conrad boasted red leather upholstery, artillery wheels, chain-drive transmission — everything, in short, except a means of propulsion. Raising the hood, the businessman found the engine compartment empty. The automaker remonstrated. True, he acknowledged, the car had no engine; and, further true, his company had never actually built an engine, but the experts who had reviewed the plans the company did have for the engine they intended to install just as soon as they actually built one had spoken favorably of them. That was good enough for the businessman, and the deal was struck.

Two decades later, that businessman was directing one the world's great corporations, General Motors. In 1903, however, Alfred P. Sloan was just one more besotted young fool, anxious to get behind the steering wheel and head off down all the adventurous roadways his country had yet to build. As Sloan wrote in his autobiography: "Humanity never wanted any machine as much as it desired this one." The great love affair of the twentieth century — Americans and their automobiles — was in first full infatuation.

Americans brought to the motorcar all the unsteady judgment of new love. Automobiles would be cost-effective. As early as 1900, one enthusiast wrote, "Experts all agree that for hauling lumber, coal, stone and farmers; produce, etc., over reasonably good roads, the automobile insures a saving of from 25 percent to 40 percent as against the horse and wagon." Automobiles would add to civic beauty. Journalist Ray Stannard Baker wrote, "It is hardly possible to conceive the appearance of a crowded wholesale street in the day of the automotive vehicle. In the first place, it would be almost as quiet as a country lane — all the crash of horses' hoofs and the rumble of steel tires will be gone. And since vehicles will be fewer and shorter than the present truck in span, streets will appear less crowded." And automobiles would get the girl. *The Independent* wrote: "The man who owns a motorcar gets for himself, besides the joy of touring, the adulation of the walking crowd; and the daring driver of a racing machine that bounds and rushes and disappears in the perspective in a thunder of explosions is a god to the women."

Within the auto world, the demand this excitement created was the single compelling fact. One early investor in Detroit wrote, "Every factory here... has its entire output sold and cannot begin to fill orders.... And it is all spot cash on delivery, and no guarantee or string attached of any kind." Demand was a vacuum that drew in the mechanically adept and the entrepreneurially eager. William Crapo Durant was a prospering carriage maker who made an early leap for the horseless world; there, he was for a time allied with Raymond Olds. When Olds needed a design for the coming year's vehicle, Durant drove his own Buick Model 10 to the Oldsmobile plant. There, he directed workmen to hoist the Buick's wooden body off its chassis, set it up on sawhorses, and cut it in half twice — front to back and side to side — with a crosscut saw. Workmen then set the sections on the ground. Durant kicked them around with his foot until he liked the proportions. There, he announced, there is your new Oldsmobile.

Those who got in early got in cheap. Henry Ford started with a dozen workers and $28,000 in paid-in capital. Low capitalizations made it difficult to achieve quality; mindless demand made it unnecessary. For the early automakers, Sloan observed, life was "a race to produce cars and get them sold before their scanty capital gave out." In 1901, a highly-regarded toolmaker named Henry Leland received an order to build gasoline engines to an automaker's design. Through improved machining and tighter tolerances, Leland tripled the engine's horsepower. When the improved version was presented to the automaker, however, its business manager told Leland he couldn't use it. Company cash flow was low, demand was brisk; to halt production just to incorporate an engine with triple the horsepower might push them into bankruptcy.

Leland, Durant and Sloan helped make Detroit the hub of the motoring world. They had other ties. In 1909, Henry Leland, as president of Cadillac, purchased an improved ignition system from a moonlighting inventor in Ohio. In 1919, William Durant, founding president of General Motors, hired that inventor as his vice president for research. In 1947, Alfred P. Sloan joined with that research chief to found one of the world's major centers for cancer research. In

1903, however, that future research chief, Charles Kettering, was an undergraduate studying electrical engineering at Ohio State University: he was twenty-seven years old, and had never ridden in an automobile in his life.

Charles Kettering was born in 1876 in mild rolling hill farm country sixty miles northeast of Columbus. He was the fourth of five children in an otherwise unremarkable family. They were poor: Charley, his family name, spent ten years attending the same one-room school, got a new pair of boots each autumn and called himself, with pride, a hillbilly. He grew to be a lanky, large-featured young man whose most notable attribute was very weak eyes. Like James Cox, Charley Kettering wanted off the farm and, like Cox, saw the classroom as his avenue. By age nineteen, he was a teacher at a county school five miles from home. To the classroom, Charles Kettering was a gift. He drew students to evening presentations on electricity and heat and magnetism and gravity. Once, a barnstorming "scientist" came through Loudonville with an X-ray machine: Kettering packed up his students and took them off to get a look at the bones in their hands. A local minister objected: peaking inside the body was God's prerogative, not man's. Parents rallied to Kettering's defense, with one stating that Kettering's classes were the first thing in which his son had shown any interest in school.

Kettering left the classroom to study electrical engineering at Ohio State, then left OSU when his eyes were not equal to the demands of study. Dejected, he landed in Ashland, as a pole digger for the Star Telephone Company, a low budget local exchange. The post of company engineer fell vacant and, there being no other applicants, was given to Kettering. He wrote off for a copy of Kempster B. Miller's *American Telephone Practice*, then tackled problems with a combination of improvisation and persistence. It was in Ashland that he met and began courting Olive Williams, a postmaster's daughter with a love for music and vast tolerance for Kettering's habits of work. In 1901, Kettering returned to Ohio State. There, twin concessions to his weak eyesight allowed him to complete his education: the engineering department waived the mandatory mechanical drafting class his eyes could not have mastered and his roommates read each day's lessons to him out loud each evening, a practice that continued until his graduation in 1904.

Shortly before that graduation, Kettering's physics professor received a letter from a former student asking him to recommended a graduating senior for technical employment. The professor recommended Kettering, then leaned on Kettering to go to Dayton, visit National Cash Register and meet Edward Deeds. Deeds was a round-faced young man who, at thirty, was already the assistant superintendent of NCR, a post he had achieved in part through John H. Patterson's peculiar standards for advancement. In his first days at NCR, Deeds told the plant superintendent there appeared to be loose brick near the top of the company chimney. The superintendent dismissed Deeds as a busybody. The chimney in question had double brick walls; Deeds waited until Sunday when the brick would be relatively cool, donned protective gloves, placed a wet sponge on his nose and, with a camera, climbed the chimney ladder between the two brick walls. He photographed the loose brick, then presented his evidence. The action showed the kind of pluck that John H. Patterson admired in his younger subordinates, and fixed Deeds' star as rising.

In April 1904, Kettering took the train to Dayton — farther from home than he had ever been — met Deeds, saw NCR and signed on as a member of its Inventions department at the then high salary of $50 a week. Kettering soon presented his first new product: the OK Credit System. It addressed a minor nuisance in retailing. In a store, a customer at any cashier station might wish to make a purchase on credit, but only a centralized credit clerk had authority to approve the transaction. Kettering's system linked a telephone to a solenoid-activated stamping device. With it, a cashier phoned a credit request to the clerk; if the customer's credit was good, the clerk activated the solenoid, which stamped approval on the sales slip at the cashier's station. It was typical Kettering work: a rearrangement of existing components to perform a new task.

Kettering's major achievement at NCR was the invention of the electric cash register. Clerks using a cash register closed each transaction by turning a crank to ring up a sale. Each year, as new features and gadgets were added, registers became progressively more difficult to crank. By established engineering standard, an electric motor powerful enough to crank a cash register would need to be nearly as large as the register itself. Kettering believed he could ignore that standard: a motor can do more than its rated work, he knew, so long as it is called upon to do so only intermittently — as in totaling up a sale. With intermittent use, the motor has time to cool and avoids burning out. Kettering's invention combined a small electric motor with an overrunning clutch that returned the register's dials to "zero" after each sale.

Kettering spent five years at NCR, acquiring twenty-three patents and displaying the traits that would mark his career. First, he took the broad view. Businessmen, he held, think of researchers as firemen to be summoned to extinguish whatever blaze breaks out in the Monday morning meeting; rather, Kettering argued, the proper aim of industrial research was to build a corporation's mastery of its technical field and, hence, its options for the future. Second, he fixed his view on the marketplace. Of his time at NCR, he said: "I didn't hang around much with other inventors or the executive fellows. I lived with the sales gang. They had some real notion of what people wanted." Finally, Kettering could motivate. A Kettering contemporary at NCR stated, "I think that Ket was worshiped by all the men that ever worked for him.... He had men work down there, they'd work all night if they started on a job, he'd work right there with them."

These qualities caught the wind of Kettering's almost manic inventiveness. An NCR patent attorney who worked with Kettering recalled: "He would come in with an idea that he developed in his mind, and wanted to know whether there was anything like that ever been done and we'd make a [patent] search on it. Sometimes a sketch was on his cuff. Might be on his shirt bosom. It might be on a theater program.... He'd sit down at the theater and he'd design on his theater program. He'd be at the theater with his wife, and he'd be sketching an invention while she was enjoying the show."

That wife was the former Olive Williams. With Kettering established at NCR, the couple was married on August 1, 1905; they then departed for a honeymoon at Niagara Falls. While waiting to change trains in Crestline, Ohio, Kettering spotted a man trying without success to start his automobile. With time to kill and curiosity to satisfy, Kettering wandered over and offered his assistance. The electrical engineer soon spotted the problem — some loose wiring in the ignition — and put it right. As recompense, the automobile's owner offered the bridal couple a brief spin around town. Charles and Olive hopped onto the rear seat, which Olive later recalled faced backward. It was Charles Kettering's first ride in an automobile.

Your old friend,

A. I. Root.

CHAPTER TEN

The apiarist

Amos I. Root began publishing *Gleanings in Bee Culture*, a bimonthly journal on all matters apiary, in Medina, Ohio, in 1872. The magazine read like a continuing conversation that Root carried on with himself and his readers: in a given issue, he reported on Root's Automatic Reversible Honey-Extractor, presented the "Poultry Department" by A. I. Root, and included "Special Notices by A. I. Root," in which he chided farmers for their resistance to the automobile and chided his state's governor for his susceptibility to the Saloon League, all in distracted prose that took some paragraphs to track down and bag its point. In his issue of October 15, 1904, the "Our Homes" section closed: "We want a machine that will float as easily and safely as the bees, the butterflies, and the carrier pigeons. May the Lord be praised, this is already in sight."

With that statement, the editor's natural loquaciousness was checked. Amos I. Root had a secret to keep, and keeping it did not come naturally. "We are told it is hard for women to keep a secret," he later explained, "and I think I must be to some extent feminine in my make-up." His situation was this: "For 32 years," he stated, "I have been ransacking the world — that is, so far as I could consistently — watching periodicals of almost every sort, and leaving no stone unturned to furnish information of interest and value to the readers of *Gleanings*. I have especially tried to have our own journal up to date in scientific matters." In mid-September 1904, Root ransacked his way towards Dayton, driving 200 miles over unlikely roads to a field known as Huffman Prairie, eight miles northeast of the city. There, on Tuesday, September 20, 1904 — a cloudy day that turned to rain — A. I. Root had seen Wilbur Wright fly.

Root was ecstatic. Flight was then still a rumor. Ten months after Kitty Hawk, no authoritative — indeed, no comprehensible — account of the Wrights' flying had appeared in print. Root tracked that rumor to a field outside Dayton. He confirmed it. In time, he would publish in *Gleanings in Bee Culture* the first eyewitness account of human flight. Root's editorial impatience traced to the fact that the Wrights had welcomed him to Huffman on condition that he print nothing of what he saw there until they gave the go-ahead.

Root appreciated the need for secrecy. In his younger days, he had been the first in town to order a French velocipede, forerunner of the bicycle. When the vehicle arrived, neither he nor anyone else could manage to ride it; in consequence, Root wrote, "the story of 'a fool and his money' was hurled in my face so many times I almost dread to hear it even yet." Root then rented the largest hall in town, and "with one trusty boy who had faith, as a companion," learned first to ride in a straight line, then to turn corners and finally to make complete circles of his hall. He then reemerged cycling through the streets of Medina to reclaim his reputation. The Wrights' circumstance recalled his own: "Well, these boys wanted just the same kind of privacy to try their flying-machine that I needed for my velocipede."

The Wrights found that privacy in a pasture outside Dayton. Kitty Hawk is a name well-known — deservedly so, for it is where flight was born. Undeservedly, Huffman Prairie is a name known only to a few. The Wrights' Kitty Hawk aircraft, a long-term associate said, "was just to prove their calculations." With it, they showed that powered flight was possible; at Huffman Prairie, they made flight practical. The prairie was an eighty-five-acre field whose owner made it available to the Wrights for their flying experiments on condition that they shoo the cattle pastured there into an adjoining field before attempting to fly — an activity the owner gravely doubted would occur. Soon after settling in, Wilbur wrote Octave Chanute with an assessment of the site: "In addition to the cattle there have been a dozen or more horses in the pasture and as it is surrounded by barbwire fencing we have been at much trouble to get them safely away before making any trials. Also, the ground is an old swamp and is filled with grassy hummocks some six inches high, so that it resembles a prairie dog town."

The field was tiny: within its confines, the Wrights could not fly even 1,000 feet in a straight line. Constriction suited purpose: a major goal for the Wrights in 1904 was to learn how to make controlled turns in the air. Progress was slow. As at Kitty Hawk, their craft gained takeoff speed by sliding down a wooden runner into the wind. Huffman's winds were lighter than those along the Atlantic, so they had to lay out up to 200 feet of track, pointed in the direction from which they anticipated the wind, and wait for a sufficient breeze. Long waits were followed by short flights — not until their forty-ninth attempt of the season did they make a flight longer than Wilbur's best at Kitty Hawk. In September, to improve launch conditions, they constructed a twenty-foot-high derrick from which a 1,600-pound weight was hung. The weight was roped to the aircraft: when the weight was dropped, the rope lurched airplane and pilot into the air.

It was frustrating work. On one flight, Orville was unable to pull out of a turn; he crashed, damaging the engine, both landing skids and both propellers.

Repairs took a week. Their next flight abruptly ended when the plane darted to the ground, breaking the upper spar, the skids and a propeller. They were ready again six days later when the stake used to restrain the 1600-pound drop weight slipped and the aircraft began launching itself with Orville only half on board. They aborted the takeoff, but several struts were broken and Orville wrenched his shoulder. The following day they made five more trials: Wilbur managed one good flight of eighty-seven seconds; three others failed at take-off, and on the day's final attempt the aircraft's tail was broken. Tail repaired, three trials were made the next day: two never got off the ground; on the third, a wing touched down and a propeller snapped.

Their efforts to get airborne took place in a virtual vacuum. The Wrights had debated how to bring news of their invention to public notice. In considering that question, they were wedged between their natural modesty, their wish to gain due credit for their labors, and their belief that no reporter could possibly get the story straight. They opted for direct demonstration. At Huffman on May 23, 1904, Wilbur and Orville unveiled the world's first flying machine to a small crowd that included a dozen invited reporters. Their timing was bad. Their season at Huffman had just started and neither they nor their craft had yet had much of a shakedown. While those assembled watched, the aircraft scooted down its launch rail. At takeoff, the engine misfired and, a reporter wrote, the craft "plowed along the prairie sod." Before a somewhat smaller audience three days later, Orville got airborne, though briefly. The Wrights' intention that day, a local newspaper reported, "was to have made a circle of the field, and like a bird, alight with the wind." Sadly, the story continued, "the failure of the machine to go further than 25 feet prevented this." Moved, perhaps, by the desire to say nice things about local people, the uncomprehending reporter of a second paper characterized Orville's eight-yard journey as "an unqualified success."

By the time Amos Root arrived at Huffman Prairie on September 20, the Wrights were in better control of their craft and their circumstance. Wilbur and Orville attempted 105 flights at Huffman Prairie in 1904; most were fitful, fretful voyages. With a naturalist's sense of metaphor, however, Root caught the Wrights' broader purpose at Huffman. It was in that field, he wrote, that the aircraft "'learned to fly,' very much like a young bird just out of its nest learns by practice to use its wings." After they became practiced on short, straight flights and on simple turns, the Wrights attempted a complete circle of their small field. Wilbur later wrote, "At first we did not know just how much movement to give in order to make a circle of a given size. On the first three trials we found that we had started a circle on too large a radius to keep within the boundaries of the small field in which we were operating. Accordingly, a landing was made each time, without accident, merely to avoid passing the boundaries of

"Well, sir, we pulled that fool thing around over the ground of Huffman Prairie about thirty or forty times, hoisting it up on the derrick so it would get a good start, and we were all hot and sweaty and about played out. What was the use of our wasting our time over such a ridiculous thing any longer? But once more we pulled her up again and let her go. The old engine seemed to be working a little better than normal. Orville stuck his head and nodded to Wilbur and Wilbur turned her loose. *And by God the damn thing flew.*"

-Charlie Webbert

the field." On the fourth attempt — made on the afternoon of September 20, 1904, with Amos I. Root on hand — Wilbur flew the first controlled circle ever made by an aircraft.

Root wrote of the experience:

> When it turned that circle, and came near the starting-point, I was right in front of it; and I said then, and I believe still, it was... the grandest sight of my life. Imagine a locomotive that has left its track, and is climbing up in the air right toward you — a locomotive without any wheels... but with white wings instead.... Well, now, imagine that locomotive with wings that spread 20 feet each way, coming right toward you with the tremendous flap of its propellers, and you have something like what I saw.... I tell you friends, the sensation that one feels in such a crisis is something hard to describe.

Root did describe it, though not until the January 1, 1905, issue of *Gleanings in Bee Culture*. Then — the Wrights having lifted their embargo of the news — Root ushered in the new year with the announcement that heavier-than-air flight had been achieved. Freed to tell the story, the editor took his time. "Dear Friends," he began, "I have a wonderful story to tell you — a story that, in some respects, outrivals the Arabian Night fables — a story, too, with a moral that I think many of the younger ones need and, perhaps some of the older ones too if they will heed it."

Actually, Root had several morals. First, he commended the Wrights, who "instead of spending their summer vacation with crowds, and with such crowds as are often questionable," had gone to the seacoast: "You and I have in years past found enjoyment and health in sliding down hill on the snow; but these boys went off to that shady waste on the Atlantic coast to slide down hill too; but instead of sliding on snow and ice they slid on air. With a gliding machine made of sticks and cloth they learned to glide and soar." Halfway down a North Carolina sand dune, Root digressed into another moral. When he had first considered issuing a beekeeping publication, he stated, he read everything on the subject, even hiring translators to guide him through European journals. The Wrights, he noted, had shown a similar diligence in studying flight, a diligence he now recommended to his readers: "If you wish to make a success of anything... find out what the good and great men have done in this special line before you." Root then charted the Wrights' progress — from unpowered glides over the North Carolina sand, to the addition of the engine, to their work at Huffman — included his description of Wilbur's turn for home; he speculated on the prospect of flights over the North Pole, and concluded with a stern admonition that no drinking man should ever be allowed to pilot an aircraft.

Root remained in touch with the Wrights. In the April 1, 1905, issue of *Glean-

ings, he reported the Wrights were building a machine able to carry a passenger, a role for which he nominated himself: "They did not say the passenger might possibly be A. I. Root (for, say, 'one trip') but my imagination caught on to it nevertheless." For once, Root had it wrong. For 1905, the Wrights were not concerned with carrying passengers. Rather, they wanted to address a danger their flights of the previous year had revealed. On several occasions, and for no apparent reason, their aircraft had suddenly ducked from its flight path and darted for the ground. The problem occurred when the aircraft was banked for a turn. Wilbur wrote to George Spratt: "When turning a very small circle with the outside wing much elevated it is hard to bring the inside wing up again." In other words, it was easier to bank the wings for a turn than to restore level flight.

Orville found the words for flight in *Paradise Lost*: "so easy it seemed once found, which, yet unfound, most would have thought impossible."

To gain information on the phenomenon, they began courting that danger — flying in small circles to see what would happen and what might be done about it. The solution came through the closest thing to a piece of luck the Wrights ever enjoyed. While Huffman Prairie was edged on two sides by trees, the prairie itself was treeless except for a single forty-foot honey locust several hundred feet inside the Wrights' normal flying circle. In mid-September 1905, with Orville flying, the aircraft suddenly tilted up and began skidding toward that tree. Orville, almost by instinct, pointed the aircraft sharply down; to his surprise, this reestablished his control of the craft. The problem was another manifestation of stall. The Wrights flew at only slightly above their aircraft's stall speed. Circling for a turn increased the centripetal force on the lower wing; at times, the load this placed on that wing exceeded the lift it was producing. The result was a partial stall, a loss of control and the sudden, dangerous drop. By aiming the craft down, Orville regained the airspeed needed to move back above stall point. This was the final piece to the puzzle the Wrights had been assembling since their first five-foot glider of 1899.

At the close of the year, Wilbur wrote, "When we had discovered the real nature of the trouble, and knew that it could always be remedied by tilting the machine forward a little so that its flying speed would be restored, we felt we were ready to place the flying machine on the market." The last flights of 1905 at Huffman confirmed this. Freed from anxiety over danger from inexplicable drops, the Wrights undertook longer and longer journeys. On October 5, Wilbur remained aloft for thirty-eight minutes, completing lap after lap — twenty-nine in all — of their course over Huffman Prairie. The main requirements for longer flights were a larger gas tank and a more interesting flight path.

The Wrights were ready for the market, but the market was not ready for them. They were Americans, patriots and Republicans — in November 1904 they had made a special celebratory flight over Huffman to mark the election of Teddy Roosevelt — and to their thinking the natural customer for their invention was the United States government. Likely, Orville later stated, they would at that time have given their government a world monopoly on flight, patents included, for $10,000, a sum representing their costs out-of-pocket and reasonable compensation for their time and troubles. Their government, however, was not interested. By common saying, build a better mousetrap and the world will beat a path to your door. That saying presupposes the existence of mice and someone who wishes to be rid of them. When the Wrights began their work, Wilbur observed, human flight was a commonplace metaphor for impossibility: faced with a particularly farfetched scheme, someone might reply, "Well, you might as well try to fly as do that." The very public failure of Secretary Langley and the very confident pronouncements of Professor Newcomb had done nothing to alter this view. Flight may have been a dream since Icarus, but the U.S. government wasn't buying any used myths from a couple of bachelor bicycle builders with no particular pull in the Third Congressional District of Ohio.

Three times the prize was offered, three times refused. On March 1, 1905, Wilbur — anticipating success — wrote the War Department to offer for sale one aircraft, suitable for scouting. Several months passed before a Major General Gillespie insouciantly replied that "as many requests have been made for financial assistance in the development of designs for flying machines," the government had "found it necessary to decline to make allotment for experimental development of devices for mechanical flight." No funds would be forthcoming, he added, until a craft has "been brought to the stage of practical operations without expense to the United States." Wilbur wrote back to say that his aircraft was fully practical. It could, he stated, carry an operator and fuel sufficient for a flight of 100 miles. The government was unmoved. Wilbur tried a third time: "We have no thought of asking financial assistance of the government," he stated flatly; still, he and Orville needed to know the criteria by which the government would judge an aircraft a success: "We cannot well fix a price, nor a time for delivery," he wrote, "till we have your idea of the qualifications necessary to such a machine." General Gillespie wrote back that the government "does not care to formulate any requirements for the performance of a flying machine or take any further action on the subject until a machine is produced which by actual operation is shown to be able to produce horizontal flight and to carry an operator."

The inventors of the aircraft then sent up trial balloons to the British and, subsequently, the French. Somewhat archly, Wilbur defended this step in a letter to Chanute: "We have no intention of forgetting that we are Americans, and do not expect to make arrangements which would probably result in harm to our native country." Wilbur did not doubt that the military use of their invention could change the course of empire. Just after Christmas 1905, he wrote again to Chanute: "The idea of selling to a single government as a strict secret has some advantages but we are very much disinclined to assume the moral responsibility for choosing the proper one when we have no means of knowing how it will use the invention."

Of the roadblocks in the way of a sale, the easiest to explain is that no one much believed the Wrights had flown. In March 1905 — by which time Wilbur and Orville had made over 150 flights at Kitty Hawk and Huffman — *The Criterion* printed an extensive article speculating on the possibility of human flight. Flight could happen, most experts quoted agreed, but enormous obstacles remained. The Croatian-born electrical genius Nikola Tesla stated, "But what we must have — and what we shall have some day — is a motor which will weigh the one-hundredth part of the motor we now use." The article mentioned the Wrights only in passing, as having "amplified in several very interesting directions" the work of Octave Chanute. Doubt extended to the Continent. Chanute wrote the Wrights: "I enclose a letter... indicating that the Germans doubt your achievements, as do the French."

Closer to home, understanding was no better. While Dayton papers from time to time carried brief and unenlightening notices of the Wrights' activities, they never acted as though a new world was being born almost on the doorstep of their presses. In his autobiography, James Cox, publisher of *The Dayton Daily News*, wrote, "Reports would come in to our office that the ship had been seen in the air over Huffman Prairie just east of the city, but our news staff would not believe the stories. Nor," he added acidly, "did they ever take the pains to go out and see." Derision followed doubt. While *Scientific American* published the Wrights' claims to flights of a half-hour and more, it added:

> Unfortunately, the Wright brothers are hardly disposed to publish any substantiation or to make public experiments, for reasons best known to themselves. If such sensational and tremendously important experiments are being conducted in a not very remote part of the country... is it possible to believe that the enterprising American reporter, who, it is well known, comes down the chimney when the door is locked in his face... would not have ascertained all about them and published them long ago?

The enterprising American reporter had already done just that. At the time the above was written, he was in Medina, Ohio, writing about bees.

NCR was the inadvertent training school of American business: Patterson hired the brightest, taught them the day's best business methods, then, often as not, booted them out the door. He fired some because they threatened him, some because they bored him and others just for practice.

the feud

John H. Patterson cast his net broadly. *The NCR Weekly*, a house organ, was, its masthead stated: "Published in the interests of all concerned in all the N.C.R. Companies. Owners, Makers, Office Forces, Sellers, Users, Non-users, Clerks, Cashiers, Customers, Servants, Children and others, if there are others." Indeed, only two groups permanently escaped the grasp of Patterson's benevolence, his competitors and his executives. Patterson trained thoroughly. Arguably, he had the best orchestrated production and sales system of the time, and in the days before MBAs it was to NCR that bright young men headed to learn how to run a business. They were amply rewarded. Patterson paid well, all down the line and dizzyingly at the top. One thirty-year-old executive reported earnings of $50,000 a year in salary and bonuses, a sum undiluted by inflation and all but untouched by taxes.

For the ambitious there was another lure. Patterson built the National Cash Register Company with a talent for organization, a flair for salesmanship and an absolute genius for firing people. He could fire spectacularly: one NCR executive returned from a business trip to find his desk and chair on the company lawn, gloriously ablaze. He could fire en masse. Once, dissatisfied with the performance of his cost accounting department, he marched its members — ledgers under arms — to the boiler room. There, ledgers were consigned to the flames, employees dismissed to oblivion. Patterson believed in system, not individuals. He undergirded that view with the simple dictum: "When a man gets indispensable, let's fire him." Rarely did he wait that long. A subsequent NCR chief executive cited in his autobiography a magazine's claim that between 1910 and 1930, one-sixth of the nation's top executives had been trained — and fired — by Patterson. Dismissal came without warning or recourse. "There are just two things," Patterson told the soon-to-be-departed. "Everything you say is wrong. Everything you do is wrong." When one discharged executive sought an explanation, Patterson replied, "No, I won't explain anything to you, because if I started to do that I might take you back."

For those in the lower ranks, dismissal created a continuing corporate updraft, carrying to the top those who for whatever reason caught Patterson's eye. With Edward Deeds, presidential favor had been gained by his daring ascent of the company smokestack and his photographic proof of loose brick. For another junior executive, Stanley Allyn, the blessing came when, heading down an NCR corridor, he overheard Patterson say, "That young man has the most efficient walk I have ever seen." Allyn joined NCR as a $10.91 a week accounting clerk; in three years he was assistant comptroller; three years after that, he was a director of the company. Those who fell within Patterson's favor did not rise unscathed. While in Dayton, executives were subject to Patterson's compulsion to instruct, instructions received through a flow of presidential memoranda that specified the recommended width of their ties, the recommended percentage they leave as tips, and the recommended leisure pursuits for their families. While traveling, they were unprotected against Patterson's whims back at headquarters. Allyn reported returning from business trips to find that in his absence Patterson had dumped the contents of his desk into the trash, something the NCR chief did to encourage his executives "to start clean."

A titled Englishman once stated that horseback was the closest anyone could get to God. At NCR, horsemanship was less a matter of godliness than a prerequisite of job security.

True passion he reserved for his own health. "When I began the work of the National Cash Register," Patterson told one assembly of NCR boy gardeners, "I smoked from five to seven cigars a day, and I drank when other men drank. But I found that if I was going to make a success of the business I must use all the strength, all the ability I had, and so I threw away my cigars and turned down my glass." And much else besides. The NCR president sprang from fad to fad. An early favorite was Fletcherism, the brainchild of Horace Fletcher, a millionaire who once lived solely on potatoes for fifty-eight days. Fletcher argued that food should be taken in very small bites, then masticated thirty-two times — once for every tooth in a fully occupied mouth — before being swallowed. Post-Fletcher, Patterson made pilgrimages to Battle Creek, Michigan, and its gospel of bran and enemas. Bran yielded to the teachings of Luigi Cornaro, a sixteenth-century Italian who lived to be 104, ostensibly through moderating his diet.

The NCR president's desire to improve himself was matched by an urge to improve others. His diet plans, his business methods, his ideas of things in general were not simply of benefit to him, he believed, but would benefit any who would adopt them. His well-paid executives were inclined to follow Patterson's lead; the rest of the world, including the city of Patterson's birth, was not. John H. Patterson regarded himself as Dayton's leading citizen, yet the city's genially corrupt government kept ignoring all his counsel and advice. True, some of what he advocated was peculiar: the NCR president, for example, wanted cats and dogs banned from Dayton as agents of pestilence. But his relations with the city were not helped by the fact that, house pets aside, Patterson was on many points irritatingly right — local government did need

reform, the canal was a stagnant mess, cultural amenities were lacking. And the city had done worse than ignore his advice, it had spurned his generosity: when Patterson offered Dayton 120 acres for a public park, city officials turned him down.

In 1907, Patterson learned — or concluded — that the railway spur he wanted for NCR would not be laid without bribes. Outraged, he summoned 1,000 civic leaders to a Monday meeting in the NCR auditorium. There, those assembled were led in mass singings of "America" and "Old Folks at Home." Then, by one newspaper account, "Mr. Patterson stepped lightly to the front of the stage.... His hair was clipped closely, and the silver was evident. His moustache is a little whiter than a year ago. His complexion, always on the order of strawberry, was clear. His eyes sparkling. His manner easy." Eyes sparkling and manner easy, Patterson proceeded to deliver a two-and-a-half hour tongue lashing. He denounced the city of his birth: "Dayton is known now, and justly, too, I believe," the NCR president said early in his remarks, "as being the worst city in the state, and turns out more criminals than any other city in the state." He denounced the city's leadership: for its unwillingness to instruct the citizenry: "This is a malarious climate in the summer time, and we ought to teach people not to eat anything sweet or sour. That may sound crazy, but it is the truth, and I believe it." He denounced all persons present: for their lack of civic mindedness, their tolerance of corruption. "Every man here is a miser," he said, "for not having done more for the city."

Accusations made, Patterson pointed the finger of blame. First, he singled out by name local political figures and the city officials he considered responsible for rejecting his offered park land. Then, he broadened his indictment. As one newspaper cautiously stated: "Mr. Patterson at this point gave a list of names that he said would go down in infamy." Those Patterson declared guilty learned soon enough of their crimes. Many were in the audience; as Patterson called out each name, the miscreant's picture was projected by stereopticon equipment onto a large canvas screen for all to see.

Dayton, the NCR president claimed, had failed its heritage. The city had been founded by great men, but even these had despaired of its future. One early leader, Patterson asserted, had advised Patterson's mother to abandon Dayton and seek a place "where the people have a higher ambition than to have a good time, to eat the choicest viands, to drink the choicest liquor, to smoke and chew, and hunt and fish." It was advice, the city's self-proclaimed leading citizen stated, his mother always regretted not having taken. And, Patterson said, it was advice that he would take now. Reaching for the rod of punishment, he announced that he was leaving Dayton. Leaving and taking NCR and its 3,800 jobs with him. Leaving and heading for points east. Buffalo, or Bridgeport. Maybe Schenectady. NCR's departure, he stated, "will be a lesson to the people in all other cities of what they ought to do to retain their factories in their midst."

Word that the city's premier employer planned to strike camp and lead his people through the wilderness to Schenectady wiped all other news off the front pages of the city. Dayton, finding itself jilted in a courtship it had not known was in progress, leapt to the role of ardent suitor. Patterson withdrew into a prominent sulk. In the days following his Monday address, NCR organized tours to let the ordinary citizens of the city see the gem of industry that was being cast aside by the foolishness of the city's leaders. Most had never seen the behemoth up close: thirteen buildings of the most modern design, thirty-five acres of floor space, all set on a landscaped 140-acre campus; its workers turned out nearly 2,000 cash registers a week, and for their efforts were compensated $3 million a year, by far the largest payroll in the city. Company general manager Hugh Chalmers told one group of visitors that NCR held ninety-six percent of the domestic market for cash registers, "and all this money is gathered outside the city of Dayton, brought in here, and paid to the people employed here in Dayton," who in turn passed it on to the city's landlords, grocers and retailers.

At week's end, Patterson presented an encore. NCR issued a condescending summons to the event: "It is especially desired that the proprietors of the various manufacturing institutions of Dayton, also the ministers of Montgomery county outside of Dayton, and also 100 prominent farmers outside the city of Dayton, be present.... We trust that this meeting will be largely attended and that no vacancies will be seen at the tables." Those arriving found the NCR president in no very sentimental mood. Strung overhead, a banner proclaimed, "The object of the N.C.R. is to make the most money with the least trouble."

Patterson took the stage as one scorned: "For eleven years I have appealed to you, but nothing but ridicule came from you," he told the audience. Ridicule of his employee welfare system. Ridicule of his proposals for civic improvement. Ridicule of his urgings on health and diet. He repeated his charges of Monday, then added fresh ones: "If the ministers will preach eating less food of the wrong kind and the wrong drinks, there will be less knocking. Knocking comes from a diseased liver and if people's livers are out of order they will be knockers." The move east, Patterson asserted, offered NCR great advantages: lower taxes, a better labor market, readier access to export markets and — no deference to those on hand — "higher class visitors." NCR's departure, Patterson added, "will be the best thing that ever happened to Dayton. As long as we stay here, of course, it will gain people, but what are people? If Dayton had 10,000 less people than she has now they would be better off."

One local newspaper summarized the drift of Patterson's remarks with a triple-deck headline, bannered across page one:

IF THE NATIONAL CASH REGISTER COMPANY
LEAVES DAYTON IT WILL BE BECAUSE THE
PEOPLE OF THIS CITY HAVE DRIVEN IT AWAY

The subheads in a second newspaper added:

Criticisms, While Apparently Harsh, Are Based Upon a Pro-
found Sense of Honor and a Lofty Ambition, Similar To
That With Which the N.C.R. Company Has Established
the Model Factory of the World, and Which Mr. Patterson
Believes To Be For the General Betterment of Man-
kind — Dayton May Yet Hold the N.C.R.

That last phrase was key. Patterson was prepared to leave Dayton, but it would
take two years to organize his company for the move. For that period, he was
placing the city on probation. Most Dayton newspapers rushed to assuage the
NCR president; one Republican paper stated, "Mr. Patterson's entire address
will convince the fair-minded individual that his assertions were not the result
of the ravings of exasperation and disgust without careful consideration, but
the thoughts of the sane, and safe, man, carefully weighed as to their final effect."

Over at the *Dayton Daily News*, however, Patterson's performance reduced
James Cox to ridicule. Ridicule took the form of a large ad — placed by a nonexistent Dayton Protective Association — inviting all citizens to a "Grand Meeting at the Glue Factory." At that event, the advertisement stated, "The [com-
pany] president will tell when, how, where and what his reasons are for permitting himself to remain one week in this reduction plant climate, where the
malaria bugs sing in the gloaming and the drinking water is thick with 4,000-
legged bacteria...." The event's program, the ad announced, included the band
playing "That sweet soul-stirring romanza — 'Dayton is a Rotten Old Town,'"
tours of the buttermilk foundations and — a knock at Patterson's fascination
with landscape gardening — free distribution of souvenir flower beds. The ad
closed with the mocking tag line, "Here to Stay, But Coax Us."

For James Cox, it was a monumental case of bad timing. The whole of the
city's anxiety over the threatened loss of its chief employer halted in its tracks,
converted to anger, and descended upon him and his newspaper. The front
page of the rival *Journal* gleefully headlined:

COWARDLY ATTACK UPON DAYTON'S MODEL
INDUSTRY, ITS PRESIDENT AND ITS METHODS,
CALLS FORTH SCATHING DENUNCIATION

As a unit, the business men and citizens of Dayton, thoroughly disgusted and aroused by the unwarranted assault, resented in no uncertain tones the calumnious utterance and rebuked the venomous appeal.... There exists no "Dayton Protective Association" except in the minds of a few perverts and cantankerous manipulators whose doctrine is "Prey, Prey, Prey."

Rebuke from a fellow editor, however, was nothing compared to the wrath of John H. Patterson, who was soon piling James Cox knee-deep in lawsuits.

Eccentricities aside, John Patterson, sixty-three in 1907, was something of a national figure, largely a benevolent one. Reformers regarded him as a rare business advocate of workplace improvements; to most businessmen, he was the owner of a notably successful enterprise, whose product sat on the front counter of the day's boom in retailing. Cox, thirty-seven when he and Patterson squared off, was as stubborn as the NCR president, though not as proud. He, too, was becoming a figure of substance. His *News* was now returning him an annual profit equal to its original purchase price. Cox had used his profits to branch out; he acquired a county-seat newspaper twenty miles away, his first step toward media empire.

In his conflict with Cox, Patterson's natural belligerence was fanned by the personal trainer, Charles Palmer, he had brought with him from England the previous year. If Patterson was a crank, then Palmer was the crank's own turn. Cox later described him as "a man of insignificant personality and poor education who excited general distrust, but [who] had established an ascendancy over

Designed by architects Frank Andrews and Stanford White, landscaped by the Olmsted Brothers, NCR looked like something between a college campus and a movie set — yet was so well orchestrated that the whole vast undertaking was able to turn on the dime to provide flood rescue and relief.

Mr. Patterson that amounted to hypnotism." Palmer claimed the capacity to read faces; Patterson sought reports on many of his executives, firing a number in consequence. Patterson placed Palmer on NCR's Board of Directors and sustained his meddling in the company's day-to-day affairs; at one point, Patterson sent his sales department an approving telegram that read: "Mr. Palmer and I congratulate you."

Patterson — or Palmer — decreed that a man who could not command a horse could not command men. Soon, NCR executives were roused at dawn, mounted on horseback and sent riding through the 300-acre company park. One Patterson biographer dryly observed: "Probably nothing like this ever happened before in an American business institution." Patterson erected a reviewing stand, where he, Palmer and a clutch of high company officials could watch as his executives — locally dubbed The NCR Roughriders — cantered past. Those dragooned included NCR inventor Charles Kettering. Kettering was a farm boy, but no horseman. Approaching the reviewing stand on a balky steed named Midnight, he nearly fell from his mount. Turning to Edward Deeds, Patterson said, "We ought not to have a man like that around here." Deeds agreed to dismiss Kettering; then, aware that Kettering was likely his most valuable employee, immediately hired him back. Others met less generous fates. One rider broke a leg in a fall; another was thrown and killed. The death brought fresh criticism from the *Daily News,* and fresh libel suits from Patterson.

As Patterson battled Cox, Palmer sowed discord within NCR. He issued decrees banning cigars, tea, salt, pepper, butter and eggs from sales meeting lunches. General manager Hugh Chalmers decided it was time to draw the line. Chalmers was revered at NCR; he had worked his way up from office boy to second-in-command, yet when Chalmers criticized Palmer, it was Chalmers who got the sack. Cox editorialized: "Behind the resignation of Hugh Chalmers rests a story which partakes of so many unusual features as to depict a situation absolutely anomalous in the commercial world. It is the story of an English lackey, a butler, a valet, who has completely practiced the art of hypnotism and so dominated the mind of his master as to sunder all friendship — his family, business and social."

Patterson upped the ante. He announced he had not time enough both to direct his company and to pursue his lawsuits against Cox; therefore, he was shutting down NCR. The thousands thus idled were soon crowding into mass meetings where they and other townspeople heard Patterson praised and Cox buried. At one gathering, a ringing tribute to Patterson was voiced by the company executive who had broken his leg falling from a horse. Other executives issued a toadying statement of support for Palmer: "The simple rules of health and exercise which have so often been referred to and ridiculed have been beneficial to us and of great value to the company."

Neither Patterson nor Cox left much space for backing down; neither inclined to compromise. The dispute was pushing Cox to the wall. Few in Dayton were anxious to join him in tangling with the city's leading industrialist, and his own resources were limited. Cox paid a call on his banker: what was the latter's opinion of John H. Patterson's business judgment? Very high, his banker replied. Cox then observed that Patterson was suing him for well over

$1 million; given this implicit opinion of Cox's worth, would the banker increase his newspaper's $15,000 credit line? His banker declined.

The affair had its ludicrous aspects. Persuaded, either by himself or by Palmer, that his life was in danger, Patterson secured the services of four mounted riflemen, who escorted him and Palmer to and from NCR. Riflemen notwithstanding, the matter ended not with a bang but with a deposition. As the trial of Patterson's libel suits approached, attorneys for both sides began taking statements. At one session, an attorney for Cox asked about gifts Patterson was alleged to have made: one to a judge who had ruled in Patterson's favor; another to labor officials at a time when a strike was brewing. Patterson's attorneys requested an adjournment. After lunch, his attorneys returned; Patterson did not. The NCR president had disappeared. Two days passed. Then, a cable arrived from the middle of the Atlantic, where Patterson was shipboard for Europe. In that cable, Patterson directed that all lawsuits be dropped and that NCR assume Cox's legal expenses. With pardonable understatement, Cox later wrote: "This was a surprise to Patterson's attorneys, our attorneys and myself."

For the next three years, John H. Patterson managed his company from New York City. When he returned, Charles Palmer was nowhere in sight. Patterson was rarely predictable. In 1908, when James Cox ran for Congress, Patterson endorsed him. For Cox, the dispute with Patterson was a near-run thing. In his autobiography, he noted: " if his attack... had not been so ruthless things might have turned out badly for us." For Patterson, the more serious matter was that of Chalmers. Chalmers was a gifted executive; he later headed the Chalmers Motor Car Company. He was not, however, the forgiving sort. Leaving Dayton, he vowed, "I will not be even with the old man till I have put him behind bars." In that wish, Hugh Chalmers would come to within one natural disaster of success.

However perplexed the Patterson-Cox feud and the firing of Chalmers may have left the NCR forces in Dayton, in Europe the company's wheels kept spinning. In October 1907, Wilbur Wright wrote to his sister Katharine from Berlin, where he and Orville took long walks each evening through the city:

> About the most amusing thing we have seen in these walks was the (National) Cash Register office.... The room was full of people going

about playing with the machines as though they were toy pianos or something of the kind.... I joined in like any Dutchman and punched a couple of tickets as souvenirs of the occasion.... The signs explained so clearly and convincingly the advantages of cash registers in selling all kinds of goods, that we came near getting one to help sell our flying machine.

The Wrights were in Europe, trying — thus far without success — to find a buyer for the world's first airplane. All other matters waited, flying included. On October 16, 1905, a full two years before their evening strolls in Berlin, Wilbur had flown a single lap of their flight path at Huffman Prairie, landed near the hangar and climbed out of the plane. Neither brother had been airborne since. They had a flying machine to sell, and they had their terms. The Wrights held that however difficult it had been for them to unlock the secrets of flight, those secrets could be easily filched by others once their machine was presented in public. They insisted, therefore, that a prospective buyer commit in advance to purchasing an airplane if in actual test flight that aircraft met the criteria for a flying machine established with that customer.

Negotiations wrangled along. The French were Byzantine, the Germans insistent, the Americans obtuse. If governments remained unwilling, the Wrights were prepared to look elsewhere. In 1907, Wilbur wrote: "Although we are not now, and will not be for some time, ready to begin the exhibition part of our program, yet we are desirous of getting into communication with parties that would be able to handle that part of the business when the time came." He sent those somewhat stilted sentences to Barnum & Bailey.

In their dealings with governments, the Wrights played their hand, to quote Mark Twain, with "the quiet confidence of a Christian holding four aces." To the moral determination one might expect from two sons of a bishop of the United Brethren Church, they added the certainty that they alone held the keys to flight. They could be patient. As Wilbur wrote to Octave Chanute:

> If it were indeed true that others would be flying within a year or two, there would be reason in selling at any price, but we are convinced that no one will be able to develop a practical flyer within five years. This opinion is based on cold calculation.... Even you, Mr. Chanute, have little idea how difficult the flying problem really is. When we see men laboring year after year on points we overcame in a few weeks, without ever getting enough along to meet the worse points beyond, we know that their rivalry & competition are not to be feared for many years.

Actually, it was to the Wrights' advantage that Chanute did not fully understand what they had done. Chanute had spilled the beans. In April 1903, he gave an illustrated lecture on the Wrights' breakthrough in aeronautical control to the Aero-Club de France; he then helped publish other information — including scale drawings of the Wrights' 1902 glider — which the brothers had full reason to regard as proprietary. In Chanute's limited defense, he may have believed that the flying problem was still a long way from solution and that he was merely cross-pollinating the American and European strains of inquiry. He was wrong twice: the flying problem had been solved, and he was giving large pieces of that solution to the Wrights' erstwhile competitors.

Chanute's description of the Wrights' work sparked a rebirth of European interest in heavier-than-air flight. The race, such as it was, was between the Wrights and those Europeans, mostly French, who copied them. The imitators were confident; their copies were poor. Aviation historian Charles Gibbs-Smith says of the Wrights' European rivals, "There was not one pioneer at that time — and they all revealingly spoke, wrote, or tried to build flying machines — who had more than a faint conception of the difficulties involved." Not until November 1906 did any European craft remain aloft for as long as twenty seconds. Curiously, no European aspirant adequately incorporated the key to the Wrights' success, the control system as explained by Chanute; in consequence, no one in Europe approached the smooth control, the gracefully banked turns or the figure eights the Wrights readily accomplished. However haltingly, though, the Europeans were taking to the air, and doing so in public. As the Wrights by their own choice remained grounded, they became the target of skepticism, and contempt. One French aviator, Ernest Archdeacon, stated the case with Gallic pride:

> The famous Wright brothers may today claim all they wish. If it is true — and I doubt it more and more — that they were the first to fly through the air, they will not have the glory before History.... The first authentic experiments in powered aviation have taken place in France; they will progress in France; and the famous fifty kilometers [Wilbur's flight at Huffman] announced by the Wrights will, I am sure, be beaten by us as well before they will have decided to show their phantom machine.

Archdeacon attached his name to the Prix Deutsch-Archdeacon, to go to the first aeronaut to complete a circular flight of over one kilometer. It was a feat the Wrights had accomplished at Huffman several hundred times. On January 13, 1908, the prize was claimed by a Frenchman, Henri Ferman, with the Wrights still on the ground.

Electrical engineering was the turn-of-the-century's hot field; the automobile was the hot industry. Charles Kettering would take those two lines, cross them and parlay that crossing into a legendary technical career. Before doing so, he produced the electric cash register, his major accomplishment at NCR.

CHAPTER TWELVE

The summer of 1908

In the summer of 1908, General Motors was incorporated, the Model T introduced, and Charles Kettering began the career that would enrich the former and leave the latter obsolete. That summer marked the infant automobile industry's first coming of age, during which it found its organization, its archetype and its genius. In retirement, Charles Kettering observed that well over 99 percent of the automobiles ever produced in the United States had been made subsequent to his entry into the field as an automotive engineer — and with trifling exceptions every one of those vehicles bore the imprint of Kettering's work.

Charles Kettering began that summer still in the employ of National Cash Register. His tenure there was uncertain. Kettering was among the most endearing of men; indeed, it was a tribute to the contrariness of John H. Patterson that the NCR president simply couldn't stand him. For many at NCR, the company was a door through which John H. Patterson pitched them out; for Kettering, that door revolved. Patterson fired him for slipping from his horse. Twice while Kettering was directing work on electrifying the cash register, Patterson strode in and fired everyone in the room. By one account, Patterson for a time discharged Kettering on sight. The reason for the NCR president's animus is not known. Possibly Kettering offended Patterson's advanced sense of order. Patterson ran an extremely sanitary ship — he had a crew of nine just to wash windows, a crew of eight just to clean cuspidors — while Kettering's laboratory looked like a pack rat's garage. At one point, Patterson had the glass half-walls of Kettering's lab painted over black, so the visitors who daily trooped through his otherwise immaculate complex would not catch a glimpse of the mess. Kettering owed his continued employment to Edward Deeds: whenever Patterson fired the inventor, Deeds hired him back. Patterson couldn't drive Kettering off; it took Deeds to lure him away.

The bait Deeds held out was the automobile. Popular enthusiasm for the motorcar was still a swelling tide. In 1907, *Harper's Weekly* declared that the auto industry was certain to expand: "There is one reason for this which must not be overlooked — that is, the fact that the automobile is essential to comfort and happiness." Essential to comfort and happiness, a statement written when there were still fewer than 100,000 cars on the road. Those who could afford to do so were buying *Harper's* judgment and spending accordingly. *Horseless Age* cautioned, "Extravagance is reckless and something must be done before utter ruin follows in the wake of folly... Many owners of houses worth $5,000 to $15,000, which they have acquired after years of toil, are mortgaging them in order to buy automobiles." Deeds had himself purchased an automobile; he felt the tug of the new technology — and in the summer of 1908 he pointed Kettering toward the commercial possibilities. Deeds suggested to Kettering they could cash in by coming up with an improvement for the automobile. "There is a river of gold running past us," Deeds told Kettering. "Why can't we throw out a little dam and sluice some of it our way?"

One of the minor mangers of the modern world — Deeds' barn — where a moonlighting inventor began to remake the automobile.

Kettering agreed to get his feet wet. Still an NCR employee, he gave the effort his evenings, his weekends and virtually the whole of his and Olive's savings, $1,500 used to buy milling equipment and a lathe. Deeds matched the investment and threw in the barn behind his home as a workplace. In mild irony, the barn was of a type known as a "gentleman's carriage barn" — designed to shelter the horses and carriages that Kettering's work within did so much to make obsolete. As a first project, the pair chose to tackle what Deeds considered to be a major flaw in his own vehicle — its unreliable ignition system. The ignition system provides the spark that ignites the fuel mix compressed in the cylinders. Common for the time, the system on Deeds' car combined a magneto with dry-cell batteries. At roadway speeds, the magneto performed well, generating the required spark; at low speed, however, its output sputtered. Drivers then threw a switch to draw current from the batteries. These dry cells were costly; they were also of limited capacity, requiring replacement every few hundred miles.

The fault with Deeds' ignition, Kettering concluded, was its vibrating coil, which produced a constant shower of sparks, much of it wasted. Kettering designed a stationary coil that concentrated the spark, providing discrete jolts of electricity timed to each compression of the cylinder. When Kettering needed help building the prototype, he recruited two of his ablest NCR subordinates,

Bill Chryst and William Anderson, to join the after-hours effort. Chryst and Anderson were the first enrollees in the Barn Gang, a cluster of NCR expatriates whom Kettering filched to assist on his projects. In May 1909, Kettering mounted the prototype on Deeds' car; Edward and Edith Deeds then field tested the device by driving to New York City and back. Kettering's ignition system extended battery life tenfold; further, it operated without the frequent tinkering most ignition systems then demanded.

As businessman of the pair, Deeds approached Henry Leland, president of Cadillac. At sixty-five, Leland was setting the pace in a young man's game, holding Cadillac to the auto industry's most exacting engineering standards. In 1908, those standards brought him the high prize of automaking — the Dewar's Cup — for his demonstration of the interchangeability of parts in automobile manufacture. A sale to Leland, Deeds believed, would make their system's reputation. In response to Deeds' importuning, Leland dispatched his chief engineer to Dayton. Kettering's new ignition performed admirably on a test drive. A flurry of conferences ensued; then, in July 1909, Leland abruptly placed an order for 8,000 of Kettering's systems.

The order caught Kettering and Deeds flat-footed. They had no production facilities, no financing, no papers of incorporation, not even a name for their partnership. Interested in development, not manufacture, they subcontracted the entire production run, then incorporated their own efforts as the Dayton Engineering Laboratories Company. Kettering did not greatly care for the name, but Barn Gang member Bill Chryst — who liked the way National Biscuit Company chewed down to "Nabisco" — thought "Delco" had a nice ring to it. On September 1, 1909, Charles Kettering resigned from NCR; he was going to be an inventor.

In the summer of 1908, the Wrights' determination to present their aircraft on their own terms paid off.

The U. S. government had finally issued an "Advertisement and Specification for a Heavier-Than-Air Flying Machine." That advertisement sought an aircraft that could carry a pilot and passenger for 125 miles at forty miles per hour and "be able to land without damage." If such a craft was presented, the government committed itself to its purchase. With this announcement, the Wrights readied an aircraft for public view. Actually, they needed two aircraft, as they were also concluding negotiations to make demonstration flights in France.

The brothers began by heading to Kitty Hawk for the first time in five years, there to brush up on their flying skills and to break in their new Wright Flyer. In 1903, when the Wrights had wished to share their invention with the world, the world had been indifferent. Now, with the Wrights anxious to keep their invention under wraps until the official trials began, the world sneaked in for a peak. A small clump of reporters edged its way toward the Wrights' camp in hopes of flushing out their fabulous bird. One reporter, witnessing his first flight, wrote:

> In the excitement of this first flight, men trained to observe details under all sorts of distractions, forgot their cameras, forgot their watches, forgot everything but this aerial monster chattering over our heads. As it neared us we could plainly see the operator in his seat working the upright levers close by his side. When it was almost squarely over us there was a movement of the forward and rear guiding planes, a slight curving of the larger planes at one end and the machine wheeled at an angle every bit as gracefully as an eagle flying close to the ground could have done.

The reporters' reaction was a foretaste of how the larger crowds in France and America would react.

Wilbur went first. In France, circumstances were against him. He was alone, apart not simply from Orville but from all familiar faces. His aircraft, carefully packed by Orville in America, was damaged by French customs officials apparently innocently curious to poke through the packing crates to see just what they contained. He was faced with communicating in his uncertain French with indifferent French workmen on how to ready for flight a machine many of whose parts had as yet no accepted name in either language. To distract him further, he badly burned his arm on the engine. On August 8, 1908, at Les Hunaudieres, south of LeMans, and before most of the leading figures of French aviation, Wilbur made his first flight.

And suddenly, it was a three-dimensional world. Wilbur's aircraft was in the air not as some clanking intruder, but as a craft at home in the sky. His initial flight lasted barely two minutes. Wilbur was nonplused; he wrote calmly of that flight to Orville, "Last Sunday I took the machine out for the first time and made a couple of circles." On the ground, however, there was consternation: French aviators were stunned by the ease, grace and control with which Wilbur handled his craft. Aviator Rene Gasnier conceded, "We are as children compared with the Wrights." For the crowds that gathered as Wilbur's flights continued, it was a moment of transcendence. People wept. People jumped in place. People hugged each other. From London, *The Times* reported: "All accounts... published in this morning's papers from the correspondents on the

Innocents abroad. Orville powers a fragile craft that neither brother believed would have much application to war past a row of spike-helmeted German soldiers.

spot, attest the complete triumph of the American inventor ... the enthusiasm was indescribable." That enthusiasm remained as the throngs swelled. Wilbur wrote to his father of one seventy-year-old man who for a week daily made by bicycle the sixty-mile round-trip journey from his home to watch the flying. The rich and titled rushed to witness the event; Wilbur wrote home, "Queen Margherita of Italy was in the crowd yesterday. Princes & millionaires are as thick as fleas."

Triumphing in France, Wilbur sent older-brotherly advice to Orville, who was readying his own machine at Fort Myer, Virginia: "I advise you most earnestly to stick to calms until after you are sure of yourself. Don't go out even for all the officers of the government unless you would go equally if they were absent." Orville confessed himself to Katharine less certain of success than were the news reporters who gathered around him and wrote of his "air of perfect confidence." He began flying on September 3. Initially, all was success. Faced with the fact of a man mastering the sky, onlookers became incoherent. One observer recalled seeing a well-dressed man walking somnambulistically from the field crying "my god, my god, my god" over and over. On September 9, Orville — flying before an audience that included three cabinet members — remained aloft for sixty-two minutes, a world endurance mark, which he bettered the following day. For a time, he and Wilbur on opposite sides of the Atlantic swapped records for longest and highest flights.

One part of the Army test required Orville to make a flight with a passenger. On September 17, he took off carrying Lieut. Thomas Selfridge. One hundred feet over the Fort Myer field, Orville's aircraft lost thrust. Later investigation concluded that one end of a propeller blade had developed a longitudinal crack; the blade flattened, robbing the aircraft of power. As Orville attempted to regain control, the aircraft pitched downward. His later view was that had the mishap occurred at a higher altitude, he would have had time to aright the craft and land safely. As it was, he crashed. Both he and Selfridge were knocked unconscious. Selfridge died of his injuries later that day; Orville sustained a broken leg, several cracked ribs and a back injury from which he never fully recovered.

In the summer of 1908, James Cox declared his candidacy for Congress. Cox liked to claim he was pushed; more particularly, he wrote that county Democratic boss Ed Hanley leaned on him to stand for election in Ohio's Third Congressional District, which centered on Dayton. Reluctance was likely feigned. For Cox, politics was his natural call-

ing; mixing it up inside the ring was far more congenial to his nature than pitching in editorial brickbats from the stands. Moreover, Cox may have needed new worlds to conquer. He had made of *The Daily News* a solid financial and journalistic success, the emblem of which was the new headquarters building he opened in 1908. Its opening gave Cox a chance to pay off a remembered snub: pressed in his feud with Patterson, he sought out his banker to request a longer credit line. The banker had declined, saying newspapers were unreliable undertakings. Cox thought otherwise. To proclaim that view, he directed that the new *Daily News* office be designed to resemble a bank. Ten thousand Daytonians toured the building its opening day.

Soon, the publisher those thousands came to visit was seeking their votes for Congress. The Cox campaign had its assets. William Jennings Bryan, the Democratic presidential candidate, came to Dayton as keynote speaker at Cox's opening campaign rally. To this, Cox added the improbable endorsement of John H. Patterson. As publisher of the district's leading newspaper, he was assured of editorial support from himself, and he had newsboys to organize into a drum corps, the Cox Juniors, that marched enthusiastically in campaign parades. And Cox was fortunate in his enemies. Third District Republi-

cans were squabbling, presenting Cox with a divided opposition and a three-way race. He ran strong in Dayton and its surroundings; strong enough elsewhere. At thirty-eight, he was a congressman.

Election achieved, Cox focused on what one southern senator once defined as a politician's second responsibility; namely, to get reelected. Cox gained office while getting only fourteen percent of the vote cast at the National Soldiers' Home, residence to thousands of Republican-leaning Civil War pensioners. In Congress, Cox directed the advantages of office against this Republican bastion. He introduced 871 private pension bills to grant or extend the pension rights of individual constituents, most of them at the Home. Further, by a deft bit of legislative maneuvering, he gained an increased appropriation for the Home itself. Funds for its operation were channeled through an omnibus bill that also included the appropriation for the zoological gardens near Washington. Early in the discussion of the bill, Cox inquired why the appropriation for the zoo was being increased; the requisite Republican committee chairman replied: "It's the high cost of living. We have monkeys in the zoo to

His banker turned James Cox down when the publisher needed a loan — when fatter days followed, Cox snubbed his nose by building a newspaper office that resembled a bank. The one-time upstart of Dayton journalism was there to stay.

feed." During later debate on the measure, Cox moved an increased appropriation for the Soldiers' Home: its residents, he detailed for the House, were less well fed than federal prisoners at Leavenworth, yet the Republican party — the supposed friend of the veteran — appeared more concerned with the nutrition of zoo monkeys. Neatly trapped, House Republicans had little option but to support Cox's amendment, which they unanimously did.

Having done for the Soldiers' Home, Cox proceeded to do for his home city. He wanted a new post office for Dayton, one that would be both "an architectural ornament for the city" and a substantial trophy for a junior congressman to bring home. He inserted authorization for such a post office into a bill that, by procedure, was not intended to carry any new appropriation. If a single congressman raised a point of order against the authorization, Cox's post office would be eliminated from the bill. He canvassed the House and found two congressmen intending to raise just such a point. The pertinent section of the bill came to a vote one day shortly before noon. Cox sidetracked one of the expected objectors by arranging to have him invited to lunch — and safely off the floor — by a senior member whose invitation was sure to be accepted. Even more neatly, he outflanked the second. By arrangement with Cox, the presiding member turned the speaker's gavel over to the other likely objector; this made him acting speaker and, as such, ineligible to call upon himself to raise his objection. Dayton got its post office; Cox got the credit.

Constituency interests aside, Cox was progressive. He supported efforts to reform the House, spoke on its floor in favor of free trade, introduced legislation to regulate the employment of children in the District of Columbia and backed Sen. Robert LaFollette's campaign to reform railway rates. He was progressive, yet clubable. He golfed, he dined out, he made himself amenable to leaders of both parties. Cox wrote engagingly of his colleagues, one of whom, Victor Murdock, recounted to Cox the rigors of campaigning in Kansas. Speaking at one stop, Murdock told those assembled that his opponent had accused him of all manner of misdeed and defect, including insanity. Raising himself up, Murdock challenged the crowd: if anyone here thinks I'm crazy, stand up.

"And by Gad," Murdock told Cox, "you know they all stood up."

Cox did for his constituents; inadvertently, his constituents did well for him. Cox was Dayton's congressman when the Wright brothers returned to Washington in 1909 to complete the Army test trials disrupted the previous year by Orville's crash and the death of Lieut. Selfridge. In 1905, Wilbur and Orville did not get so much as a polite reply from the government to which they were offering the secret of flight. In 1909, the mountain came to Mohammed. On June 26, the entire Senate adjourned to watch the Wrights. Proceeding with his usual caution, Wilbur told the Senate the day was too windy; they would have to come back. After a series of postponements, Cox's colleagues began to blame the delays on him. He wrote: "As the House, in its usual routine, assembled at noon I was asked many times, somewhat sarcastically, whether we ought to adjourn to go out to Fort Myer."

Cox was present when the Wrights completed the final significant test, the speed trial with passenger, similar to the flight during which Orville had crashed the previous year. Cox recorded the reactions after Orville passed out of view on his way toward Alexandria, Virginia: "Seconds grew into minutes and minutes seemed to be hours. The audience was in great suspense. Beads of sweat broke out on the forehead of Wilbur Wright. In our imaginations, anything could have happened. Finally, the ship broke into the skyline and came rushing to the finish with a speed that seemed tremendous." Wilbur was the first to reach the landed craft; the Army review team member who rode as passenger said it was the only time he ever saw Wilbur Wright smile.

What you don't
see is what you get
— a 1912 Cadillac,
with no place to
insert the
hand-crank.
Working on the
self-starter,
Kettering believed
there would be a
hand-crank for
backup; at
Cadillac,
Henry Leland
decided otherwise.
When Kettering
inquired why there
was no crank slot,
Leland replied that
maybe he had
more faith in
Kettering's
invention than
Kettering did.

before the flood

The aircraft the Wrights flew in France and Virginia and the automobiles upon which Charles Kettering tinkered in Dayton shared a fault: both were hard to start. In 1908, the Wrights still used their catapult device to launch themselves awkwardly into flight; automobiles relied on an almost as cumbersome a method, the hand crank, to get them started.

The hand crank could be more than cumbersome; on occasion, its use proved fatal. Early in 1910, a woman stalled her car on Belle Island Bridge in Detroit. A passing motorist named Byron T. Carter stopped and offered to crank the engine back to life. Cranking a car, one contemporary wrote, "required the strength of Sampson, the cunning of Ulysses and the speed of Hermes." On this particular occasion, the gods were against gallantry; the crank snapped back, breaking Carter's jaw; complications set in and he died. The death greatly troubled Cadillac president Henry Leland: Carter had been a friend and the recalcitrant automobile had been a Cadillac. Leland reportedly vowed to his staff: "The Cadillac car will kill no more men if we can help it." Injuries from crank starting were common: in the preceding year, six Cadillac workmen had sustained broken arms from back-snapping cranks. The difficulty of crank starting was the then commonly given reason why women should not sit behind the wheel: Cincinnati's Mayor Markbreit claimed, "No woman is physically fit to run an auto." Leland put the matter to his newfound inventor in Dayton: could Kettering devise a safer, easier way to start an automobile?

Once started, an internal combustion engine runs so long as it is fed fuel and spark that power its rotation. The engine, however, has no means of starting itself; its initial rotation must come from some other source — like the pull cord commonly used to start lawn mowers. Alternatives to crank starting had been tried, but with little success. Spring-loaded and compressed air systems existed, but these offered only "one chance" starting. Acetylene explosions were used to jerk pistons into movement, but this fouled spark plugs. Cadillac engineers investigated electrical starting, but had concluded the motor required for starting would need to be nearly as large as the engine it was trying to start.

Typically, Kettering took the large view. Given one problem, he proceeded to solve three. He never doubted that a small electric motor could start an automotive engine: at NCR, he had electrified the cash register with a motor far smaller than that theoretically required. His key insight was that a single motor could both start the engine and, once that engine was running, do double-duty as a generator. As a generator, it could produce spark for ignition and current for incandescent headlights — thus permitting elimination of the unreliable magneto/dry cell ignitions and the acetylene headlamps. Further, with the addition of a storage battery, the system could store excess electricity to permit future starts. Asked to eliminate the hand-crank, Kettering devised an integrated system to start the car, ignite the fuel and light the lights — tasks all accomplished by the electricity the system itself generated and stored.

In September 1910, Kettering scrounged parts to test his thinking. "I made some calculations," he said later, "drove over to the Myers and Robbins factory in Springfield, and selected the frame and armature core of a quarter-horse-power motor. I set up a Cadillac engine and, from the Mine and Supply Company in Columbus, got some sprocket wheels and chains used in conveyor work." Earlier efforts at electrical self-starting had failed, Kettering believed, because the starting motor had been mounted directly on the engine flywheel. Thus, the motor was geared to the engine at one to one, with no mechanical advantage to make its task easier. In his own system, Kettering placed the motor astride the engine, then used the sprocket wheels and chains to gear it to the engine with a mechanical advantage of eighteen to one. His cobbed-together creation looked rather like a refugee from an agricultural implements auction, but it started the engine. Demonstrated in principle, self-starting now had to be made workable in practice. Kettering directed the system's design; his Barn Gang machined and assembled the components.

There were problems. Kettering wanted the system to provide current for headlamps. The only incandescent filaments then tough enough to handle the jouncing of a car's front end were six-volt bulbs. But a six-volt current would not be nearly strong enough to start the engine. Kettering resolved the dilemma by coupling four six-volt batteries with a switching mechanism: for starting, the mechanism aligned the batteries in series to produce twenty-four volts; once started, it realigned the batteries in parallel to produce the six volts needed by the headlamps. Automotive voltage regulators did not yet exist — yet, without voltage regulation, the generator would at high engine speeds produce bursts of electricity strong enough to burn out the battery plates. Kettering improvised. The self-starter's motor had two wire coils: a large one for starting, a smaller one for generating. By winding these coils in opposite directions, the smaller acted as a brake upon the larger, keeping its current to a level the battery could tolerate. "Reverse winding" was a little known technique: Kettering called it to mind from an article he'd once read in a popular electrical magazine on a railway car lighting system.

Time pressed. Leland wanted self-starting for his 1912 models; to meet the requirements of production planning, he needed to know by February 1911 if Kettering's system would work. A crudely-assembled prototype was tested on Deeds' car on December 17, 1910. For a finished version, all the electrical and mechanical components had to be completed and assembled in eight weeks. Fourteen-hour days became standard; one technician recalled: "We didn't know anything about 5 p.m. All we knew was light and dark." Much of the work was tedious; to ease the monotony, one crew member brought in a phonograph and his only record, "When You and I Were Young, Maggie," a saccharine ballad of which all grew heartily sick but which they were too busy to replace.

Piece by piece, the system came together. The switching mechanism that realigned the batteries from series to parallel was completed on New Year's Eve; the clutch the driver would use to engage the system was finished on January 4; the final design of the generator was detailed January 10. They worked rapidly, but too large. Leland shipped a Cadillac in which to mount the prototype. On January 14, when the crew tried to install the self-starter, it was too big to fit. Amazingly, no one had thought to track down a Cadillac, raise the hood and measure the available space. Word then arrived that Leland planned to leave for Bermuda on February 17, setting that date as the deadline. Under the pressure, the Barn Gang held together by its youth (all were under thirty); by Kettering's fierce optimism; and by the fact that, as Kettering put it, they didn't have a job, a job had them. The final redesign was installed in the Cadillac on the afternoon of February 16. Kettering drove it to the Dayton railway station, killing the engine every few blocks so he could test the starter again. He loaded the world's first self-starting vehicle on the train for Detroit, then presented it to Leland the following morning. The Cadillac president drove it, approved it in principle and departed for Bermuda. Following further refinements, Cadillac made its commitment: Henry Leland ordered 12,000 self-starters for his 1912 Cadillac.

As with their ignition system, Kettering and Deeds hoped to subcontract production. That proved impossible. A key item on their list was storage batteries, thousands of them. No battery manufacturer had ever heard of Delco. And only one battery company representative bothered to respond to Kettering's request for estimates. That salesman made the call less in hope of finding a live prospect than out of curiosity to meet the man who had placed the largest order for storage batteries in history. He found Kettering in that unlikely barn, sat through a demonstration of the self-starter, then ran off to browbeat his superiors: Delco, he said, had no offices, no production facilities, no credit rating, but they had something. By threat of resignation, he forced his firm to accept the offer. Elsewhere, the partners were less fortunate. Some suppliers refused orders so large from so small a firm; others simply could not meet the technical standards the self-starter required. Reluctantly, Kettering and Deeds were pushed into direct production. They rented a floor of the Beaver Power Building on the fringe of Dayton's downtown, signed on O. Lee Harrison — the battery man who had accepted their order — as first sales manager, and hired a dozen workers to build self-starters.

Kettering's self-starter was introduced on the 1912 Cadillac to international praise. In Britain, the system won Henry Leland his second Dewar's Cup. In France, "le Delco" became the generic term for any automatic starter. Elsewhere, only Henry Ford downplayed its significance. Ford told Kettering the Model T would never adopt a self-starter; Kettering, in reply, placed his faith in the power of consumer preference. "Mr. Ford," he said, "that is something you yourself will not have anything to say about." So it proved: self-starting was so popular that if Henry Ford had not incorporated one, people would have stopped buying Fords.

From its initial dozen workmen, Delco boomed. Just eighteen months after setting up shop, Kettering and Deeds were employing 1,200; in another year, over 2,000. The self-starter had begun as an idea; now it was a business, a large one. At NCR, John H. Patterson may have intuited that for all his value to the company, Charles Kettering was simply not an organization man. In truth, Kettering had no very great tolerance for management. At Delco his secretary received standing instructions to tell unexpected callers he was dead. Kettering may have left NCR because he chafed under organizational restriction; now he had a company of his own, already a third the size of NCR, and growing.

In 1910, Amos I. Root, the bee man, returned to the Wrights' flying field at Huffman Prairie. With the casual

nonchalance of an old friend, he stepped past the "very plain notice" announcing "Positively No Admittance" and wandered in the direction of the hangar erected on the grounds. When Root had first sought out the Wrights in 1904, the field had been all but deserted. Now, there was a throng. Looking back toward the road that ran along its edge, Root noted: "an ice-cream wagon came on the grounds; the popcorn boy was in evidence." The Wrights and flight had passed that fundamental American test of the seriousness of a phenomenon: people could make money selling food to the curious. On most days several hundred, on some days over a thousand, arrived by automobile or buggy or by the interurban line that ran to the Simms Station stop near the field to gawk and gaze and smile in wonder as the Wrights and their instructors put the student pilots at the world's first flying school through their paces. Root described the scene:

> One of the students took a seat near the engine. Two others took hold of the propellers to do the cranking, and the fourth young man sat on the ground and held the machine till the propellers got up to full speed. The starting-ground is simply a smooth piece of grass descending a few rods. At a signal from the man in the machine the boys let go, and off it started. The rubber tires, as they bumped over the ground, made some little jolting, especially when the machine got up speed. Very gradually the rubber wheels touched more and more lightly on old mother Earth, and pretty soon the beautiful and wonderful fabric slid off into the air, and then it was as still and smooth in the running as a boat going through the smoothest water.

The fascination that drew Root drew students to the school. One early student, Bernard Whelan, had been in Dayton earlier that year when Orville Wright flew over the city. Watching that flight — "And Mr. Wright was plainly visible in the pilot seat" — Whelan said, "I just got enthused." He headed for Huffman. There, he and others got their first lessons on flight control aboard the "kiwi bird," a flight simulator consisting of the wings of a defunct Wright Type B Flyer, set up on a trestle and continually agitated by a motor-driven cam. Lessons were not cheap. Recalling the experience a half century later, Whelan said, "It was the only thing I know that cost more then than it does today. It cost sixty dollars an hour to take flight training at the Wright school. That's a dollar a minute. And they didn't sign you up for anything less than four hours." Students were trained that quickly. The most famous of them — "Hap" Arnold, who commanded the U.S. Army Air Force during the Second World War — soloed after three hours, forty-eight minutes of flying time, ten days after leaving the ground for the first time.

The Wrights delegated most of the teaching to instructors. Orville, at the field on one errand or another, characteristically checked up on student progress. Whelan recalled, "I heard him say more than once: 'Have you done any mushroom hunting?'" Huffman Prairie was a marshy refuge for wild mushrooms, often hunted by local residents. Whelan explained:

By mushroom hunting, he meant very low flying. And he was of course an expert pilot himself and he would fly and make turns and figure eights around the field with the lower wing almost in the weeds, you know. And the reason he wanted you to have some of that was that low flying like that, your mistakes show up very quickly ... You have to be very alert not to drag the wings or make some other error. And that's why he wanted you to have some mushroom hunting.

Lessons were expensive, as were aircraft. In his account of his 1910 visit, Amos Root wrote, "I might mention that there has been some criticism in regard to the price — $7500 — for each finished and fully equipped machine. But even at this price they are at present unable to supply the demand." The aircraft used by students or sold to private buyers were assembled by hand at the Wrights' factory in west Dayton; completed, they were loaded onto an old horse-drawn hay wagon and transferred to Huffman at midnight, to avoid the jostlings of the curious.

The plant was small. Fred Kreusch hired on in 1909 as the Wrights' third employee, after answering their advertisement for a machinist. "[Wilbur] asked me my experience, what I had done, and why I wanted to make a change," Kreusch recalled. "So I told him that I would like to see about the airplanes." Tom Russell was hired the following year, after establishing that he could get along with the Wrights' head machinist, Charlie Taylor, which not all could. Eventually, there were a dozen or so employees, who took three days to assemble each aircraft. As employers, the Wrights kept a certain distance. "I always addressed them as Mr. Wright," Kreusch stated. And as employers, they had their own ideas as to what constituted employee motivation. One

year, Russell recalled, the Christmas bonus was "about a pound box of choco-lates. Oh, boy we used to laugh at that... Well, [we all] said, now we're sissies."

Comparing the brothers, Tom Russell stated, "Orville wasn't as sober as what Wilbur was. No, Orville could take a joke... but Wilbur, I never saw him crack a smile." The crew called Wilbur "Eagle Eye." Said one, "I used to say he could see through a brick wall. I know sometimes when the motor wouldn't be func-tioning right, he'd come over and he'd be on this side of the motor and he'd say something over there was wrong, and he wasn't even on that side. He looked like he was looking through it." Wilbur's visits were few. In three years, ac-cording to employee William Conover, Wilbur may have spent no more than an aggregated month on the premises: "Orville was there all the time. But then Wilbur was not. Wilbur was in New York, taking care of the lawsuits."

The lawsuits were patent suits. Almost from the moment the Wrights achieved flight, the fruits of their accomplishment were being stolen. The Wrights' patents were basic to flight. A patent, however, does not enforce it-self; it merely provides the basis for a lawsuit. The suits were many, the litiga-tion torturous, the underlying issue was clear: those who had contributed noth-ing to the creation of flight did not see why it was not theirs to exploit for free. Real money was involved. In 1911, an English aviator named Claude Grahame-White picked up $100,000 barnstorming in an aircraft that was a knock-off of the Wrights,' yet he offered not a dime in royalties. Pride of creation was also at issue. In the flurry of the new, the public was little able to judge who had contributed what to the creation of flight. Octave Chanute muddied the wa-ters. As time passed, Chanute exaggerated his own contribution and deni-grated that of the Wrights; he issued the absurd statement that "wing warping" — the central feature of the Wrights control system — had been on the aviation scene long before Wilbur and Orville arrived. Chanute stated: "Personally, I do not think the courts will hold that the principle underlying the warping tips can be patented."

The Wrights were clear-thinking people, and to them the issue was clear: at considerable time, money, energy and risk, they had developed the only work-able system for maintaining in-flight control of an aircraft. That system was patented. Those who wished to use that system must either be licensed by or pay royalties to them. Wilbur stated: "It is our view that morally the world owes its almost universal use of our system of lateral control to us. It is also our opinion that legally it owes us." A man planted firmly in the right, possessed of strong character and a well-drafted patent, must, however, still face the rancorings of the public. Having for years disbelieved in the possibility of flight, the public could not now get enough of it. When, in May 1910, Wright rival Glenn Curtiss flew from Albany to New York City, the *New York Times* devoted four full pages to the achievement. Few Americans had yet seen an aircraft fly.

When they did, they were transfixed. One early pilot said of an exhibition crowd: "There wasn't anyone there who believed an airplane would really fly. In fact, they'd give odds. But when you flew, oh my, they would carry you off the field." Money — prize offerings of up to $50,000 — and the spotlight of public attention were being claimed by exhibition flyers. The public was not interested in patent fights; if the Wrights wished to maintain their preeminence, they must do so in the air.

Wilbur and Orville began to train a flying team to match skills with their rivals. The first pilot trained was Walter Brookins, a neighborhood boy they had known since he was four years old and who had been a student of Katharine Wright at Dayton's Central High. Others clamored to join, among them Wright employee Tom Russell, who sought out the Wrights' general manager:

> I says, "I understand that Walter Brookins has learned to fly" ... I says, "Is there any chance of me getting in on learning to fly?" He looked at me quizzical-like. He says 'no,' and opened a drawer down there and he pulled out a stack of applications. There was three thousand of them. He says, "You would be on the end of that." He says, "But my advice to you is, don't do it." He says, "Because every fellow that's learned to fly now will be dead." He says, "They'll be killed." Because he says, "These planes right now are in their infancy and they are not foolproof by any means." And he was right on those aviators.

The planes were not foolproof; neither were the pilots. The crowds that packed out to see them perform were not long satisfied with aircraft flying lazy circles in the sky; they wanted some risk and some dare. The early barnstormers were willing to supply it. Once on Long Island, Wright pilots Arch Hoxsey and Ralph Johnstone insisted on taking off in a gale. Their aircraft had top speeds of forty miles an hour; the gale was gusting at up to eighty. The best progress they could make was to fly forty miles an hour backwards. Both lived to tell about it. Both were soon dead — Johnstone when he failed to pull out a dive at an exhibition; Hoxsey when he plunged from 17,000 feet. Within two years of taking their training, five of the Wrights' first nine exhibition flyers were dead.

So the Wrights pulled out of exhibition flying. They were losing, frankly, more than their pilots. At the international flying meet at Reims in 1909, pilots flying competitors' models broke every record the Wrights held: altitude, distance and speed. In 1910, the first international meet held in America confirmed that result. The Wrights were winning the patent litigation, but losing the war — losing the chance to shape the future of aviation technology. Perhaps they were fighting on too many fronts: operating a flight school and an

John H. Patterson employed thousands at NCR; the Wrights, about a dozen at their aircraft factory. When one NCR toolmaker applied for a job with the Wrights, Charlie Taylor asked if he worked in an NCR dust coat. "No," the applicant said, "it might get snagged when you're working close to machinery." "Good," Taylor says, "anybody wears one of those coats, I figure they're not workers."

aircraft factory and an exhibition flying team, all through the skirmishes of the patent wars. In 1911, Wilbur Wright stated: "During the past three months most of my time has been taken up with lawsuits." The brothers had hoped, he wrote, to sell their invention for enough to free them from monetary care, so they could pursue aeronautical research; instead, they had been forced to spend their time on business and legal matters: "When we think what we might have accomplished if we had been able to devote this time to experiments, we feel very sad, but it is always easier to deal with things than with men, and no one can direct his life entirely as he would choose."

Wilbur lamented the work he and Orville might have done, yet perhaps they had nothing of great significance left to contribute. In 1905, the Wrights presented the world with an astonishing creation: a heavier-than-air machine that could take flight, choose direction and land safely all under the control of an operator. With this creation, they accomplished the task they had set for themselves. They had not sought to build the perfect aircraft, but one that would fly. In their fidelity to that task, their aim became their limit. The Wrights saw, correctly and before others, that an aircraft must be fully controllable by

its pilot. To gain control, they accepted a machine of inherently unstable design; in consequence, their aircraft needed constant course correction in flight. The Wrights saw, correctly and before others, that lateral equilibrium could be maintained by warping the wings. Others realized that such warping encouraged the aircraft to slide sideways; they developed ailerons, the variation on the Wright principle used to this day. With his 1908 flights in France, British aviation expert Charles Gibbs-Smith writes, Wilbur brought the Europeans the Wrights' essential message of controllability. He adds: "Thus freshly alerted and inspired, [the Europeans] exercised the perennial privileges of the pupil, first to learn from the master, then to criticize, and finally to improve on him.... Although they were to hold their own until 1911, the Wrights were slowly but surely overhauled, when the small stream of successful flying machines had broadened to a swift-moving river."

On May 2, 1912, Wilbur Wright complained of a temperature after returning home from a picnic with his father, Orville and Katharine. By all accounts, he had been worn down by the patent litigation, which jeopardized his fortune, his work and his name. Four weeks later, he was dead from typhoid fever. The hundreds of tributes included none more fitting than these words from his father: "A short life, full of consequences. An unfailing intellect, imperturbable temper, great self-reliance and as great modesty, seeing the right clearly, pursuing it steadfastly, he lived and died."

James Cox's *Dayton Daily News* ran a page-wide headline above the account of Wilbur's simple funeral. Above that headline, even larger type announced that aviator Phil Parmalee, one of the first of the Wright flyers, had been killed in a crash. Aviators, then, were what astronauts were to become: known, and mourned, singly and by name. Tributes to the co-inventor of flight came in from around the world, from prime ministers and newspaper editors and fellow experimenters — including the rather sour comment of Sir Hiram Maxim, he of the ill-fated four-ton "flying machine," that Wilbur was "one of [!] the foremost men in the art of navigation." In Dayton, even the cash registers fell silent. For ninety minutes surrounding Wilbur Wright's internment all retail business in the city ceased; for a briefer period, street cars came to a rest.

In his own first letter to Octave Chanute, Wilbur had confessed himself "afflicted" with the idea that flight was possible. No one understood better than he himself what that affliction had cost. Several months before his death, Wilbur wrote:

> If there be a domineering, tyrant thought, it is the conception that the problem of flight may be solved by man. When once this idea has invaded the brain, it possesses it exclusively. It is then a haunting thought, a walking nightmare, impossible to cast off. If we now consider the pitying contempt with which such a line of research is appreciated, we may somewhat conceive the unhappy lot of the investigator whose soul is thus possessed.

Private burial took place at Dayton's Woodlawn Cemetery. The six pallbearers included two from the Wright Company, two from the Dayton Aero-Club and two — Edgar Ellis and Charles Alinger — from what the *Dayton Daily News* described as "the only organization of which the decedent was an active member," the Annual Club of Ten Dayton Boys. Its members were no one in particular, men of local ambition, largely from the same West Side neighborhood as the Wrights. But they, along with the Wrights' immediate family, mechanic Charlie Taylor and a scattering of witnesses at Kitty Hawk, had been the only ones to believe that Wilbur and Orville had flown. Wilbur was the first club member to die. The night before his burial, the club's surviving members gathered and added this inscription to their twenty-seven-year-old leather-bound meeting book:

> The youngest member of our club is gone. The silent laugh, the witty

sayings, the desirable company of Wilbur Wright shall be for us no more in the world. To repeat the countless words of praise that have been his from every civilized nation, would be vain. That he has been to the world, is all known. What he has been to us, no one else can ever know. It is enough to say that our hearts are bowed down. Therefore, resolved, that we extend to the bereaved family our sincere sympathy & the answer that none outside of themselves can feel loss more than we do.

Among the honorary pallbearers at Wilbur Wright's funeral was James Cox, who was then closing in on the Democratic nomination for governor. From his first term in Congress, James Cox returned with fatter rations for the veterans at the Soldiers' Home and a new post office for Dayton — trophies sufficient to give him a lock on re-election in 1910. He was returned to office by a healthy 12,000-vote margin. Cox headed back to Washington, however, with an eye on events in Columbus: the forty-year-old newspaper publisher and congressman had set his sights on Ohio's governorship.

To gain that office, Cox began floating leftward toward the strongest current then running in Ohio politics, that of progressive reform. Cox was not a conviction politician. Not like Cleveland mayor Tom Johnson, a nationally hailed model of municipal reform who fought a nine-year knuckle-by-knuckle battle with the city's traction companies; not like Toledo's radical mayor, Samuel "Golden Rule" Jones, who announced an electoral victory with the words, "I am elected in spite of six hundred saloons, the street car company and the devil." Cox was a pragmatist, and what he in 1911 pragmatically began to do was to cultivate the common ground he shared with the state's progressives; namely, the view that Ohio's existing constitution so limited the powers of government that the state was unable to govern effectively. In an age of industry, Ohio had no power to regulate wages and hours or to compensate injured workmen. In an age of organized finance, Ohio had no authority to inspect banks or ban the sale of fraudulent securities. In age of cities, Ohio's municipal governments lacked broad powers: they could exercise only such authority as was approved piecemeal by the legislature. The state's reach was further curtailed by its being consistently shortchanged on tax collections: oddly, taxes due to the state were set in each township by a locally elected assessor. Cox characterized the typical assessor: "His chances of re-election were determined by the amount of property he overlooked." Ohio's progressives held that only a more powerful state government, directed by a strong executive, could provide Ohio's citizens with a government appropriate to the age. Cox shared the progressives' perspective: as a businessman, he believed in concentrating executive power; more particularly, he intended the executive in whose hands that power was to be concentrated would be him.

To help plan his rise, Cox signed up John A. McMahon, one of Ohio's leading attorneys, as senior advisor. McMahon was of a distinguished family: his

father had reportedly turned down separate offers from Andrew Jackson of a cabinet post, support for a senate bid and appointment to the U.S. Supreme Court. His uncle was Clement Vallandigham, the Dayton congressman who led the Peace Democrats during the Civil War. McMahon briefly held Ohio's third congressional seat himself, then left Congress to practice law. He had his pick of clients. Leaving once for Europe, John H. Patterson instructed his executives to take any legal matter that arose in his absence to McMahon and do whatever he advised. An executive asked what they

should do if McMahon was unavailable: consult who you like, Patterson replied, just don't take the advice. Though well-stocked with forebearers and admirers, McMahon lacked an heir, a political one. One national magazine writer commented: "It had been the dream of McMahon's life that his son should be a prominent office-holder, but he has never been able to do anything with his son." James Cox looked to be likelier material. The adoption was mutual. For Cox, it repeated an earlier experience: in Paul Sorg, he had found a mentor to advance his fortunes in business; in John McMahon, he found someone to play a like role in politics. McMahon was seventy-eight, and an old-school conservative; Cox, forty-one, inclined to progressivism; ambition bridged the gap.

Circumstance gave the progressives, Cox and McMahon their opportunity. Under the Ohio constitution, the electorate has the option, each twenty years, of calling a state constitutional convention. When that option fell due in 1911, voters authorized such a convention, then elected a solid progressive majority to do its work. It was a heady gathering, which placed before state voters forty-two proposed constitutional amendments — including amendments that would grant the state authority over hours and wages, over banks, securities and insurance companies; establish judicial reforms and the direct primary; enact women's suffrage and a set of conservation measures and abolish capital punishment.

Still a congressman, Cox campaigned statewide on behalf of the amendments. His speaking tour made him better known around Ohio; his public advocacy of constitutional reform helped allay whatever suspicions progressives had of his commitment to reform. Tying his campaign to constitutional reform also tied Cox to political success: in a special summer election, voters approved thirty-four of the forty-two proposals. (The defeated measures included women's suffrage — which Cox said he voted for, though he did not publicly endorse — and abolition of the death penalty.) When Ohio's Democrats met in convention, Cox's nomination was unopposed. As in Cox's first bid for Congress, his opponents did themselves in. Former President Teddy Roosevelt's "Bull Moose" candidacy had split the Republican Party down to precinct level. In a three-way race, Cox claimed Ohio's governorship with forty-two percent of the vote.

Three weeks after the election, 1,076 Dayton business and civic leaders gathered at the city's Memorial Hall to pay Cox tribute. Speeches were made; toasts raised. Cox was never personally popular in Dayton; his rise had been too much a tale of him against all. Still, as one national political writer stated, "The business men of Dayton, if not political enemies, have for Cox a genuine admiration as a successful man.... They look upon him as a unique and marvelous human mechanism which has an uncanny faculty of performing well any task to which it may be set." Mindful of that faculty, speakers began pointing to Cox's larger possibilities. The Reverend W. A. Hale stated, "Why you are only a boy, and we expect to see you president of the United States some day." Others picked up that theme, amplified it and passed it on. In his own remarks, Cox begged off: "I have no false notions about being a child of destiny or that my present successes mean that I will become president of the United States." Where the White House was concerned, Cox was not particularly in need of destiny. He was competent, supremely confident — and, only forty-two, the governor of Ohio.

Some seek election to be something; others, to do something. The former want the honor of the thing, the prominence of spotlight and office; the latter seek office to further an agenda. Cox had an agenda. The day following his inauguration, James Cox presented state legislators with a detailed and forcefully argued package of fifty-six proposed reforms. State bodies to regulate banks, review insurance offerings and prohibit the sale of fraudulent securities. A state civil service. Pensions for widowed mothers, increased pensions for the blind. Prison reform and minimum ages for employment. A road-building program. Home rule for cities. Tax breaks to encourage forest conservation. Adoption of initiative and referendum, recall and the direct primary. Within three months, all fifty-six had been voted into law.

Admittedly, the Republican split had given Cox heavy legislative majorities with which to work: Democrats held an eighty-seven to thirty-six edge in the Ohio House and twenty-six to seven in its Senate. Large majorities, however, often prove unmanageable. Cox's success — his domination of the legislature from his first days in office — owes itself as much as anything to the simple assurance with which he wielded power. He had an acute sense of circumstances and men. One national reporter wrote, "To the logical exactness of a mind legally informed he adds the feminine intuitions of a super-reporter." More prosaically, the leader of Ohio's Anti-Saloon League stated: "The governor has the rare facility for lining up more representatives and senators for a bill in which he is interested than anyone with whom I ever came in contact."

Second, Cox was an extremely able administrator. He was a progressive, but a business progressive: the values he invoked most frequently in his opening address to the legislature were those of system, simplification and efficiency. Government operations, he told the legislature, have a seeming natural tendency to expand. Since a private corporation is "subject to the hazards of business," it must size its operations to its success. Government, however, "because its revenue is both regular and certain," operates "without this spur of necessity." In consequence, Cox said, governments place little emphasis on efficiency. As an example, he noted that of the twenty-five agricultural activities conducted by the state, fourteen were duplicated and eleven were triplicated. His intention was to ride herd — and to import experts to do likewise. He replaced locally elected tax assessors with professionals, who added $1.6 billion to the state's tax rolls; he recruited professional managers for the state budget, who achieved a ten percent cut in the state's general appropriations: these two measures let him call the legislature back into session to sharply reduce the state's nominal tax rate.

Much enacted under Cox was standard Progressive fare; in the area of workmen's compensation, however, he took the lead. Under the doctrine of "assumed risk," Ohio workers had little recourse if injured on the job. Assumed risk held that if a workmen freely undertook a task, he was not entitled to an award of damages if he was injured in its execution. In one case, a workman died after rescuing several fellows from a defective vat that had filled with gas; a judge, citing assumed risk, dismissed his widow's suit for compensation. Cox argued that "assumed risk" was simply at odds with popular notions of fairness; it therefore undermined respect for government. Further, he claimed that under the existing system of private workplace insurance, injured workers pressed by necessity often settled for little to avoid delay, and that too large a share of settlements went to lawyers' fees. Cox gained passage of a workmen's compensation law that became the nation's standard: through it, employers paid into a central fund an amount reflecting their number of employees and the hazard of their operations. Workmen's claims were made against this fund and granted or refused by a state-appointed panel. The system produced a favorite, if ghoulish, Cox anecdote. A workman badly injured in a plant that straddled the Ohio-Pennsylvania line dragged himself to the Ohio end of the factory so as to be eligible for compensation. Because of the interstate nature of the case, the matter eventually reached the governor: Cox ordered an award made.

Beyond his stated motives of efficiency and fairness, Cox pushed workmen's compensation for another reason: behind his pallid, analytical demeanor, he was a sentimentalist. The three achievements of his governorship in which he claimed the most pride were workmen's compensation, school reform — which consolidated the one-room schools that still dotted Ohio into larger, more adequately financed operations — and prison reform. In his first month in office Cox went to the state penitentiary in Columbus to present to the inmates his plans for prison reform. One, which he secured, was the abolition of contract labor. A historian writes, "When he told the inmates 'the state doesn't want to mint any dollars from your tears,' there were cheers, stamping of feet, smiling and weeping, among both the convicts and the officials."

Cox's warmhearted remarks juxtapose oddly with the cold eye he turned to the one segment of his constituency that claimed to have received little from his reforms. That constituency was organized labor. Labor wanted Cox to lead the charge for the eight-hour day; instead, he helped sidetrack such legislation in committee. To grant labor's wishes would have meant building its power. As one of Horatio Alger's boys, he was perfectly willing to aid those whose feet kept slipping from the bottom rung of the ladder he so adroitly climbed. Power, however, he did not intend to share.

In the fall of 1912, attorney John McMahon moved from senior advisor in James Cox's gubernatorial campaign to U.S. federal court in Cincinnati, where he was defending John H. Patterson. One of the NCR president's systems had caught up with him. Patterson had a system for training salesmen. A system for answering complaints. A system for rewarding employee ideas. These and his larger, highly organized systems of production, marketing and sales had brought Patterson the bulk of the market for cash registers — indeed, in 1911, NCR rang up the sale of its one-millionth machine. Only a few competitors remained, and Patterson had a system for eliminating them. The NCR president, one contemporary observed, considered himself "divinely appointed to make cash registers." Competitors were not opponents; they were transgressors, to which Patterson assigned no very sentimental fate. "The best way to kill a dog," he often said, "is to cut off its head."

NCR cash registers were solidly built. Each year, as Patterson's salesmen pushed new and improved versions onto the nation's retailers, old but still highly serviceable registers found their way into a growing second-hand market. The fact that second-hand dealers were making money off the very cash registers John H. Patterson had built was more than the NCR president could bear. In 1903, he set up a dummy corporation, gave it a million dollar budget and the focused mission of driving the independent second-hand dealers from the marketplace. His organization used all the leverage an all-but-monopoly enjoys when it takes on a corner store. Starting in New York City, it opened its own second-hand stores — ostensibly unaffiliated with NCR — across the street or around the block from targeted independent operations. From this vantage, it would undersell the competitor, harass its customers and bribe its salesmen until the competitor gave up the game and accepted a buyout offer.

Such tactics were extended beyond the second-hand businessmen to customers for new registers. Business historian William Rodgers writes:

> Men especially trained in persuasion and tactics of intimidation... would swoop down on the prospective purchaser of a Hallwood or other competitive cash register and "warn" the customer that the machine was no good, that it infringed NCR patents, that the manufacturer was being sued, and that anyone who bought and used a Hallwood machine would, likewise, be sued.

If the merchant had already strayed and signed a contract to buy a Hallwood — or, for that matter, a Globe, Century, Ideal, Latimer, Peck, Navy, Osborn, Simplex, Sun, Toledo, Union, Weiler or any number of others — Patterson's "knockout men" would urge the merchant to cease payment on the contract, with the promise that NCR would cover any legal costs that ensued, thus depriving the competitor of income from the sale.

To undercut his competitors' reputations, Patterson's production lines turned out "knockout machines" — crude reproductions of competing models, often bearing a facsimile of the competitor's nameplate, sold cheap and designed to fail. And Patterson took to the courts, routinely filing suit against competitors for alleged libels of Patterson's character, or for real or alleged intrusions of the mesh of patents with which NCR surrounded its products. At one point, NCR had seventy-five patent infringement suits outstanding, the contesting of which drained off the resources of his smaller adversaries. Patterson also used litigation to hamstring a competitor's plans. In one case, he wrote: "If a patent is granted to the Lamson [Cash Register] Company, we will bring suit. If we lose, we will take it to the Court of Appeals. It will take five or six years of litigation and probably cost Lamson $100,000 before they would have a legal right to use their special key arrester and key coupler..." Lamson eventually succumbed, settling on Patterson's terms. In so doing, Lamson's owners accepted from Patterson this humiliating restriction on their future endeavors: "In case we desire to re-enter and continue the business of the manufacture and sale of cash registers, the states of Nevada and Montana offer, in our judgment, an ample and sufficient field for all of us."

Such tactics outlasted all effective opposition. And such tactics eventually landed John H. Patterson in federal court. On February 22, 1912, he and twenty-eight high-ranking NCR executives — virtually the whole of the company's upper management — were indicted on three counts of violating the Sherman Antitrust Act: conspiring to create a monopoly, unlawfully monopolizing the trade in cash registers, and holding and carrying on a business created by a monopoly. The indictment was the first full-bore explosion at NCR since 1907, when Patterson, under the sway of his trainer, had bounced his second-in-command, Hugh Chalmers. Chalmers had departed NCR vowing that he would not be even with Patterson until he put Patterson behind bars. With the 1912 indictment, Chalmers returned to exact his revenge: he took the stand as a key government witness to NCR's alleged wrongdoing. Patterson proclaimed his innocence — then lined up the best legal team he could, headed by a former U.S. solicitor general, seconded by John A. McMahon. Pre-trial maneuvering delayed the start of testimony until November, when those indicted took up residence in an entire floor of Cincinnati's Sinton Hotel, simultaneously running the company and appearing in court.

The government spent two months building its case. Big fish like Chalmers outlined NCR's efforts to disrupt its competition. How $5 from the sale of each new cash register was reserved for a "competition" fund, to be used to run others out of business. How NCR agents were supplied with "knocker cards" to be filled out whenever a rival machine was "wiped out of an agent's territory." How one company publication boasted that 174 rival registers had been "knocked out" in a single month. How "knocker" machines were built and targeted at American and Peck. A stream of lesser witnesses told of how they had been entangled in these schemes. A former sales agent for American Cash Register told of being trailed and harassed by NCR agents; a succession of retailers testified that NCR had coerced them into canceling contracts with competitors. A former salesman for the Union Register Company told of encountering an NCR office store window in which three Union machines were draped for mourning beside a placard that read: "The Union Cash Register company died today; buried tomorrow."

Patterson's partisans claimed the whole thing was a put up job — the prosecuting attorney was a relative of President Taft and anxious to build Taft's reputation as a trustbuster; the trial judge was a friend of a man who lost money investing in a now-defunct NCR rival. The company, one friendly editorial stated, had "committed no greater wrong than thousands of business men are guilty of every day and hour of their lives." Indeed, that editorial continued, if NCR had done wrong, it had done so only in response to patent infringements perpetrated by the very same smaller fry who now cried "foul" at the government's convenience. That view — that NCR's actions had been provoked — was one the trial judge refused to let Patterson's attorneys explore when cross-examining government witnesses. Nor did the jury hear exculpatory words from the defendants themselves. All twenty-nine declined to take the witness stand. In Dayton, many doubted whether Patterson could do wrong in anything; elsewhere, a few doubted the government's motives in bringing the case. Those doubting, however, did not include the jury. Shortly before midnight on February 13, 1913, it returned verdicts of guilty on all counts against Patterson and all but one of his co-defendants.

At sentencing, trial judge Howard Hollister said the Sherman Antitrust Act established a fairly simple standard; it was, he said, "the standard that any fair-minded reasonably conscientious man applied to his own conduct." NCR had transgressed that standard, the judge added, not inadvertently or occasionally, but as a matter of concerted and continued corporate policy. From the bench, Judge Hollister delivered a diatribe at those just convicted. Patterson, the judge asserted, was of the deluded belief that the nation's entire cash register business belonged to him; he had built up NCR "not through the merits of his product and the extraordinary efficiency of his organization, but by harassing, annoying, interfering with, discouraging and pursuing his competitors." Patterson's co-defendants, he speculated, might have been moved to their misdeeds by mercenary motive: "I am aware that a large salary will tempt a man to do things that he would rather not do." He cited several of the salaries, very high by the day's standards, that Patterson paid to those convicted, including the "$18,000 to $20,000" paid to Edward Deeds. All the convicted, the judge concluded, had "contributed to the breaking down of the ancient standards of fair dealing between traders, not only required by law, but inspired by the finer instincts of every fair-minded man."

Rebuke delivered, Judge Hollister handed down sentences: for John H. Patterson, a $5,000 fine — and a year in jail. Fines, alone, for most of the others.

Attorney McMahon called the sentence of jail time in an antitrust prosecution "astounding." Patterson was unabashed. His supporters might see him as more sinned against than sinning; Patterson's own view was simpler — he was sinned against. *The Cincinnati Enquirer* reported from the courtroom:

> The self-possession and coolness of the defendants as they received prison sentences from the Court was remarkable. President John H. Patterson, who was the first to stand before the court, if anything, was more calm than any of the spectators in the courtroom. He received his sentence... and one year in Miami County Jail without a quiver and, after thanking the court, withdrew to his seat.

Facing prison, John H. Patterson needed either a reversal on appeal, or an act of God. He got the latter.

flood

The rains began Easter weekend, five weeks after John H. Patterson was sentenced to prison. Rain comes to Ohio early each spring, but these began, continued, intensified and intensified yet again. Of the deluge on Easter Monday, March 24, 1913, *The Dayton Daily News* reported:

> It seemed as if the windows of heaven had been opened. The rain descended in floods. The sky would lighten, the sun seem at the point of shining. Then another black mass of clouds would sweep across the sky. There was a lightning and mad rain. Time and again throughout the day the process was repeated.

That evening on the west side of Dayton, Bishop Milton Wright recorded in his diary: "I apprehended a flood. Felt the danger of it."

Dayton had lived with the danger of floods since its founding. Indeed, the watershed of the Great Miami River above the city was almost sculpted for flooding: the land is more steeply sloped than that of any other river system in Ohio, the region's heavy clay soils shed more readily than they absorb, and the valley's farmers had cleared the brush and other growth that might otherwise slow runoff. To these conditions, March 1913 added a fourth: the ground was already sodden from snow melt when storms dropped seven to eleven inches of rain over the whole of the 3,500 square mile catchment. Little of that rainfall was absorbed; the rest ran off into rivulets and gullies and creeks to be gathered by the Great Miami's tributaries and directed at Dayton.

Upon reaching Dayton, the Great Miami makes a fishhook-shaped curve to the west and southeast before resuming its southerly flow. The city's business district sits on land flat and inviting within that curve. In 1913, that downtown was protected by levees rising twenty-three feet above the river bottom; so long as the river remained below that level, and so long as those levees held, the river would continue its semicircular way around the business district. Once through or over those levees, however, the Great Miami would cast off its loop to the west and take the shortest route south: directly through the downtown. When Bishop Wright "apprehended a flood" on Monday evening, the water under the Main Street Bridge was running eleven feet deep; it was rising, however, nearly a foot an hour.

Before dawn on Tuesday, John H. Patterson — at liberty and in Dayton while his attorneys framed his appeal — inspected the levees on the south side of the river. Water flowed black and sullen; at points, to within five inches of the top of the levees. Returning to NCR, the sixty-nine-year-old president summoned his executives to an emergency meeting, convened at 6:45 a.m. Dayton, he told them, would soon be flooded. Patterson issued marching orders: his carpentry crews were to build rowboats for use in rescuing those who would be stranded by floodwaters; his commissary was to bake thousands of loaves of bread and cook hundreds of gallons of soup; others were to gather cots and beds for makeshift sleeping arrangements; twenty riders on horseback were dispatched to gather in supplies from farming communities to the south. In fifteen readily obeyed minutes, John H. Patterson reorganized his company to cope with a disaster that had not yet occurred.

Disaster was not long in arriving. Within minutes of that meeting's adjournment, the first trickles of water began sliding over the city's levees. The first major break came near the confluence of the Miami and Mad rivers, just northeast of the downtown. So tumultuous were the waters in the main channel that, to one observer, the Mad River seemed unable to enter and appeared to be backing up in its tracks. At 8:30 a.m., 100 yards of levee near the railway yards yielded. *The New York Tribune* published an account based on eyewitness description:

> Suddenly... the levee fifty feet from him crumbled with a roar, and a huge cataract swept the railroad yards, picking freight cars up as if they had been shoe boxes.... A two story house stood a moment in the path of this inrush... and a woman and a child screamed inaudibly from a second story window. Then the house toppled over, mother and child disappeared from view, and within three minutes only a pile of loose wreckage remained.

The waters slammed a triple row of railway cars against the ground floor of the Delco factory on East First Street. Forty-three early arriving workers were already in the building. Instantly, they ceased attempting to move equipment out of the flooding basement and fled to the security of the second floor. Within an hour, the first floor — which housed the machine shop, shipping department and assembly areas — was under water. The Delco workers were stranded for two days, joined by the thirty people they pulled from floating debris into their second floor refuge.

Company vice president Charles Kettering did not reach Delco that morning. The flood was between his home and his factory. Instead, Kettering attended an emergency meeting north of the flood, where he volunteered to get a telegram bearing news of the disaster through to Ohio Governor James Cox. Kettering later gave this account:

> I had a buck-board automobile out at the curb, with no top, no dash, no fenders, and no body excepting a slat bottom and a seat for two. Bill Chryst of the Delco factory was with me. It was raining and sleeting but we had on our rubber coats, hats, and boots. We had an idea that if we went far enough north, we would find a bridge across the river. We rode for hours, it seemed. I have no idea how long. We came to a railroad bridge and drove across it. At the other end we got water in the carburetor and the car stopped on the submerged track. I climbed out and lifted the hood and wiped the water out of the carburetor with my handkerchief and got the car going. Then we started northward again. We drove some distance and finally saw a light ahead.... When we reached it we found it to be a railroad train dispatcher's tower, and he had a telegraph key open, and a limited line of communication available.... That was how it happened.

Kettering's daring was unnecessary; Cox already had the news. That morning,

The flood cleared the shelves of goods, then restocked them with debris. One reporter wrote, "Nearly every store in Dayton was a mere black dripping cavern." The flood destroyed $800,000 worth of pianos, $900,000 of leaf tobacco hanging in warehouses and 47,000 books at the Dayton public Library.

he received a call from the managing editor of the Cox-owned *Dayton Daily News*, who reported the levees were breached and water was gushing into the streets. While that call was in progress, rising waters wiped out telephone service. By evening, water claimed the first floor of the *News* building; one-ton rolls of water-saturated newsprint floated up out of the basement and invaded the accounting department.

The breaks in the levee sent a wall of water five feet deep through the downtown, tossing debris through storefront glass and wiping the goods off shelves. *The Daily News* later reported: "Unbelievable was the rapidity and the force of the current in the main channel. Drift shot past with the speed of a limited train. Timbers splintered against the solid concrete of the bridges with the impact of a head-on collision." A guest at the downtown Beckel Hotel speculated: "It seemed to me that the main current of the Miami River must have diverted through the principal streets of Dayton." This, indeed, was very nearly the case. In consequence, this observer recorded, "Before noon on Tuesday, Jefferson and Third streets were raging, roaring torrents of a depth of 12 to 14 feet.... Down both streets poured a mass of drift, now a lot of chairs and tables from some home, now counters, shelving, barrels, boxes, crates of fruit from some grocery; several pianos, piles of lumber, and every few minutes some struggling drowning horse." It was a bad week for horses. Fourteen hundred drowned. When a frantic horse tried to clamber aboard a rowboat packed with

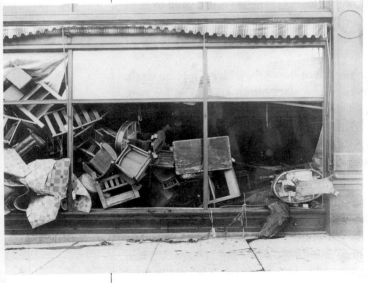

survivors, one of those on board drew a pistol and shot the animal dead.

People saved themselves however they could. In one residential area, floodwaters rose to within several feet of a sturdy telegraph wire that ran from a largely submerged pole to near a second floor window. By Tuesday evening, forty people floating by on debris had managed to snag that wire, then work themselves to safety; one of those thus saved was a devout temperance worker, who had bobbed along in the waters clinging to a drifting whiskey barrel. On one hilltop, a throng that had found safety there heard a strange chopping sound; suddenly, the shingles of a house roof flew upward and a human head appeared: the homeowner had taken refuge in his attic; now, as the attic filled with water, he was desperately chopping his way to safety. On Warder Street, the Adams family hurriedly evacuated as water swirled around their home. Mr. Adams, Sunday school editor of the *Otterbein Press*, loaded himself, his wife and their infant children, Charles and Lois, into a rowboat brought around by a relative. Immediately, a current caught the boat, ran it up against a tree and capsized it. Weighed down by her heavy overcoat, Mrs. Adams lost hold of her two children, who fell into the water. Several blocks downstream, a man in a boat spotted eleven-month-old Charles bobbing along and called out to the oarsman in a boat nearer the child. The second boatman snagged Charles' coat with his oar, then flipped him into the back of his boat.

On Hawthorn Street, Orville and Katharine Wright had overslept. Orville had returned from a business trip to Europe the previous week and was not yet back into a routine. In consequence, brother and sister had just thirty minutes to move belongings to their second floor before evacuating. By nightfall, six feet of water stood in the Wrights' home. In the confusion, a neighboring Samaritan came by in a canoe and paddled off with the eighty-four-year-old Bishop Wright, leaving his whereabouts unknown to his children. In abandoning home, Orville abandoned on a shelf in the shed near the house the irreplaceable collection of photographic negatives he and Wilbur had taken at Kitty Hawk and Huffman Prairie.

Early Tuesday afternoon, fires caused by exploding gas lines broke out in the downtown. There was little way to fight them. Flames spread to the Ball Candy Company, where 131 women workers, marooned by the waters, used empty candy pails to bail water onto the flames until rescue boats arrived. One Dayton resident, an eight-year-old at the time of the flood, recalled years later: "My Sunday school teacher always talked about the way the world would end — with fire and water, about Noah and the flood. And I thought that was happening." Fire was Orville Wright's chief concern that evening. From the safety of high ground, he watched as buildings near his office on Third Street burned. The 1903 aircraft sat disassembled in packing crates behind the shop; of greater anxiety to Orville was that his office on the building's second floor contained his and Wilbur's lives' work — all the records of their glider trials, their wind tunnel work, their study of propellers. Orville went to bed Tuesday night believing the whole of it would be lost to the flames.

The situation that looked dreadful Tuesday evening to those near it looked worse from a distance. On the high ground of Germantown five miles away, twelve-year-old Rodney Miller was summoned to the house by his mother. He later recalled: "Mother called to us, 'Boys, it looks like the town is going to wash away,' and she was right. You could see just the north end sticking out of the water.... The rumors were terrible: 10,000 dead? 12,000? There was no way of finding out." The lack of reliable information fueled speculation. Across the nation, Wednesday morning's newspapers spread the news of disaster across page one. *The New York Times* headlined: "Dayton, O., Engulfed, Thousands May Be Dead." One of its news accounts began: "Dayton is tonight nothing less than a seething river three miles wide, a mile and a half on each side of Main Street, its principal thoroughfare. It is estimated that 2,000 to 5,000 people have perished." An Albany, New York newspaper reported the disaster with its most purple prose: "There is duplicated in varying degrees, the heroism and martyrdom of the Titanic, the horror of Johnstown and the hopelessness of San Francisco after the earthquake."

The facts were bad enough. Fifteen square miles of Dayton lay under six to eighteen feet of water. Fourteen thousand homes were destroyed or damaged; 50,000 people — nearly half the city — were at least temporarily without shelter. The flood had inundated commercial generating facilities, so survivors were without light. They were short on food, as well: everything not canned or jarred was sodden or contaminated. They were threatened by pestilence: the waters had gathered in and were dispersing the contents of over 4,000 privies. And, they were without central direction: local government collapsed in the first hours of the flood. At the center of this catastrophe, coolly cantankerous and issuing orders to all, was John H. Patterson.

The Dayton flood brought much individual heroism, much remarkable and lifesaving improvisation. What sets it apart from other disasters is the role played by a private businessman and the company he directed. John H. Patterson's National Cash Register sat on high ground beyond the southern reach of the floodwaters; the NCR complex had its own generating capacity, its own supplies of fresh water and the only telegraph line still operating in the city. To these assets Patterson threw in his thousands of employees, disciplined and waiting to do his bidding.

By 10 a.m. on flood Tuesday, the first of the NCR rowboats was launched into the floodwaters. They were stubby, flat-bottomed craft, cut square across bow and stern, with two notable virtues. They built quickly: by the time Patterson's carpentry crews hit their stride, they were turning out a fresh boat every eight minutes; 275 in all, consuming over 50,000 board feet of NCR lumber. They rode steady: the boats remained upright in the churning waters as they were rowed house to house to collect those who had taken refuge on rooftops, awaiting rescue in the near-freezing rain. By later count, nearly 9,000 people — though not all by NCR — were retrieved from the rooftops and second story windows of the city.

Those collected by NCR were taken to the factory. There, they exchanged drenched clothes for dry ones, were served hot meals and freshly brewed coffee, examined by company medical personnel and given space to bed down for the night. One reporter who hurried to the scene, Arthur Ruhl of *The Outlook*, noted the contrast between the stricken city and the factory complex: "To step from the silent, sodden city into this humming Babel, where everything seemed to be had for the asking, was like stepping from the infernal regions to one of those sanitary socialistic Utopias pictured by Mr. H. G. Wells." Sanitary, yes. The Dayton flood was probably the first natural disaster whose survivors were served paper cups filled with distilled water and handed all but mandatory doses of malted milk. The difference, of course, between what H. G. Wells might imagine and what John H. Patterson could provide was that Patterson's little empire worked. At NCR, thousands were fed and fed well; thousands slept in reasonable comfort throughout the complex — with Patterson turning

an uncharacteristically blind eye to evidence of cigarette smoke. At the emergency hospital set up on the fourth floor of the administration building, hypothermia victims were warmed, fractured bones set, broken teeth extracted and women gave birth. The first child born was a boy, named "John H." for the NCR president; the second, also a boy, was named "Cash." Short for cash register.

Floodwaters crested as Tuesday moved to midnight, then began an exceedingly slow retreat. Much of Dayton spent that night on its rooftops or in the second floors of unheated houses, waiting for Patterson's flatboats or the rowboats of neighbors or, at minimum, dawn. Upon awaking Wednesday morning, the several hundred people stranded in the Beckel Hotel realized that the crashing sounds they had heard during the night had come from nearby buildings, collapsing as they burned. With fire moving their way, escape was made to buildings a secure distance from the flames.

> We got out on the roof of the Beckel Annex.... We took ladders along, and from slippery roofs got to open windows, passed through buildings, and from windows to roofs again. We reached a ten foot alley. A ladder was pushed across it to the next building and we crawled over, one at a time.... Among those taken out safely was a woman with a broken arm, and Mr. Bennett, the proprietor of the hotel, was carried from his death-bed.

On Wednesday, several of those trapped in the Delco factory heaved a large steel washer across the street to men in another building. The washer trailed a length of twine used to pull a heavy wire across. By this means, a supply line was established to other buildings in the vicinity. One proved to be a coffee

"People who had been caught on the streets clambered quickly into trees or up telegraph poles.... One great tree with spreading boughs was so thickly populated... that it looked like some great Christmas tree hung with huge dolls."

— *from Delco's flood history; above, Delco, where coffee signaled returning civilization.*

It pays to advertise. A hastily-built rowboat carries both an older couple — and the rescuer's initials. On flood relief and rescue, NCR spent almost $2 million, two-thirds of the company's profit for the year, all unreimbursed.

warehouse; coffee beans were sent back to Delco, where an automotive engine hooked to a dynamo provided electricity for brewing coffee, the first sign of returning civilization. Wednesday found all members of the Adams family still alive, though not yet reunited: Mr. Adams had saved himself by clinging to a tree, from which he had been taken suffering shock. On Wednesday, as well, Orville Wright learned that the papers in his second-floor office had survived: the heavy rains of the previous night had prevented the fires from reaching his and Wilbur's years of research. Orville and Katharine still had no news of their father; in his diary, Bishop Wright — using the plural to include his late wife — recorded, "Our children advertise for me." Such advertising was informal: all the city's newspapers were flooded out of their pressrooms. For many, NCR became the clearinghouse for posting notices and gaining information. *The NCR Weekly,* converted to daily publication, bannered its issue of Wednesday with what was hardly news to anyone within reach of its circulation: "DAYTON CUT OFF FROM WORLD."

It very nearly was. In Columbus, Governor James Cox began directing relief efforts to alleviate what he described, in a telegram to *The New York Times,* as "the worst calamity that has ever befallen this State." His home city of Dayton was the hardest hit: Cox declared the city a disaster area and ordered in the National Guard. He secured an emergency rescue and relief appropriation from the state legislature, obtained for Dayton one million rations from the federal government and urged governors of adjacent states to respond with tents, cots and other supplies. On Wednesday morning, Cox outlined these and other measures in a telegram — and sent it to John H. Patterson, who for all intents and purposes was now ruling Dayton. Six years previously, Patterson had tried to run editor Cox out of the city; now, Governor Cox bypassed local officials and granted Patterson "full authority to act for and in behalf of Dayton." National guard members posted around the city were informed, "All orders signed by Mr. Patterson will be honored by all posts of the National Guard." When at week's end President Wilson's representatives — Secretary of War Lesley Garrison and Major General Leonard Wood — reached Dayton, they made their headquarters at NCR and slept as Patterson's guests at his Far Hills estate, enjoying the hospitality of a man the government they represented had recently declared a felon.

Their host, John H. Patterson, was entirely in his element: sixteen-hour days of organizing this, directing that, coordinating something else. Patterson wired

The New York Times: " Situation here is desperate. All of the people, except those on outskirts, are imprisoned by water. They have had no food, no drinking water, no lights and no heat for two days." He called for "motor boats and the people to man them," fire engines, motor trucks and automobiles, provisions, clothing and medical supplies. Patterson reached across his scattered empire to pull resources into its threatened core: by Thursday evening, the first of three relief trains financed and filled by NCR's New York office was en route to Dayton.

Cox's grant of authority aside, Patterson had effective charge of only half the city. The flooding split Dayton in two. Patterson and NCR ministered south and east of the waters; to the north and west, 15,000 people were homeless, cold, wet and hungry. They were by turns housed, warmed, dried and fed by a spontaneous rescue effort that was all the more remarkable for being without the organizing center NCR provided to the south. Lacking Patterson's carpentry crews and his quickly assembled boats, residents managed rescue as best they could. A *Dayton Daily News'* account:

> W. G. Sloan, the well-known colored ball player, was in the rescue work continuously from Tuesday morning until Friday on the West Side. He took the Caleb family of five persons from a raft on which they had been floating, tossed in the heaving and rushing waters for 48 hours. With Frank Thoro and George Crandall helping, Sloan saved 317 people during 68 hours of continuous work. He carried five cans of fresh water. Most of the rescue work was done with a steel bottom boat which they commandeered at the point of a revolver from a selfish owner at the handle factory, who was not using it himself and refused to allow it to be used by the rescuers.

Supplies flowed in from all sides. Again, one account:

> A relief train from Detroit was halted by a broken bridge over the Mad River. In this emergency the farmers of the neighborhood with their teams and wagons — 130, not counting the buggies and other lighter vehicles driven by women — loaded the supplies onto their wagons, crossed the river on a highway bridge which was still standing, and reloaded them on a train waiting on the other side of the river. One observer wrote, "You could stand on the south side of Mad River and look as far to the west as the eye could carry, and along that winding road see horses and wagons loaded with provisions."

On one thing, the NCR president enjoyed a monopoly — press coverage.

Patterson's efforts were sincere. At a personal level, he turned his apartment in town into a dormitory for nurses and directed that "selected" refugees be housed at his Far Hills mansion. There, a few of those rescued by Patterson's rowboats found themselves eating at the same large round table where Prince Hohenzollern, Jane Addams, Olga Petrova, Lord Northcliffe, Ilya Tolstoy, Booth Tarkington, Jacob Riis, William Howard Taft and others had held forth. Patterson backed sentiment with money. For all of this — the 50,000 board feet of lumber for flatboats, the sleeping accommodations and meals for thousands, the distilled water, paper cups and malted milk — NCR was picking up the tab, with no reimbursement sought and no tax deduction available.

Still, Patterson saw no very good reason why all this sincerity should go to waste. He began in the cash register business with a machine no one wanted; he turned that machine into something no retailer could do without, and he knew something about the uses of publicity and the care and feeding of the press. In *The Outlook,* Arthur Ruhl reported:

> Newspaper reporters, shot off by their city editors without time to get so much as a toothbrush or a collar, found themselves sleeping in brand-new brass bedsteads, under down quilts, and rattling round in tiled bathrooms, where everything was supplied to them, even — if they had time to use them — with buffers to polish their finger-nails. When their clothes gave out, they were given new ones — clean linen, overalls, pajamas, anything they needed.... Men smeared with mud were asked, as they went to bed, to send their clothes to be pressed, and there were large signs posted in the lower corridor stating the clothes pressers and barbers worked all night and accepted neither pay nor tips.

The 1913 flood was a widespreading disaster. Dayton was its largest but not only target. Piqua, upstream; Middletown and Hamilton, downstream; and cities elsewhere in Ohio and Indiana were likewise reeling. Dayton was, however, the focal point of press coverage of the flood. Forty-eight newspaper correspondents (including the eighteen-year old Ben Hecht, future co-author of *The Front Page*) and fifty-two Western Union employees reached the city; more specifically, they reached NCR, with its operating telegraph lines, its down quilts and its barbers who worked all night for neither pay nor tips. In Dayton, reporters did not seek out Mr. W. G. Sloan, "the well-known colored ballplayer," for interviews; rather, they paid attention to the pronouncements of Mr. John H. Patterson. The 1913 flood was reported largely from and with the assistance of NCR; to a large extent, what the outside world heard was that it was John H. Patterson who took on the waters, and whupped them. For example, Arthur

Ruhl in *The Outlook* wrote "What Dayton might have done without John H. Patterson and the highly trained and flexible organization ... can only be a matter of speculation, inasmuch as 'The Cash,' as they familiarly speak of it in Dayton, was for days the stricken city's brain, nerves, almost its food and drink."

Thursday morning, the skies turned cold, drizzle turned to a substantial snowstorm, raising further the discomfort of those without homes, heat or food. The flood was receding: only the three city streets closest to the river still held water. That retreat, however, revealed what looked to be the sullen work of a retreating army: debris and destruction was everywhere. Local historian Charlotte Reeve Conover, who lived through the flood, wrote: "The wreckage in some cases reached to second story windows; street cars, grand pianos, painted manikins in party dresses from department-store windows, deceased pigs, bales of hay, furniture — all rapidly gluing themselves together with a foul paste composed of the rinsing of garages and paint stores, of country backyards and city cess-pools." Most remarkable was the mud. The headmistress of a private school wrote:

> I have calculated that in our house alone we have one hundred tons [of mud]. In this, as in most houses, are plastered and buried dishes, silver, books, chairs, furniture. Every drawer is glued with mud, within and without. People put the hose through their pianos, onto their upholstered furniture. We ooze at every pore. The back yards are full of mud — the front yards, steps, sidewalks, streets, basements. Men wade above their knees in mud.

Organized cleanup began the Saturday following the flood; within a week, nearly 4,000 men were engaged on the task. Work was directed by the Army Medical Corps and largely carried out by Patterson's Citizens Relief Commission — whose principal members included two of Patterson's recently convicted co-defendants, along with the owner of Huffman Prairie and the author of the "Here to Stay, But Coax Us" advertisement. Debris was piled onto railway flatcars run into the flooded districts on interurban lines, then hauled away. The flood destroyed 45,000 library books, $900,000 worth of tobacco warehoused in the city and 1,500 pianos. The pianos were taken the river's edge, doused with kerosene and burned. The Dayton Bicycle Club volunteered for what was the most loathsome task — collecting and carting off to the fertilizing plant the bloated bodies of the 1,400 dead horses found once the waters receded.

Very slowly, the city cleared itself out. On Warder Street, the Adams family was without heat or running water, so the "flood babies" were sent to stay with relatives upstate. Mr. Adams began to shovel the mud out of the downstairs, room by room. When the waters has risen in his dining room, they carried to the ceiling a table and the bowl of peanuts that sat upon it; when the waters receded, the table returned to the floor, the peanuts still dry. Charles Adams reported, "Dad worked outside in the mud, then came in and ate the peanuts." The peanuts were an incidental help, as the city was nearly out of food: grocer's shelves were empty and wholesalers had nothing with which to resupply them. In one oddity, $150,000 worth of sugar had, prior to the flood, been stored in burlap sacks in a warehouse; when waters receded, the burlap sacks were still there, but the sugar was gone, dissolved in the waters. For several days, two-thirds of the city's population was

James Fox sweettalked the boss's daughter, then formed Ahrens-Fox, the Cincinnati company that built the world's best fire trucks. After the Dayton flood, Fox himself got sweettalked out of one of his trucks by an inventor with weak eyes, strong will and a stupendously flooded basement.

being fed through relief kitchens. Help poured in from all quarters: 232 municipalities contributed relief; the Pennsylvania Railroad sent a full work train to Dayton, with mechanics who worked to get the water and electrical works back into operation; and the Bartenders' League of America announced it would give food, medicine, shelter and clothing to any needy member of Bartenders' Lodge No. 222 (Dayton).

At Delco, the screw machinery on the first flood floor was "so thickly covered with slimy mud as to be almost unrecognizable." Company vice president Charles Kettering got himself to Cincinnati, where he talked the owners of the Ahrens-Fox Company into lending him one of the splendid fire trucks they built, even though he had never driven one. Kettering barreled the seven-ton vehicle back to Dayton, where its high pressure hoses blasted Delco's equipment clean of mud. Thirteen days after the flood, Delco resumed partial operations, powered by electrical transformers dispatched to the factory by Cadillac.

The Dayton Daily News was the first newspaper in the city to resume publication. As governor, James Cox responded vigorously to his home city's needs: he was Ohio head of the American Red Cross, and for his labors that March received the national organization's "Man of the Year" honors. Apparently, he responded to his own interests, as well. A rival editor charged that Cox had a second-hand press tracked down in Columbus, loaded by National Guardsman onto a relief train to Dayton, and then set up for operation on the sidewalk outside *The News* building. In his autobiography, Cox acknowledges the press, he acknowledges the sidewalk, but he doesn't say how the first reached the second.

Throughout the city, people totaled up their losses. The death toll itself proved to be almost unimaginably low: eighty-four persons drowned, thirteen more dead from exposure. The low death figure was attributable in part to the fact that the levees had broken before the mass of office and retail workers had arrived for work and in part to what Governor Cox termed "the remarkable capacity of the human being to save his own life." Property loss, however, was staggering: $67 million as money was then counted, equal to perhaps $1 billion as values are reckoned today. Orville Wright wrote to an associate: "My personal losses have been slight, somewhere between three and five thousand dollars. Hundreds of families and merchants in the city lost practically everything they had. This is probably the greatest calamity that has ever happened to an American city, as insurance policies do not coverage damage by flood." His losses included nothing irreplaceable. Flames had stopped a few doors from his office and its priceless trove of aeronautical data; the packing crates containing the 1903 airplane had been smeared with mud but were otherwise intact; and the photographic negatives from Kitty Hawk and Huffman — including the shot of Orville leaving the ground on man's first flight — survived on the shelf in the shed where Orville had left them when he and Katharine abandoned home.

Any porch in a storm. A horse and mule fortunate to scramble to the security of a roof when waters were high were stranded there when the flood subsided.

Bishop Milton Wright stayed elsewhere while the Wright home was cleaned. On Friday, April 4, he returned to Hawthorn Street, recording in his diary: "I walked home after dinner. Found Orville drying his bonds." That same day, the commander of the Ohio National Guard issued an indignant denial of the report in a Cincinnati newspaper alleging that the Guard had executed seventeen looters the previous evening following drumhead courts martial; the guard's commander wished all to know that they hadn't shot anyone. That same day, Governor James Cox, that commander's commander, raised John H. Patterson to the rank of colonel. This was the same rank Patterson's illustrious grandfather had held, though, admittedly, John H.'s commission was in the commissary department. Orville Wright, for one, fully shared in the praise of Patterson's efforts; he wrote to an associate: "I do not suppose there has ever been a similar calamity where relief was so promptly afforded with so little waste. Dayton was very fortunate in having a man with the ability of Patterson to take this work in hand."

The flood made John H. Patterson a national hero. Speaking in Dayton to a throng of the homeless, the commander of the Salvation Army predicted that God would reward Patterson. Others appealed to more secular authority. Calls went out to Woodrow Wilson for a presidential pardon of Patterson's antitrust conviction. One out-of-state editorialist wrote: "Mr. Patterson may technically be a convict, but at heart he is a man who loves his kind and whose conduct shames the spirit that cries out for his incarceration." Patterson would have none of it. He sent a curt wire to the President: "I make haste to assure you that these messages and efforts are without my knowledge or consent. I am guilty of no crime. I want no pardon. I want only justice." He was unrepentant. Early in the disaster, he dispatched a telegram to his New York office for delivery to and publication in *The New York Times*. In that telegram, John H. Patterson stated that if Howard C. Hollister, the judge at the antitrust trial, set foot in Dayton, he, Patterson, would throw him in jail. The NCR executive receiving this message discretely destroyed it.

Snow covers
rooftops
during the
calm that
followed the
storm.

Arthur Morgan, his son Ernest relates, spoke often of the image of a wild duck, flying with broad even strokes toward a blue speck on the horizon only it could see. Arthur Morgan, his son said, was that voyager — and the speck he sought on the horizon was utopia.

the seed man

Some while after the flood, a mathematically inclined employee at Delco calculated that the water falling in the storm of March 1913 weighed 33 billion tons, sufficient to fill a reservoir twenty-five feet deep, a mile wide and 174 miles long. The writer concluded: "No work that could have been constructed by the hand of man would have been sufficient to withstand this tremendous rush of water." The writer in question had not cleared that conclusion with Arthur Morgan.

Late in life, Arthur Morgan was asked if he had viewed himself as an incumbent or as an insurgent. The reply was unambiguous: an insurgent, Morgan said. From the somewhat unlikely field of water control engineering, Morgan quite consciously directed his life and work against all the standard ways of thinking that, to Morgan's mind, were responsible for the sorry state of human affairs. Summoned to Dayton after the 1913 flood, Morgan would demonstrate what better thinking, amply supported, could create: the nation's first regional flood control system, one with no moving parts, requiring no human intervention and that has never spilled a drop.

Arthur Morgan was born near water, half a block north of the Ohio River in the city of Cincinnati in 1878. His father dabbled — attending occasional surveying classes in nearby Lebanon, selling notions on the streets of Cincinnati, and one day packing the family up to seek opportunity in the northwest. St. Cloud, Minnesota, was the end of the line, the northernmost navigable point on the Mississippi River. There, Morgan spent a sickly childhood — meningitis nearly killed him, measles weakened his sight, and he early formed the belief that he would not live long. The life existing around him Morgan found dismaying. For a time he attributed the low level of things in St. Cloud to its newness and to the polyglot of immigrants who settled it; then he went to Minneapolis on a Sunday school outing and was disappointed to learn that city folk seemed no better.

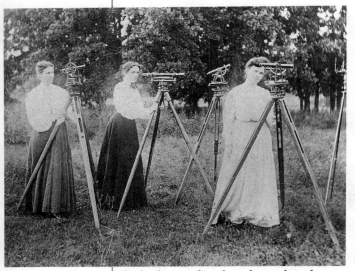

Morgan's was a divided home: his mother was hardshell Baptist, pious and determined; his father's broader outlook covered a drinking problem sufficient to keep the Morgan family dry for three generations. From an early age, he was given to theological speculation: once, waiting to be found in a childhood game of hide-and-seek, he acknowledged that while God could end his life at any time, God could not make it true that he had never lived, and was therefore not all-powerful. Adolescence brought a prolonged spiritual crisis. As he later described it, "My friends and Sunday School teachers and the minister at church and my mother told me I ought to believe the Bible wholly... I wanted to be good, and yet I wanted to think things out for myself." He was interested in botany and in Darwin and these he tried to reconcile with Bible literalism. At fifteen, he read John William Draper's *A History of the Conflict between Religion and Science*, Edward Bellamy's utopian *Looking Backward* and W. R. Alger's *Genius of Solitude*. Finally, Morgan concluded that God "gave us our minds to use, and wants us to use them. I decided that God would not condemn me for trying to be honest with myself and trying to find out what is really true." He joined a rather earnest discussion group of which his older sister was a member, and flirted not with girls but with Socialism.

The questions Morgan wanted answered — life and his place within it — were too large for him to address in St. Cloud, so at eighteen he lit out for the

Almost a parody of Thurber's "The War Between Men and Women." Above, women of the Morgan family survey the enemy's encampment.

territories, not heartfree like Huck Finn a half century before, but almost with a sense of being driven. Traveling west, he wrote home of waiting at a store to meet a man who might have work to offer. Young men lounged around the porch, he wrote, "whittling their lives away, and are probably there yet. I happened to think, "'What if I should catch the same lethegy?'" Morgan moved on; he floated a three-foot-wide log thirty miles down the Mississippi from Anoka, Minnesota, and then worked his way to Colorado. He picked fruit. He set type. He delivered goods. He mined coal. He bought fifty 30-cent editions of Ruskin, Carlyle, Goethe, Emerson and Kipling and tried selling them to miners with singular lack of success.

Honest work, all of it, but Morgan interpreted that phrase more narrowly than most. He had vowed to take no employment that "in its essential character was not a contribution to human well-being." Working for a time in a lumber camp set in the Rockies, Morgan learned the mill was sawing wood to be used to build a gambling hall at a nearby mining camp. He was opposed to gambling — years later he boasted he couldn't tell one playing card from another — so he quit. When his resources were exhausted, he returned home. But not necessarily in defeat. Back in St.

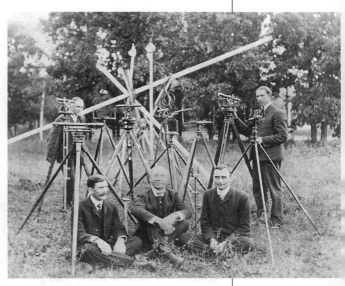

Cloud, he entered the surveying business with his father; they operated, at Arthur's insistence, under the name of Morgan & Morgan, not Morgan and Son. Morgan would be largely self-educated. As Roy Talbert, a student of Morgan's career, wrote: "John Morgan taught his son to shoot elevations with a transit and to lay lines for ditches and levees, and that was about all the training Arthur Morgan got."

Here, the men enjoy the calm before the storm.

Morgan was, however, assiduous, disciplined, naturally intelligent — and surprisingly skilled at self-promotion. Minnesota had no statewide standards for drainage control. In 1904, Morgan, age twenty-six, volunteered to draft a set for the state engineering society; the society adopted his proposals, which were then written into law by the state. Morgan was offered the post of state engineer. He declined. Wider fields were opening. Based on a competitive examination, he was one of four engineers hired by the U.S. Department of Agriculture's Office of Drainage Investigation. He left Minnesota to pursue his work; also, perhaps, he left to distance himself from the death of his first wife,

Urania, an osteopathic physician, just four months after the birth of Ernest, their only child. Later, traveling on government assignment, Morgan felt remorse over his absences and worry that were he to die, his son — left in the care of relatives — would grow up an orphan, so he wrote a series of letters to be given to young Ernest at age eight, age ten, age twelve and so on, should anything happen to his father.

Against the odds as he reckoned them, Morgan lived; the letters were never delivered, at least not in Ernest's boyhood. Remarkable letters. Never quite convincingly warm, nonetheless compassionate, filled with exacting self-examination, highly principled advice and recurring complaints about the state of Morgan's health. Thus, at age ten, Ernest was to have read: "Your duty is not to try to believe certain doctrines true, but to keep your mind and heart open, always willing and anxious to learn what is really true. If you live the right kind of life, getting a strong body and a strong character and doing your work like a hero, you are doing what is most important."

Central to the thinking Morgan tried to pass to his son was the belief that fine, individual character was the engine that drove human progress. Life, Morgan held, is limited not by the weakness of human nature, but by the meanness of prevailing pattern. Progress came when higher standards were established, established as the legacy of those few who made constant conscious efforts to present better ways of living. "The long climb of the race," he wrote, "is made by a part of the people that carries the other part upon their backs." Morgan cast himself as just such a carrier. In his fifties, he wrote a play, *The Seed Man*, about a small-scale entrepreneur — a favorite Morgan type — who prospered in the seed business and in life by aiming to put a few more seeds in the customer's packets while taking a few less cents from the customer's pockets and dealing honestly with all. The "seed" in question was not simply that which grew to be barley or oats; it was also the "seed crystal" that directs the growth of the crystals that surround. To that end, Morgan wished not just to design better patterns, he wished to be one.

Personally, Morgan was resolved to do right, as he saw it. Twice while he was working for the agriculture department, the deadline set on a project passed before the task was complete. Each time, Morgan was ordered back to Washington. Each time, he refused. They could fire him if they wished, but he would not leave a job half finished. On both occasions, he was allowed to remain. Once, in temporary charge of the agency's Washington office, he refused to release a report on the Everglades because he believed it to be a cover for a get-rich-quick land scheme. Backers of the plan maneuvered to have Morgan's supervisor dismissed. Morgan went to the press, sparking a congressional investigation that led to the "resignation" of those officials in league with the developers and to the reinstatement of Morgan's supervisor.

By the time that reinstatement occurred, Morgan was out of government. In 1910, he established the Morgan Engineering Company in Memphis, designing levees for flood control, canals for drainage, dams and bridges. The following year, he married Lucy Griscom, a young biology instructor from Wellesley, whose Quaker sense of mission and commitment to simple living would do little to soften her husband's highmindedness. At thirty-three, Morgan had completed his apprenticeship; his entry to larger spheres awaited nothing more than chance.

The Conservancy
dams, Morgan
said, were built
not with the
sculpture of
Greece in mind,
but the pyramids
of Egypt — broad
at the base,
narrow at the top;
built for longevity,
not for speed.

the conservancy

Arthur Morgan was out in his garden in Memphis on the first Saturday in May 1913, when his wife Lucy came out to announce a long distance telephone call. The caller represented Dayton's Flood Prevention Committee; his purpose was to invite Morgan to come see what the river had done to the city and to tell the committee what he, Morgan, could do to ensure it didn't happen again. The Monday following, Morgan toured Dayton; by day's end, he was placed in charge of the city's flood control planning. To Morgan, the speed of his hiring was one of the day's two singularities, both attributable to Edward Deeds.

Second to Patterson, Deeds was the leading figure in the flood prevention effort that followed the emergency itself. To him and to other business leaders, Morgan argued that Dayton faced a problem rarely handled successfully. Flood control, he told them, did not consist of piling more dirt on top of levees; rather, effective flood control must start with a full understanding of how a river system behaves and how that behavior can be accommodated while rendering it harmless to those living in its midst. Morgan wanted a solution that would be long-term and conclusive. Finding such a solution, he emphasized, would take years of research and planning, years during which a populace recently terrified by flooding would be crying out for action and, perhaps, for the heads of those who might appear to be dallying. To Morgan's near astonishment, Deeds pronounced himself in entire agreement with Morgan's approach. Morgan later wrote: "To an engineer who usually found his greatest handicap to be the difficulty of getting public support for thorough preparation, this recognition was like suddenly finding oneself in an engineer's utopia."

Deeds was also responsible for Morgan's rapid hiring. The week previous, he had been approached by local Democratic boss Edward Hanley, who informed Deeds that the city council was about to name its own flood control engineer, one more likely to be politically expedient than professionally competent. If Deeds' committee wanted a professional, Hanley advised, it had better act fast. Deeds sought the advice of the city engineer — who recommended Morgan for the post.

To initiate flood control, the Flood Prevention Committee set itself the daunting task of raising $2 million from the recently devastated city. The money was to be raised in a two-week effort whose guiding spirit was John H. Patterson. Morgan had his doubts about Patterson, who he termed "a peculiar combination of original genius and dictator." Still, Morgan was to admit, Patterson knew how to raise money. Donations to the campaign were totaled up and displayed on a thirty-foot-high wooden cash register placed at the southeast corner of the old courthouse, a few steps from where Abraham Lincoln had attacked slavery in 1858. On the campaign's final Sunday afternoon, the total registered stood over $400,000 short of the goal. Patterson personally summoned 500 Dayton men and women to a meeting he said would "undoubtedly be the most important ever held in the city," to be convened at NCR's sales training school, the Hall of Industrial Education. All those invited had already given to the campaign. Patterson wanted more. To set the proper tone of mission, the assembly was led in the singing of "Onward Christian Soldiers," with words projected by stereoptican slide onto a large screen. To pump enthusiasm, the Masonic and NCR bands played martial hymns. To remind all present that each generation is called upon to make its sacrifice, a drum corps of Civil War veterans beat out a continuing tattoo.

Preliminaries accomplished and mood ripe, John H. Patterson took the stage. Six years previously — and before many of those now present — Patterson had excoriated Dayton as "known, and justly, too, as being the worst city in the state." Now, supported by the inevitable stereopticon slides, he painted a picture of the city as little less than Edenic — or would be, provided only that the snake in the grass, the Great Miami River, could be charmed with adequately financed flood control. To help achieve the city's security, he announced, he was doubling his already substantial contribution to the campaign. Who would join him? Who of those present would, for the love of Dayton, likewise double his or her contribution? One man called out affirmatively. Instantly, a Patterson assistant ran to the spot and planted near the contributor a plaster lath and cardboard sign announcing, "I am a doubler." Then a second. Then a third. Each was rewarded with a placard until the hall resembled the floor of a political convention. In less than an hour, nearly $600,000 was raised.

Patterson then proposed that all present parade behind him to the huge cash register at the courthouse, where that evening's contribution would be added to the total. The suggestion was something less than spontaneous: the procession found its route flanked by crowds of cheering onlookers, drawn to the line of march by promises of a victory parade, while overhead the fireworks

Patterson happened to have on hand lit the sky. The march swelled, joined by onlookers on foot and others in horse-drawn wagons, one of them filled with schoolchildren chanting, "We want, we want, we want who?" — a question that brought the ringing response: "John H. Patterson." One Dayton newspaper reported, "When the head of the parade reached the waiting throng at Third and Main, pandemonium reigned supreme. Sky rockets whizzed, red fire blazed and smoke of gunpowder worthy of a scene of carnage floated out over the throng."

The signal action above was not Patterson's, but Hanley's. In urging Deeds to hire an expert, the local Democratic leader ensured that flood control, the city's most pressing problem, would be tackled not by elected officials answerable to the citizenry, but by a privately-constituted committee of businessmen answerable largely to itself. Hanley's action marks an acquiescence to the rise in Dayton of a business and engineering elite that regarded the city as something between a foster child and a test case. Flood control would be their creature — the product of the salesmanship of John H. Patterson, the civic leadership of Edward Deeds, the political cooperation of James Cox and the technical skill of Arthur Morgan. These men were hardly of a piece, but they believed in the values of efficiency, order and technical expertise that were then rising to ascendancy in American life.

In short, the values they shared were those of the engineer. The rise of such values followed the development of more complex industrial technologies; equally, it reflected a simple flexing of the newfound muscles of the rising professional classes, whose own claims to deference were rooted in their own claims to expertise. Popular fiction saluted the trend, presenting engineers as romantic adventurers on civilizing quests. In *The Winning of Barbara Worth*, which sold 1.6 million copies in 1911-1912, Harold Bell Wright asserted, "there can be found no finer body of men than our civil engineers." Informed opinion endorsed planning and order: Walter Lippmann wrote, "There are more and more people in the world who hate waste, and can't rest until they end it.... The spectacle of people foozling and fuddling without a plan, without standards; the whole idea of wasted labor and wasted materials is a horror to them." To the possibilities of engineering and planning, Dayton in 1913 offered an opening in time. That year was near the high water mark of progressive reform, the need for which appeared to be given greater urgency in Dayton by the flood, which called out for great measures just as it showed the inadequacy of previous methods.

Those acting in Dayton for flood control had, or secured, government friendly to their ends, and means. In Columbus, James Cox was firmly in control. In Dayton, John H. Patterson judged the months after the flood to be the moment to overthrow the municipal government of which he had long disapproved.

The state legislature had at Cox's urging recently enacted municipal Home Rule legislation, permitting various alternatives for city government. Patterson chose the most "businesslike" option — the city manager form, in which an elected council hires a professional manager to run the affairs of the city — then orchestrated the campaign for its adoption. Dayton was committing itself to the rule of experts, and the experts knew it.

Experts proceed from facts. Within two weeks of his appointment, Morgan had fifty teams of surveyors out in the valley making topographic surveys and marking the high points flood waters had reached. Study was barely begun, but Dayton was already impatient. A letter to a local newspaper read, "Every day you hear people say, 'Why don't they do something?' What the people want is action. Action speaks louder than words." The action most wanted was crews of men piling ever higher the dirt atop the levees, while other crews cleared the river channel of obstructions.

Morgan was in no hurry to act. He did not share the popular understanding that a well-tended river channel will not flood. A river's channel, Morgan wrote in *Scientific American*, "is the mechanical result of flowing water, and has no necessary relation to extreme flood flow." The Grand Canyon, he observed, was the result of eons of erosion; no conceivable rainfall would cause the Colorado River to overflow the chasm it had cut in that rock; conversely, some rivers flood quite easily. One such was the Great Miami.

Morgan wanted to know more about the Great Miami. Its peculiar characteristic was the variability of its flow: it is generally calm, often sluggish, and once in a great while a torrent — something like the dry streams of the southwest that turn from sandy to rampaging a few hours after a cloudburst. Morgan contrasted its behavior with that of the Seine at Paris; the Seine drains a region six times as large as does the Great Miami, but the largest recorded flood in Paris was only one-third the size of Dayton's 1913 deluge. Morgan wanted to know more about rainfall. To learn it, he commissioned the first ever comprehensive study of rainfall in the eastern United States, gathering the then staggering total of a half-million facts to chart the location, intensity and duration of the 160 largest storms on record. Morgan wanted time, as well, for the exhaustive recruiting of a staff he thought up to the challenge. In all, 3,000 applicants were reviewed for professional positions with the Conservancy: the hardest post to fill, Morgan said later, was that of editor of the newsletter he wished to publish: he could not seem to locate an engineer who could explain technical matters in straightforward language.

Facts are gathered to answer questions. Morgan posed a question so basic its answer had never seriously been sought: how much flood control is enough? The Great Miami averages a flow at Dayton of 2,000 cubic feet a second; on flood Tuesday, flow peaked at 250,000. Engineers then termed 1913 a 100-year flood, the greatest likely in a century. Morgan aimed for a system that could withstand a 1,000-year flood. To gauge how large such a deluge might be, he dispatched an engineer to a castle on the Danube where the high water marks of floods had been recorded since the great flood of 1065; to this data, he added partially incomplete records available for 2,300 years on the Tiber at Rome. Utilizing this information, Morgan concluded that a flood control system capable of handling forty percent more water than the river carried in 1913 would protect Dayton against any conceivable flood. He decided to design for that size.

The question, of course, was what to do with all that water. Flood control for Dayton, Morgan believed, rested on finding some means to handle safely the vast amounts of water the Miami River system only rarely carried. He sought an answer through what he termed "conclusive engineering analysis" — a design approach that, in common with the research methods of Charles Kettering and the Wrights, was intended to eliminate preconception as a basis for decision. In Morgan's words, "every possibility for solution of the problem, whether promising or not, should be explored... to a point where, in comparison with other methods of solution, it either is proved to be inferior or finally emerges as the best possible solution."

In Dayton, analysis brought Morgan to a solution never tried in America and whose European precedents were few, small and centuries old. He decided Dayton could best be protected from flood by building dams with holes in them. In engineering terms, they are called "dry dams." A dry dam is built with a permanent opening in its wall, with the opening sized to permit passage of no more water than the river channel downstream can safely carry away. In normal conditions, the river simply flows unobstructed through that opening; no water is stored behind the dam. Following heavy rains, however, the hole in the dam acts as a bottleneck on the river's flow; excess water — that is, water above the quantity the riverbed downstream can safely contain — automatically backs up in a "retarding basin" behind the dam. From there, it is dissipated once the storm has passed. In Morgan's view, by storing no water behind the dams in normal conditions, dry dams would allow maximum storage of water during emergencies. Morgan's approach addressed Dayton's key requirement: the short-term storage of huge quantities of water; it also fitted the landscape. He later wrote, "The rare combination of great need for retarding basins and excellent sites for them, which by good fortune were not occupied by immovable railroads or by cities, determined the nature of the Miami flood-control plan."

To opponents upriver from Dayton, the Conservancy was a passel of city boys with a bad case of the smarts. "Morgan knows more than God," one paper stated. "God made the rivers, but Morgan thinks he can do better."

OUR SENTIMENTS

LET'S CLEAN OUT THE CHANNEL, *NOT* DAM IT UP!

By August 1913, Morgan had a draft of the plan.

Among the obstacles to Morgan's design, the first was that it wasn't legal. Ohio law had no provision to permit either the multi-county flood control Morgan had in mind or to establish the public agency to carry such work forward. As planning proceeded, the thirty-five-year-old Morgan met with the eighty-year-old John McMahon — James Cox's advisor and John Patterson's defender in court — to draft the needed enabling legislation. Meticulously, McMahon crafted what became the Ohio Conservancy Act, which authorized creation of multi-county Conservancy Districts empowered to act to achieve flood control. Under the law, Conservancy Districts could plan for flood control, build dams, levees and other works to carry their plans into effect, and levy assessments or taxes to finance construction and operations. It was an expert's law — all this would occur without direct voter approval, with authority wielded by three court-appointed trustees.

The second obstacle to Morgan's plan was the vehement opposition it brought forth in cities upstream of Dayton. To them, any effort to hold floodwaters north of that city looked like a plan to "Drown Us First." One newspaper denounced the Conservancy legislation as "more despotic and drastic than all the edicts of all the Czars that ever lived." *The Troy Daily News* asked: "Who called Mr. Morgan into the deal? Not the taxpayers of the cities who are to be robbed by this stupendous scheme of graft.... Where the feast is thought to be there the vultures gather and you may be sure rich pickings are in sight when this company (Morgan Engineering) hoves into view." Who called Mr. Morgan into the deal was a committee of Dayton businessmen determined — in cooperation with the state's governor, a Dayton resident — to write into law the legislation Mr. Morgan's plan for flood control for Dayton required. Opponents continued to argue that simple dredging and clearing of the river channel would prevent future floods. Some put forth more fanciful suggestions: one called for draining off flood waters through massive concrete pipes placed below the river; another proposed drilling innumerable holes, so that floodwaters could escape into supposed subterranean cavities; a third urged replacing the current river bottom with one made of concrete, so flood waters would be speeded out of the region.

Edward Deeds, NCR superintendent and Delco president, led the public fight for passage of the Conservancy Act. In the valley, he undertook a speaking tour which, at some small hazard, included stops at those cities in strongest opposition. In Columbus, he opened a headquarters to coordinate the lobbying of legislators and the currying of reporters. Concerned that typographic errors in the bill might turn into loopholes in court, Deeds, Morgan and several others from Dayton proofread the printers' galleys of the proposed law, a task they finished at 6 a.m. the morning the bill was to be introduced. In the end,

Deeds' arguments were probably less persuasive to lawmakers than the simple fact that the size of the 1913 catastrophe argued for large measures and the even simpler fact that Governor James Cox wanted the bill passed. By substantial margins, the Ohio Conservancy Act passed by the legislature; Cox signed it into law on February 7, 1914.

Opponents were unreconciled. *The Troy Daily News* reported passage of the bill with the headline, "All Troy Mourns." Shortly thereafter, the newspaper directed a ditty, "Just Jim Cox," at the governor:

> Oh Jimmy Cox, my Joe Jim
> When we were first acquaint,
> I thought you were a statesman, Jim
> But now I know you ain't;
>
> And now you want another term
> To carry out your plan,
> Just wait until November, Jim
> And you will get the 'can.'

Ditties notwithstanding, James Cox emerged from the Conservancy fight with his confidence intact. Several months after signing the bill, Cox underscored this in a lengthy assessment of Ohio politics that the Ohio governor sent to William Jennings Bryan. The three-time Democratic presidential candidate was then serving as Woodrow Wilson's secretary of state, a post that did not dampen his interest in who was up and who was out in Ohio politics. In Cox's own reckoning, he was himself highest among those "up." "I shall carry Ohio this fall," Cox predicted to Bryan, "by a larger majority than I did two years ago" — when he had racked up the largest margin in state history. "I have the physical strength to make this fight and the moral sustaining force because I know the laws [passed by his administration] are right."

To Bryan, Cox rattled off his successes. Workmen's compensation. Centralized tax assessment. And — a point likely to please the Prohibitionist Bryan — new liquor commissioners who had pulled the licenses of all who ran "disorderly houses," thereby putting "four thousand unworthy characters out of business within a month." True, Cox added, the opposition clung to its traditional depravity: insurance companies had plunked down $250,000 to try to overturn workmen's compensation; other adversaries had hired agents to scour the state arguing that Ohio "had been turned over to Socialism and that a perfect hodgepodge of legislation had been passed." To no avail. For all their bluster, he wrote, none of his opponents would state publicly which of the fifty-six reforms he had enacted they would repeal. It was a combative letter, suggesting a man who likes the thrust and parry of politics, and who is usually on the thrusting side.

Certainly, Cox had cause for optimism: his 1914 re-election campaign drew the support of most major Ohio newspapers, many progressive Republicans and Secretary of State Bryan, who made a two-day swing through Ohio on the incumbent's behalf. To this, Cox added the comforting belief that Frank B. Willis, his Republican opponent, was an idiot: "... a jovial fellow, big in heart and body, the kind that never took public service very seriously, and pretty much laughed his way through every day." The governor felt he was riding high; in fact, he was running on empty. In his 1912 campaign, Cox had trumpeted: "It's a time of unrest, and why not? It's an ambitious age." His platform of 1914 called for no new measures, endorsed neither women's suffrage nor the eight-hour day, and offered no higher ambition than to maintain "efficient business organization in the affairs of the state."

By progressive standards, Cox had done well; by the standards of others, he had done, perhaps, too much. *The Ohio State Journal* editorialized: "Think of it — 300 bills enacted by a Democratic legislature, whose primary object is, or should be, governmental simplicity." In moving power to the center, Cox had stubbed every toe that had stood on the periphery — the locally elected tax assessors put out of office by Cox's appointees; the administrators of the rural schools swept away by Cox's school consolidation. Cox suffered most by taking the middle ground on Prohibition. He sought to regulate the sale of alcohol in a state divided between those who wanted an outright ban on spirit and brew and those who wanted it passed out wholesale. Unlike previous governors, Cox strictly enforced Sunday closing: "every saloon in Ohio," he wrote Bryan, "has been closed tight on Sunday... The accomplishment of this in Cincinnati has been looked upon as a sort of seventh wonder." And in Cincinnati, German beer drinkers joined forces with Methodist abstainers to carry the county for the Republican Willis, a Prohibitionist.

"They double-crossed you," Bryan wrote to Cox after the election. "They worked the dry vote against you in the country and the wet vote against you in the city." Defeat was nonetheless a shock. Willis claimed the governorship for the Republicans by 30,000 votes out of 1.1 million cast. Cox was startled, and petulant: "Most of those in opposition were not moved by principle," he later wrote. "With them it was grievance, and they remained militant until Election Day. There was no need of hauling them to the polls. This type votes early."

For flood control in Dayton, Cox's defeat was a breach in all the as yet unconstructed dams. Newly-inaugurated Governor Willis opposed the Conservancy Act; two weeks after he took office, a bill stripping conservancy districts of the authority to build dams was introduced. Edward Deeds organized the Act's defense. He opened a headquarters in Columbus' Hartman Hotel, cajoling journalists, badgering legislators and presenting his NCR-style stere-opticon slides to all who would watch. He registered thirty-six Dayton citizens to lobby on behalf of the Conservancy Act; then dropped petitions bearing 72,000 signatures on the legislative committees reviewing the proposed amendments. Doubtless he would have done more, but this proved sufficient. In April, the state senate killed the proposal by a surprisingly wide twenty-three to eight vote. Cox's former chief legislative aide credited the outcome to Deeds.

Deeds was determined that flood control for Dayton be safely burrowed in. In June 1915, the Ohio Supreme Court upheld the constitutionality of the Conservancy Act. The following month, the Conservancy Board of Trustees met for the first time; Deeds, elected chairman, immediately announced the $180,000 personal gift of a headquarters building, to be raised not far from the site where Dayton's levees had collapsed two years previously.

To the cause of flood control, Edward Deeds pledged his energy, his money — and his swimming pool. The pool was pressed into service to help surmount the third and final obstacle to Arthur Morgan's plan, a technical one. Morgan's plan called for backing up floodwaters in retarding basins behind a series of dams. The weight of the water stored behind each dam, however, would propel water through its opening with a destructive force, like water spewing forth from a gigantic high pressure hose. Morgan's engineers calculated that at one of the proposed dams, that force would equal 165,000 horse-power — enough to tear up the downstream riverbed, erode the banks and undercut the base of the dam. Morgan's plan was to place obstacles below each dam's opening; these would pitch the emerging waters back on themselves, dissipating most of the kinetic energy. The principle this plan employed

— known as "hydraulic jump" — had, however, never been used in practice and was not well understood in theory. To gain understanding, Morgan's engineers drained Deeds' swimming pool, then built and tested within it scale models to learn how this principle could be put into effect.

Meanwhile, the detailed work of planning continued. Morgan believed that five strategically placed "dry dams" would reduce the maximum flow at Dayton to one-fifth of that during the flood. He was aware his proposal was unconventional. Morgan commented, "The thought of dams without water behind them offended some people's intuitions of propriety and pro-

Edward Deeds was of an experimenting mind — besides turning his swimming pool over to Morgan's engineers to work out the details of hydraulic jump he invited Charles Steinmetz to his farm to see if electricity could coax greater growth out of plants. Results were uneven. Deeds reported: "not so good on potatoes, but hell on lettuce."

vided a text for the opposition." That opposition gathered en masse in Dayton's Memorial Hall on October 3, 1916, when Morgan submitted his plans to the Conservancy Court. Morgan's cross-examination had not more than started, *The Dayton Daily News* reported, "before it was apparent to everyone that he had a grasp of the subject clearly beyond anything that was to be expected." Every alternative plan put forward by opponents had already been studied by Morgan's engineers; studied in depth, rejected and the reasons for that rejection made clear. "During the five days that Mr. Morgan was on the stand, there was no request for information made... that was not met with instant response. The promptness and thoroughness of the answer was always more surprising and unexpected than the question itself." The opposition was left grasping for straws: Morgan testified that the dams would withstand anything but the return of glacial ice; the following day, *The Troy Record* carried a big headline: "Morgan Admits Dams May Fail." The Conservancy Court, with more immediate concerns than the return of glacial ice, directed Morgan to proceed.

While Arthur Morgan made his case to the Conservancy Court, James Cox was back on the campaign trail, making his case to Ohio's voters. His successor in Columbus, Cox noted, had repealed none of the fifty-six reform measures enacted during Cox's term as governor. That, to Cox, resembled vindication by events; now, he wanted vindication at the ballot box: a second term as governor. Cox could be as coy as anyone in politics, claiming that his candidacy was aimed at aiding President Woodrow Wilson's re-election bid. In the end, Wilson's candidacy saved his: the president carried Ohio by 90,000 votes; Cox's margin was a bare 6,616. Cox's election was also aided by a campaign chest well-filled in Dayton. After the election, a Dayton socialist writer charged that $37,000 was contributed to Cox by "Dayton capitalists" — $7,000 each from Edward Deeds and Charles Kettering, the rest from individuals tied to the flood control effort; further, that these donations were reimbursed to the individuals in question out of the funds raised in Dayton for flood planning. The amount in question was a goodly sum for a statewide campaign; in 1912, the Democratic party reported expenditures of only $1.1 million nationally to elect Woodrow Wilson. Arthur Morgan confirms the story, though he gives the amount as $26,000. In his book on the Miami Conservancy District, Morgan writes without other comment: "In explanation it was stated that the contribution was made to protect the Ohio Conservancy law." Edward Deeds was taking no chances.

By then, Deeds was out of a job. The cause, of course, was John H. Patterson. Patterson, too, had had his day in court, and he had triumphed. U.S. Circuit Court of Appeals in Cincinnati overturned the conviction of "Patterson et al." on charges of criminal violation of the antitrust statutes. The court did so in an exceedingly long, torturously worded opinion. Narrowly, it held the trial court had erred in not permitting Patterson's attorneys to present evidence that NCR's alleged criminal activity had been provoked by the alleged criminal activity of those NCR was trying to put out of business. More broadly, the decision called to mind a verdict supposedly once returned by a jury in Scotland: "Not guilty, but don't do it again." Flood rescue and relief had made Patterson a national hero; the judges were not eager to lock him in prison. The court ordered the case be retried; it never was. Patterson returned from the federal courthouse in Cincinnati to Dayton where he was greeted by a welcoming throng of 20,000.

Patterson seemed unchanged by his brush with federal authority. He retained his faith in the power of promotion. The outbreak of war in Europe had brought on what to eyes less discerning than Patterson's looked rather like a business recession. Two weeks after his conviction was overturned, the NCR president ran a full-page "Business is Booming" ad in the *Saturday Evening Post*, then had it reprinted in 1,500 newspapers, 300 trade and religious magazines and thirty-five monthlies. The campaign's central message was: "If business was not good it was because people thought it was not good. They had only to think it was good, say it often enough, believe implicitly that it was good and it would be good." He retained, as well, his somewhat curious regard for his subordinates. In freeing Patterson, federal court also set aside the sentences of the two dozen NCR executives convicted with him. Over the next few months, Patterson fired every single one of them, Deeds included. Patterson's only comment was that he dismissed his co-defendants because "one of them got me into this mess." The triumph in Dayton of rationally-based, emotionally-detached expertise was something less than full.

Homebodies.
Orville and
Katharine Wright
were, a relative
said, like some old
married couple.
When in 1926
Katharine married
for real, Orville felt
betrayed. He was
the kindest of men
—"one of those
persons that never
complained" —
and he did not
again speak to his
sister until she was
on her death bed.

at home

Like John H. Patterson and the proponents of the Conservancy Act, Orville Wright gained vindication in court.

In 1914, U.S. Circuit Court of Appeals ruled that Orville's aviation patents were airtight; as no aircraft could get airborne without infringing them, all who wished to fly must either enter into a licensing agreement with Orville, pay royalties or remain grounded. In his biography of the Wrights, Tom Crouch speculates that at this moment Orville could have shifted from defense to offense, scattered his adversaries and built, or attempted to, an industry giant based on control of key patents. Had Wilbur lived, the effort might have been made — Wilbur's ambitions were worldly; had he had a hand on events after the court victory he might have tried to learn if the role of business tycoon was within his extensive bag of talents.

Orville had no such wish. At forty-two, he was becoming a homebody, or more of one. The court had affirmed what he wanted all to know: that it was these two bicycle-building brothers who had given flight to the world, and none else. For Orville, that was sufficient; he had no great liking for business or businessmen and little wish to become one. In October 1915, he sold the Wright Company to a group of New York investors for $1.5 million. No huge sum, but then Bishop Wright had maintained that all the money one needed in life was enough to keep one from being a burden to others, and $1.5 million was more than that.

Orville had already paid for his life's one indulgence, the home he would occupy until his death, Hawthorn Hill. The site for this Georgian-style dwelling had been selected and its plans drawn up prior to Wilbur's death in 1912; Orville, Katharine and Bishop Wright moved in some months after the flood. It was a clear move up. For forty-two years, the Wrights had lived on the less fashionable side of the river, at 7 Hawthorn Street, in an unpretentious wooden frame dwelling in an only somewhat better than average neighborhood. Orville had been born in that house; Wilbur had died there. By contrast, Hawthorn Hill was classically graceful, set on a prominent hill in Dayton's most affluent suburb. The project was Orville's more than anyone's: he designed its heating,

electrical and plumbing systems, including the shower stall with its loops of copper piping that sprayed the bather with water from all sides.

A visitor commented, "It's a beautiful home inside. I have heard stories about when they built this house — now this is typical of Orville Wright — that they put thirteen coats of white enamel on the wood work and there hasn't been a coat of paint put on since."

Like almost everything the Wright family set its hand to, Hawthorn Hill was well-proportioned, graceful, welcoming. The front pillars were added at Orville's direction, and he and Katharine helped design the entrances and balconies. The home had a huge icebox, but no refrigerator: Orville thought refrigerator ice tasted wrong.

Beautiful; hardly glamorous. The furnishings and wall coverings were subdued, Victorian. It was a quiet home, characterized by Orville's reading chair, an armchair to which Orville attached a book holder of his design: it held a book open and at a comfortable angle for reading while leaving Orville's hands free and unfatigued. Once again, Orville was living in a small world. He left Hawthorn Hill to putter in the laboratory he maintained in the city, for calls upon his brother Lorin and family, for occasional short trips to McCook Field to see what the Army flyers were up to, and for not much else. Once, Katharine rousted both Orville and Bishop Wright out of the house to march in a "Votes for Women" parade, political equality for women being one of the few social ideas of which Orville consistently approved. Always close, Katharine and Orville drew closer yet after the death of their father, aged eighty-eight, in 1917. They were companionable. Katharine wrote for Orville the correspondence that he, though a fine writer, found burdensome to undertake. They had an agreement, or so Orville believed, to share each other's lives and thoughts until death it them did part.

The year after the Wrights moved into Hawthorn Hill, Charles and Olive Kettering took occupancy of what became their permanent home. Ridgeleigh Terrace was set toward open country two miles and a bit south-southwest of Hawthorn Hill, built with the money the automotive self-starter was bringing in. Ridgeleigh Terrace was gracious and elegant: half-timbered Tudor of gray wood and fieldstone, with plaster-cast ceilings, teak paneling and a $27,000 Aeolian pipe organ Olive Kettering used to give recitals. The house showed off Kettering's gadgets: in the 1920s, it boasted what may have been the world's first home air conditioning system. It showed off as well Kettering's vast tolerance for cats, any one of which a visitor might find dozing upon opening a closet or bureau drawer in the guest room.

Where the Wrights' home was secluded, the Ketterings' was impromptu; they entertained frequently and at short notice. At one gathering, the near-sighted inventor gained brief renown as a latter-day Annie Oakley. He announced to those present that he was so fine a shot he could fire a rifle bullet at the edge of a knife blade so accurately that the blade would split the bullet in half, with each half flying off to snuff out the flame of candles set to either side. And with a casual aim, Kettering proceeded to do just that. One shot, and both candles were extinguished. The guests were amazed. One even suggested that Kettering give up inventing and take to the performing stage. So pleased was Kettering with their delight at his achievement that only reluctantly did he explain that the bullet had been a blank. The candle flames had been extinguished by tiny bellows which he, a better engineer than trick shot, had secreted in the candlestick holders.

Kettering was gregarious. He was a talker for all seasons, played an enthusiastic if unskilled violin and, on the dance floor, would "practically wear his partner out." He was casual: "Don't think he ever put on the dog," an associate said of Kettering's attire. "Not a fashion plate. A laboratory man." He was also generous. With his money, and his time. Just as on his honeymoon in 1905 —when he wandered over to help a driver start his disabled vehicle — Kettering invariably stopped to change the tire or check the engine of whoever happened to be stuck on the roadside; just as invariably, he completed the repair without

Imposing where Hawthorn Hill is welcoming, Trailsend proclaimed James Cox as a man of means.

mentioning his name. His was by all accounts a happy marriage. His wife Olive thought the world of him — "Now, Ginny," she told their daughter-in-law, "just don't argue with Charley" — tolerating while regretting the absences his frantic work habits prompted.

James Cox also settled. In 1915, following the failure of his bid for re-election, he returned to Dayton to build Trailsend, a baronial structure that dominates a substantial high bluff not far northwest of Ridgeleigh Terrace. The home proclaims its owner as a man of means, a stone and brick mansion of Georgian architecture, set among mature hardwoods. Trailsend drew its name from the local belief that it was at this spot that native tribes, their journeys for the year complete, gathered each fall. Under Cox's tenure, Trailsend was not a gathering point: Cox rarely entertained. Not long after its construction, Trailsend had a mistress to mind it. James Cox remar-

"The high character
of its meetings was
fixed from the start.
...Furthermore, the
formal and
informal talks by
Messrs. Deeds and
Kettering, the
effective leading
and prompting of
discussion by the
former, and
inimitable
impromptu
remarks of the
latter, gave an
anticipation and
zest to each
meeting."

— *Club history*

ried. The first Mrs. Cox is something of a mystery. She is not mentioned, not once, in Cox's autobiography; veteran reporters at his newspaper, curious about their boss's past, were never able to learn what had become of her. Some speculate that she committed suicide; others, that she ran off with the butler, or the night editor. Actually, Cox and his first wife were divorced in 1912, quietly if not amicably; somewhat unusual for the day, they were granted shared custody of their two children. In 1917, Cox married the former Margaretta Blair of Chicago, by whom he had two daughters.

In or out of office, James Cox had a talent for making money. It did not delay his enrichment that he was tight with a buck. A member of the house staff recalled, "He didn't pay well. As butler, I started out at $25.00 a week. Then it was cut to $22.50. He said things were tight." On other matters, Cox was more generous: he played golf with the flexible rule that he could tee up his ball, wherever it lay, anywhere on the course. As a former young man rising, he took an avuncular interest in the ambitions of his caddies; Cox urged one into the field of journalism, a field in which the caddy, James Reston, did well.

Their homes reflected private interests, personal pursuits; shared endeavors found shelter at the Dayton Engineers' Club. The club was founded in 1914 by Charles Kettering and Edward Deeds — the pair claimed its first two membership cards; Arthur Morgan got the seventh, Orville Wright the sixteenth, with John H. Patterson added as an honorary inductee. Deeds and Kettering paid for the club's permanent home, a $305,000 structure plunked down on Monument Street next door to the offices of the Miami Conservancy District, where the two enterprises could keep a modernizing eye on each other. At its dedica-

tion, Orville Wright, as second vice president, formally accepted the building from Kettering and Deeds; James Cox, as governor of Ohio, bestowed the official blessings of the state.

Membership reached 250 by 1917. It was a male setting — a members' room with fireplace flanked by elephant tusks, a billiards room with twin pool tables, meeting and conference rooms. With daily lunches, weekly dinners and monthly technical sessions, the club was a gathering spot for Dayton's ambitious technical corps. By one story, the club had a rule against laundering tablecloths until they had been reviewed by a member of the staff; the rule was intended to prevent any important mealtime scribblings from being lost in the wash.

Deeds and Kettering used their connections in the wider world to line up speakers for the technical sessions: Henry Leland of Cadillac, utility magnate Samuel Insull, Dr. William Mayo and naturalist Louis Agassiz. One speaker made an impression on Arthur Morgan. He was Herman Schneider, dean of the engineering school at the University of Cincinnati, who spoke on "Teaching Engineering versus Teaching Engineers." In his talk, Schneider detailed the educational model he had introduced in Cincinnati, under which engineering students alternated periods of on-campus study with off-campus work in technical employments. The aim, he said, was to produce a better rounded, more grounded engineer.

Morgan had been ruminating along similar lines. Like many unhappy with the ways of the world, he believed the place to start to set things right was with the young, where the young congregated, in schools. As a would-be educator, Morgan fully favored practical experience: "The schoolhouse has received too much credit," he wrote, "and the barn not enough." The college educations then offered struck him as archaic, suitable to the training of "a priest, or lawyer, or a gentleman of one or two hundred years ago." With his wife, Lucy Griscom Morgan, he discussed founding a school; to that end, the Morgans acquired a prospective site at Jacob's Pillow in Massachusetts. The Morgans were an extremely purposeful couple. While the Wrights, Ketterings and Coxes had settled into substantial homes, they — admittedly much less affluent — lived with their three children northwest of Dayton in a house set on land that would be inundated once Arthur's dams were built. Their son Ernest, then a teenager, recalled: "People in Englewood thought the Conservancy was a big swindle, a big racket and Arthur Morgan was the head crook. A gang of boys would shout threats and taunts to me. Nothing much happened. Apparently I was protected by some aura of evil emanating from my father, who was going to drown them all."

By the fall of 1917, Ernest no longer went to school with the neighborhood boys. Instead, he and his younger brother Griscom — along with Kettering's son Eugene, Deeds' son Charles and Orville Wright's nephew Horace — were enrolled at the Moraine Park School, a private kindergarten through twelfth grade that drew its enrollment from the offspring of Conservancy engineers,

As ever in charge, John H. Patterson drives the sleigh. At his Far Hills estate, Patterson ruled at table as well. He expected dining NCR executives to speak coherently, on command. When one newly-promoted was called upon, he stammered, "My soup is getting cold," sat back down, thus losing his promotion.

Delco executives and municipal administrators. The school had been organized by Arthur Morgan, who earlier that year called a meeting at the Engineers' Club to enlist interest and support. Moraine Park's resulting nine-member board was practically an interlocking directorate: Arthur Morgan, Charles Kettering, Orville Wright, Edward Deeds and five of their professional associates. Kettering provided the school with its quarters, renovating his disused 225-foot by fifty-foot greenhouse for the purpose; Morgan recruited its headmaster.

In choosing a headmaster, Morgan employed his standard recruitment procedure: cast a wide net, then flick the minnows aside. On one prospecting trip through five northeastern cities, he interviewed fifty candidates. The minnows were many. Morgan's trip notes record these comments on typical candidates:

> My first impression as he entered the room was that he might have a thick skull.... Dr. Hall says he is the best man student at Clark University.... It bodes ill for the future of Clark University if he is.

> A kind old man of perhaps 55.... Not a man we want and I told him so.

> A cultured man who probably was alive once.

> I think nearly anyone could sell him a gold brick.

After further search, Morgan urged appointment of a Colorado educator, Dr. Frank Slutz. Headmaster chosen, teachers were hired, and Moraine Park opened in the fall of 1917 with sixty students.

Morgan's influence helped make character building central to the curriculum. One Moraine Park prospectus stated: "The object of education is not primarily to impart information, but to insure to the child the qualities, character and accomplishments he will need when he is a man. As it is only by practice that men become masters in any field, opportunity must be given for boys and girls to practice those activities which it is hoped they may be masters as they mature." Learning was organized around doing — for younger students, raising chickens became a math lesson: how much feed would produce how many eggs at what market value? Two older students who were caring for cows gained permission to meet an English requirement by reading government bulletins on Holsteins; when these proved boring, that fact became an entree to literary criticism. The school was well equipped. For the juniors, there was a sand pile, a wading pool and no required classes. For the seniors, Moraine Park offered a student-run workshop, printshop, bank and chemistry laboratory; students handled the school's janitorial and secretarial tasks and kept the lunchroom's books. The aim was wholeness and balance. One student wrote in somewhat superior tones of his school's physical education program: "A coach, his assistants, and the physically favored few... make up the athletic circle of too many schools in this country.... It is certainly better to have a great number of good physical specimens than to have a few phenomenally strong men and many weaklings."

Enrollment reached 200. By all accounts, students enjoyed the place. One student, then Virginia Weiffenbach, said of her days at Moraine Park:

> We loved it. Later, with college, we realized the shortcomings; I struggled, because I was underprepared in academics. But I became a whiz at being practical. Take the [student-run] projects. I and two others gave children's parties: we took care of everything... the invites, the decorations, food, entertainment and games — "Punch 'n Judy," "Pin-the-Tail."

Morgan wrote of the school's requirements for its students, "As tools to live and work with, but not as the end of education, [students] must master the essential parts of the subject matter commonly included in school programs." Not all did. Perhaps most embarrassing, those struggling included Eugene Kettering, son of the school's chief benefactor. Kettering wrote the school's headmaster: "I feel we are neglecting the fundamentals which you will never be able to get the boys to learn after they get past a certain age."

Dayton's engineering and technical elite was a small world. Virginia Weiffenbach, the student who thrived at Moraine Park, and Eugene Kettering, who struggled there, were later married. By chance, the first man to see Virginia in her wedding dress was Orville Wright: she and he had been separately dropped off at the wrong entrance to the church; they encountered each other — she, the young bride; he, the blushing inventor — while each was trying to find a way out of the church basement.

the innocents

The Annual Club of Ten Dayton Boys continued to meet each October.

They met in the flood year of 1913, when members gathered and spoke of their experiences with the deluge, which caused "very great loss" to member Joseph Andrews and "a great deal of inconvenience" to member William Boyd, he with an invalid wife and a cellar full of water. Soon, Boyd — whose fifth wedding anniversary Wilbur and Orville had reported on a quarter century previously in the pages of their *West Side News* — was, like member Frank Gilbert, a widower. Two years later, member Edgar Ellis announced a career move, from the Trimble Paving Brick Company to the Ohio Association of Paving Brick Manufacturers. The secretary for that meeting recorded with mild dismay that no word had been received from Reuchlin Wright, "presumably on account of the fact that he has been in the Far West and did not get his notice in time to write us. His letter will no doubt come later, and be passed around among the other members for their pleasure as it is a pleasure for any of us to read from the pens and hearts of those who are absent."

By the 1916 gathering, Ellis had moved again — he was temporarily employed by the National Republican Committee. It was a year in which Republicans celebrated too soon. The GOP's candidate, former Chief Justice Charles Evans Hughes, went to bed election night believing himself victorious, only to wake to the news that late results from the West Coast had returned Woodrow Wilson to the White House. Wilson was re-elected on the slogan, "He Kept Us Out of War." He did not do so for very much longer; in April 1917, America declared war on the Central Powers. A minor consequence of that declaration was that, after thirty-one consecutive annual meetings, 1917 passed with no gathering of the Ten Dayton Boys being held. Members, the secretary recorded, were away from the city on business matters, "or otherwise tied up by war conditions."

When Europe broke into war in 1914, the conflict did not greatly engage the interest of Dayton. Its citizens were as isolationist as the rest of the America, if not more so. One local minister admonished his congregation: "Don't shout for war unless you would shoulder a musket." While some in the city took sides in the conflict, not all who did so sided with America's future allies: Dayton had a large German population, whose hearts were most open to their Fatherland. Purses, as well. In 1915, the German-language *Gross-Daytoner Zeitung* sold German war bonds to its readers. The city's leading newspaper, the Cox-owned *Daily News*, unswervingly opposed intervention. In November 1915, it editorialized: "Nor is a victory by Germany the worst thing that can happen. If the Allies were to win and their winning meant a great increase of Russian aggressiveness on the one side and of Japanese assertiveness on the other, America might live to be very sorry that Germany had not won." In December 1916, The News termed the war "the crime of all the ages" and urged that the next arm lifted in the struggle should be "paralyzed." As it happened, that next arm was America's.

America fought "the war to end all wars" with the innocent optimism and self-belief that made such a slogan possible and resonant. In Dayton, storefronts were decked out in red, white and blue buntings; patriotic speakers held forth in movie theaters before each show. When conscription was enacted, the four Dayton men who held the first number drawn included one born in Germany and one born in Hungary, both now heading "over there" in service against their native lands. When the county's first sixty-six draftees left the city, Dayton declared a full holiday to see them off. The newly-conscripted, historian James Perkins relates, were banqueted at Memorial Hall; they then paraded past thousands down a flag-lined Main Street and on to Union Station. There, each inductee received a parting gift from the local chapter of the Catholic Women's League for Patriotic Service, then embarked for basic training at Ohio's Camp Sherman.

The conflict pressed Arthur Morgan into brief service. In 1917, he, at government request, scouted a location for a major military airfield. Morgan took Orville Wright with him to help assess the ground. Orville, Morgan wrote, favored a site adjacent to the Huffman prairie where he and Wilbur had flown: "He said that there usually was an upward movement of air at the south margin of the field, due to the higher land in the south, and that this upward current helped an airplane to get off the ground. Also he said that the soil in this area was soft and spongy and cushioned the shock of landing." The government accepted Morgan's recommendation, acquiring the land that today forms

Volunteers flock to the Home Guard; others flocked to the altar. A local paper reported, "With the entrance of the nation into the war there was a drop in enlistments, as patronage of the marriage license bureau increased." Initially, married men were not subject to the draft.

a fair portion of Wright-Patterson Air Force Base, one of the world's largest military installations.

For Morgan, war was part tragedy, part simply a problem to be thought logically through. He bullet-pointed the issues in typewritten notes made prior to America's entry. Morgan feared the influence of the military: "The army spirit is cynical... The army [man] will always go just as far as the people let him." Pacifists were evasive: "The pacifist fails to see that the world never did run [on the basis of honor and mutual respect]. No large community ever held together on goodwill alone." Always at issue for Morgan was the question of personal motive: "The unarmed man and untrained man does not know when he is too decent to fight and when he is a coward." In 1915, former President William Howard Taft had organized the League to Enforce the Peace, which advocated a peace without victory and creation of an international organization to adjudicate future disputes between nations. Morgan signed on. He became secretary of its Ohio chapter; he and Lucy Griscom Morgan were in the audience at Washington's Willard Hotel when Woodrow Wilson first endorsed the idea of a League of Nations.

With America a combatant, however, peace without victory looked decidedly less attractive than victory without quibble. Morgan persevered with the League, drawing a strong, cautionary rebuke from Edward Deeds. As chairman of the Miami Conservancy District, Deeds in February 1918 wrote to his chief engineer: "There have been several criticisms lodged against you and your relations to some peace or pacifist movement. This went so far as to recommend that you, with one other, be dropped from the Engineers' Club, because of your German tendencies." Needless to say, Deeds added, he did not share this view personally, but he urged Morgan to desist from involvement in any public question that might reflect upon the work of the Conservancy. Several months later, Morgan resigned as the League's Ohio secretary. The reason for this resignation is not known; in any case, Morgan had dams to build. He had dams to build, in part, because Deeds had interceded with Treasury Secretary William McAdoo to gain government permission to sell the bonds to finance the Conservancy dams, despite a general wartime ban on non-military construction. The sale was of $24.3 million at five and a half percent — a higher rate than Deeds and Morgan had hoped for, but reflecting the then-current low ebb in Allied fortunes.

War touched everyone, including even the Annual Club of Ten Dayton Boys, whose members were now well past the age of active service. Member William Andrews, at sixty-five, became an inspector of munitions at the Davis Sewing Machine Company, which produced military bicycles, fuses and detonators. Member Edgar Ellis was general auditor at McCook Field, the Army's experimental aviation station. Member Charles Alinger, fifty-nine, was a machinist at National Cash Register. Like other Dayton manufacturers, NCR was hip-deep in war contracts, building airplane parts and Colt automatic rifles. There was a certain corporate pretense about this: NCR president John H. Patterson sailed through the First World War ostensibly oblivious to his company's participation in the conflict. Burnt by the federal government in the antitrust prosecution, he was persuaded that any manufacturer who undertook war work would sooner or later be hauled into the dock, charged with profiteering. As a precaution, Patterson refused to sign his name to any of the contracts for munitions work that came his company's way. As a further precaution, Patterson spent most of the war in discrete semi-exile in California. It was not, altogether, a splendid performance for a colonel in the Ohio National Guard, even one who held his commission in the commissary department.

By 1918, Dayton Ten member Charles Alinger had moved from NCR to the Dayton Wright Company. The company had been founded early in 1917, with Edward Deeds as president, Charles Kettering as vice president and Orville Wright as an incorporator and leading name. "These men," Wright wrote accurately of his fellows when the venture was launched, "are extraordinarily good businessmen with lots of financial backing. They are going to try to carry out some of my ideas in creating a sport of aeronautics." With war, aviation for play was cast aside, and company purpose abruptly changed to the building of combat aircraft for the government. The irony was not lost on Orville, who in 1917 wrote to a correspondent:

> When my brother and I built and flew the first man-carrying flying machine, we thought that we were introducing into the world an invention which would make further wars practically impossible. That we were not alone in this thought is evidenced by the fact that the French Peace Society presented us with medals on account of our invention. We thought governments would realize the impossibility of winning by surprise attacks, and that no country would enter into war with another of equal size when it knew that it would have to win by simply wearing the enemy down.

The aircraft had not prevented war; worse, in Orville's view, by making secrecy impossible, it had made stalemate inevitable. The two sides, he wrote, "are apparently nearly equal in aerial equipment, and it seems to me that unless present conditions can be changed, the war will continue for years."

To change that condition, the U.S. government decided to adapt the mass production techniques of the auto industry to the task of turning out aircraft in numbers sufficient to drive German flyers from the sky. As Orville wrote a second correspondent: "If the Allies' armies are equipped with such a number of aeroplanes as to keep the enemy planes entirely back on the line, so that they are unable to direct gunfire or to observe the movement of the Allied troops — in other words, if the enemy's eyes can be put out — it will be possible to end the war." In military aviation, the nation was starting almost from scratch: in the nine years ending with 1916, the U.S. Army had taken delivery on only 142 new aircraft. With war declared, Congress tried to play catchup with a mammoth appropriation of $1.6 billion for military aircraft. To perform this task, no one was better situated than Dayton-Wright: in Charles Kettering, it had the leading figure in automotive technology; in Orville Wright, it had the reigning name in aviation; and in Edward Deeds, it had a well-placed friend. In August 1917, Deeds was commissioned a colonel and placed in charge of aircraft procurement for the U.S. Army. Orders went out in all directions, though nowhere more than to Dayton-Wright, which ultimately contracted to deliver 4,000 combat planes and 400 trainers.

In war, as in peace, Charles Kettering was in up to his elbows. Kettering was fiercely chauvinistic. He was readily of the belief that the things at which he excelled — automotive technology and improvisation — would soon be filling the skies with aircraft. To their later sorrow, he, Deeds and Orville Wright were soon issuing optimistic forecasts of how soon that avenging fleet would take wing. Aircraft, however, proved difficult to mass produce. One observer of their tribulations stated, "It was much easier than at first supposed to mount guns and other items if done by competent, versatile, aircraft people. But when the auto people (unfamiliar with exacting aircraft 'tricks') started on their own to mount this equipment on foreign copies, they made a sorry mess." In theory, production strategy was to choose what was judged to be the best foreign model — the British de Haviland 4 was selected — and then resist making any design changes that would stall production. Indeed, Orville Wright told one interlocutor that at Dayton-Wright his principal contribution to the war effort "was to prevent more changes being made." The first Dayton-Wright aircraft to be shipped to France was not completed until February 1918. Ernest Dubel, a company employee, recalled:

> It was built completely by hand at South Field.... We assembled the ship in twenty below zero weather, and snow a foot deep, and Mr. Kettering tested the motor, and all the controls and equipment personally. We took it apart and made it available for the shipping men to put it into crates to ship to France.... When we were getting ready to take the ship over to the main plant at South Field, we ran into some difficulties, and we were behind schedule about two hours. When we arrived there, we didn't have time to take out for lunch. And the company sent us, what they called a box lunch. And we, including Mr.

Kettering, sat on a lumber pile and ate our midnight lunch, in the bitter cold.

Much of the nation was nearly equally cold. The winter of 1917-1918 was among the most frigid on record — January temperatures in Dayton averaged 15 degrees. For warmth, *The Daily News* urged its readers to line shoes and coats with newsprint; the Home Guard was detailed to protect coal supplies as, in one case, thieves made off with ten entire railway carloads of the fuel. In late 1917, Governor James Cox learned that coal supplies then moving to Lake Erie ports would be frozen in at lakeside for the winter before they could be trans-shipped. The coal, Cox wrote, "could not conceivably be used [at its intended destination] until probably the first of May, yet tens of thousands were without the means of resisting the most severe winter in a generation." When Cox's appeals to have the fuel reallocated to Ohio were unsuccessful, he used his powers of office simply to seize the coal.

No railway line ran to the construction site of Germantown dam — so an engine was moved there by leapfrogging ties and track down country lanes and city streets.

Governors then enjoyed great powers; Cox employed his to the hilt, along with his considerable powers of improvisation. When construction workers were needed to build camp housing at Fort Sherman, Cox had 3,000 there in forty-eight hours. When enlistment caused a shortage of farm labor, a second Cox effort enrolled 18,000 high school students in harvesting crops. In April 1918, the war department wanted to drive 40,000 trucks from Detroit to the port of Baltimore. A bottleneck was the twenty-seven-mile gap in the National Road in eastern Ohio. Cox quickly dispatched hundreds of state prisoners to provide the needed on-site muscle; he wrote, "How the red clay flew in those hills of south-eastern Ohio! The countryside shook from the explosions of dynamite that were tearing away rock and hardpan soil."

On a far larger scale, rock and hardpan soil were being torn away near Dayton. On January 27, 1918, even before the winter cold had eased, construction began on the dams of the Miami Conservancy District. By the end of March, work was in progress at all five dam sites. It was a huge undertaking — Morgan's engineers had detailed the resculpting of the Miami Valley; now, his construction crews required twenty-one draglines, sixteen locomotives and 200 railway dump cars to carry off the shavings. At the site of Taylorsville Dam, the line of the Baltimore & Ohio had to be moved to higher ground for a distance of ten miles; at the Huffman site, a cut nearly a mile long was made 120 feet deep into solid rock. At Germantown, historian Carl Becker writes:

The nearest railroad line was three miles from the site of construction and separated from it by rough, hilly country. But the District somehow had to get a locomotive and dump cars there to move heavy loads efficiently in the building of the dam.... engineers laid a temporary track, moved a train forward on it, took up the rear track and relaid it at the front.... In this fashion, a 40-ton locomotive and 12-cubic-yard dump cars traversed unpaved country roads and the streets of Germantown.

For Morgan, all things connected; all events offered opportunity for social reform. At the Conservancy, reform came close to ground level, where shovels were hoisted and dirt was flung. As a young man, Morgan wrote, he had sought work on a construction crew. The foreman to whom Morgan applied responded, "All right, get you a blanket and a woman and come along." Construction camps were typically shantytowns, housing a drifting population of workers who toiled for a few weeks, then turned up missing, headed off drunk, and surfaced at another job site when their money ran out. Morgan commented:

> This human wreckage was part of the price paid in the glorious American epic of pioneering and nation building. Each job being a temporary undertaking, it seemed uneconomical to incur the expense of decent housing and living conditions. Yet, as men went from job to job, what was temporary makeshift so far as each job was concerned was the lifetime environment for the workman who followed the big engineering-works construction business.

Morgan would do better. In place of shantytowns, he constructed five model villages, including small individual homes for workers with families. Each camp was self-governing through a local community association. Each had its own newspaper, its own baseball diamonds and playgrounds, its own community hall, with daytime classes for children and night school classes in English for immigrants and reading for those illiterate. Morgan always spoke in broad themes; at the Conservancy, he first gave those ideas broad expression. The Miami Conservancy District stands, in physical terms, as Dayton's notable civic achievement: it was paid for, entirely, by local funds; it encompassed an entire watershed in its solution. And, like many things that work all but effortlessly, it has, in Dayton, been approximately forgotten.

Work progressed less smoothly at Dayton-Wright Aircraft. There, as at the nation's other aircraft production sites, the de Havilands and other aircraft were simply not coming off the assembly line in the numbers promised. In spring 1918, President Wilson authorized a high-level inquiry into aircraft production; surprisingly, Wilson turned the investigation over to his 1916 presidential opponent, Charles Evans Hughes. Soon thereafter, Edward Deeds, under pressure, resigned his post as chief of aircraft procurement. The investigation marked the second time — the NCR antitrust indictment being the first — Deeds had run afoul of federal authority. In Oc-

tober 1918, Hughes brought his inquiry to Dayton. Dayton-Wright had a few things to say in its defense: it had produced over 1,800 aircraft, which, while well fewer than the number contracted for, was well more than any other contractor. In the end, Deeds was generally reckoned guilty of optimism in his earliest predictions of aircraft production; guilty, perhaps, of favoritism in the assigning of contracts to Dayton-Wright, but cleared of any more serious misdeed. (The result disgusted one of Deeds' main accusers, a fifty-year-old sculptor and aviation enthusiast who by one account had accused Deeds of "retardation of production, aeronautical ignorance, profiteering, and pro-German sympathy." The sculptor, Gutzon Borglund, subsequently headed west, where he spent some years carving Mt. Rushmore.)

By the time Charles Evans Hughes' inquiry reached Dayton, Charles Kettering — Dayton-Wright's vice president — was off on a different bearing. On December 24, 1917, he accepted a government assignment to produce an aerial torpedo for use on German targets. As with any new project that captured his imagination, Kettering immediately began pushing it forward. As one Dayton-Wright employee recalled, Kettering "walked out of his office over through the office where I was working and he says, get your stuff together, and go down to the garage and get in my car and I'll be down shortly." As was his habit, Kettering simply laid claim to those he wanted working directly with him. The claimed employee added, "He never told my boss, and it was the next year before my boss found out where I was gone."

The aerial torpedo — or "bug," as it came to be called — was a fourteen-foot pilotless biplane designed to deliver a 300-pound bomb to targets well behind enemy lines. Huge chunks of technical expertise were thrown at the venture: Orville Wright directed design of the biplane's body; C. H. Wills — one-time

The dams of the Conservancy were artificial bottlenecks — permitting passage of no more water than the riverbed downstream could safely carry away, backing up the surplus in retarding basins behind each dam, and requiring no human intervention to make them work.

chief designer at Ford — developed a lightweight forty-horsepower engine; Kettering directed design of the guidance system, incorporating ideas on gyroscopes contributed by Elmer Sperry. Perhaps in consequence of such expertise, the "bug" was, in the sense of the term that pleases engineers, extremely clever. Design allowed the biplane to be built from the scraps of pure-grain spruce left over from the making of de Havilands. To economize other materials, the craft had paper-covered wings and a tail of resin-impregnated cardboard. Level flight was maintained by a gyroscope, with altitude maintained by a sensitive aneroid barometer, with controls pneumatically actuated by air bellows using the suction from the engine crankcase. For the first prototype, Kettering said he obtained the needed parts "by pinching pieces out of my pipe organ and my player piano." For shipment to the front lines, "the bug" could be disassembled into a compact box; in the field, two soldiers could reassembled it in five minutes, using nothing other than a standard-sized wrench, of which two were packed in each box. Before launch, soldiers were to program the craft for an intended distance. When a small airscrew built into the wing counted the appropriate number of turns, the craft's wings were cast free and its 300-pound bomb plummeted on its target.

Flying bombs were "ahead of the curve" during the First World War; one war later German V-1s and V-2s caught that curve and followed it all the way to London.

Occasionally, the thing actually worked. In a field trial on October 22, 1918, one of Kettering's aerial torpedoes landed within fifty feet of a target 500 yards distant. Reliability was not a constant. Engine-designer Wills wrote gyroscope-expert Sperry to describe a notable launch:

> The ship went up about 500 feet and she nosed right straight up into the air and then dropped back, and went up again to about 1000 feet and tipped over backwards. The instrument board came loose and broke the hose connecting the controls. When all the controls were disconnected the ship side-slipped and started up in circles about a mile in diameter.... Mr. Kettering watched it until it was up about 12,000 feet ... There were a couple of hundred people there and they got into automobiles and started to chase it.... They finally located it twenty-one miles away and there were about a dozen farmers out with lanterns looking for the aviator. There wasn't a thing hurt on the engine, not even a spark plug broken, but the gasoline tank was dry. It would have been going yet probably had it not been for the lack of gasoline. It had traveled approximately 90 miles for it had been in

flight just on one hour. One farmer asked Mr. Kettering who drove it and he told him he did and the farmer wanted to know where he put his legs.

An Army observer at subsequent tests somewhat generously concluded that "the bug" was "at present lacking in sufficient accuracy of control." Events, in any case, were outrunning inventors; on November 11, 1918, the Armistice was signed. Practical flying bombs would have to await another war.

The collapse of the Kaiser's armies in the field came more rapidly than the Allies had anticipated; until shortly before the Armistice, Allied staffs were planning for the 1919 campaigns they thought victory over Germany would yet require. For James Cox, peace may have come not a moment too soon. The week prior to the Armistice, he was re-elected as Ohio's first three-term Democratic governor. He retained office on the strength of his performance as 'war governor,' something he ceased to be almost as soon as the votes were counted. His victory was narrow — a bare 12,000 vote margin out of a million cast, as Republicans claimed both houses of the Ohio legislature and every statewide office but his own. Perhaps it was time to get out of Buckeye politics, and into something loftier. For Democrats generally, it was an unhappy election. President Wilson had appealed for a Democratic-controlled Congress so that the party that had directed the war could make the peace, once peace came. It was a foolish act, suggesting at a time of national unity that war and peace were partisan concerns. In any case, it backfired. Republicans increased their hold in the House and, ominously for the League of Nations Wilson hoped the postwar world would enact, gained a narrow majority in the Senate.

Whatever the larger issues peace might bring, much in life was ready to resume. After a single year's lapse, the Annual Club of Ten Dayton Boys met again in late October 1918. The minutes of that meeting record: "The treasurer reported a balance from 1916 of $16.22 from which deducting the cost of the 1918 lunch — $2.85 — leaves a balance in the treasury of $13.37. No dues were collected this year as it was deemed unnecessary until the present surplus is exhausted."

Walking tall —
Cox had not yet
met defeat, his
running mate
had not yet
contracted polio.

a study in limits

Back in the days before television cast its boring pall
over the proceedings, national political conventions
were great, glorious slogging matches. Troops of delegates
— professional politicians all — marched in behind the banner of their own
state's "favorite son" and did battle along whatever lines that year drew. "Silver" versus "gold." "Wets" versus "drys." True, Republicans won most of the
elections, but Democrats had the best brawls. This they assured by their adher-
ence to the two-thirds rule, which held that to be nominated, a candidate must
receive the votes of that share of delegates. A determined minority could, therefore, block all others and, if not prevail, then at least strike a better bargain.
Nominating tactics took on the aspect of siege warfare — ballot followed ballot
as floating coalitions of factions fought for dominance. The prolonged nominating process once so depleted one Democratic state delegation of its ready
cash that its chairman gathered its members together and declared, "We need
to move to a more liberal candidate or a less expensive hotel."

When the Democrats gathered in San Francisco in 1920, they met under the
specter of an ailing, possibly dying President Woodrow Wilson and the yet
unresolved question of American entry into Wilson's beloved League of Nations. On the issue of the League, some party leaders voiced wholehearted
support, others paid mere lip service. More numerous lips had another concern: Prohibition had been enacted; urban delegates wanted it amended or re-
voked, rural delegates favored enforcement to the driest letter of the law. This

being politics, much was negotiable. *The Nation* reported, "Many delegates were perfectly willing to trade and accept a one hundred percent League of Nations in return for 2.75 percent beer."

Cox believed President Wilson hoped the convention would renominate him — that despite the stroke that had paralyzed his left arm and the traditional two-term limit, he would receive a third nomination to fight on for the League. It was a vain wish. When nominations began, a dozen names — not including Wilson's — were put forward. The strongest contenders were William McAdoo, former secretary of the treasury and Wilson's son-in-law, and Attorney General A. Mitchell Palmer, who directed the widespread arrests and deportations of suspected radicals immediately after the First World War. James Cox — as a three-term Democratic governor of a large and normally Republican state — had figured peripherally in pre-convention speculation; he placed fifth in a preference poll of Democrats conducted by *The Literary Digest*.

Cox wanted the nomination. In January, he had signaled this intention by speaking at the Democrats' Jackson Day Dinner, the event at which candidates by their presence then announced their availability. Beginning with the Ohio delegation as a base, he slowly gathered support as the McAdoo and Palmer forces deadlocked. On the twelfth ballot, he passed McAdoo to take the lead; on the thirtieth ballot, McAdoo nudged narrowly back in front. At this point, McAdoo's opponents — who believed the former treasury secretary had used his administration of the nation's war bond drives to reward potential supporters — broke into mocking choruses of "Every Vote is on the Payroll." On the thirty-ninth ballot, Palmer's remaining support collapsed and Cox retook the lead. On the forty-fourth, Cox was nominated. For the Democrats, he was an appropriate compromise: he was a cautious wet on Prohibition and, while a supporter of Woodrow Wilson, had not served in Wilson's government and could therefore likely sidestep criticism of the national administration.

As was then customary, Cox followed the action from a discrete distance. He learned of his nomination by telegraph at 4:50 a.m., at his office at *The Dayton Daily News*, where he was following events. Barely an hour later, the church bells in Middletown — near Cox's place of birth and where he had entered journalism — began ringing to mark the triumph of the local boy. It was, Cox wrote, "a quick response of a fine community, paying tribute to one whose struggles began in a humble way." Cox was not particularly humble; his struggles had, however, carried him most of the distance spanned in that fundamental American dream: born on a farm, he was just one election away from the White House. He fully expected to arrive. *The Outlook* quoted a close associate of the nominee: "Cox is literally confident, coldly and absolutely confident, that he will be elected President next November.... He believes in himself to a degree I have never known in any other man."

First Patterson, then the Wrights, then Kettering and a now a presidential candidate to call its own. Dayton at its high mark parades in honor of its favorite son. The 1920 election, which matched two candidates from Ohio, was something of a disaster for the state. Harding proved inept as President, Cox unappealing as a candidate; neither major party has nominated anyone from Ohio since.

Part of Cox's confidence lay in the fact that, to his way of thinking, his Republican opponent, Ohio Senator Warren Gamaliel Harding, was a buffoon. Harding's unequal battles with the English language were already drawing the barbs of political journalist H. L. Mencken, who dubbed him — in reference to his city of residence — "the Marion stonehead," and added, "the curious imbecility of Dr. Harding's speech of acceptance continues to engage speculation." In his moment of triumph, Cox may have given no thought to another Ohio Republican, Frank B. Willis; Cox had characterized Willis as "a jovial fellow, big in heart and body, the kind that never took public service very seriously" — and in 1914, Willis had defeated Cox's bid for re-election.

Of the decisions Cox made during his campaign, only the initial two had impact on events. The first came during the convention, when Cox's floor manager Edmond Moore asked who Cox wanted as his running mate: "I told him I had given the matter some thought and that my choice would be Franklin D. Roosevelt of New York. Moore inquired, 'Do you know him?' I did not. In fact, so far as I knew, I had never seen him." Roosevelt was a former assistant secretary of the navy, the bearer of a great political name, and not yet stricken

with polio. In New York state politics, Roosevelt was a reformer; before going ahead with the nomination, therefore, Cox wanted to know if New York's Tammany Hall organization objected. Questioned by Cox's manager, Tammany chief Charles Murphy replied: "I don't like Roosevelt.... But this is the first time a Democratic nominee for the Presidency has shown me courtesy. Tell [Cox] we will nominate Roosevelt on the first ballot as soon as we assemble." Cox's selection of the thirty-eight-year-old Roosevelt brought the future President his first broad claim to national attention.

In truth, the same could be said of Cox, who was hardly a nationally-prominent figure prior to the convention. The attention his nomination brought focused on the similarities between him and his Republican opponent. *The Literary Digest* summarized press accounts:

> No matter what happens in November the next President of the United States will be an Ohio editor who began active life in a printing-office, successfully edited and published several small-town newspapers, played an unimportant part in Congress, and never attained to a national reputation until this summer.... Neither nomination alarms Wall Street. *The Wall Street Journal* is glad that no radical was nominated at San Francisco, and the *New York Commercial* declares that "business will be safe with either" Cox or Harding. The conservative *New York Times* (Dem.) is glad that the two Ohioans are business men and both without 'any radical inclinations."

Press profiles gave almost as much space to Cox's business success as to his political career. By 1920, Cox's newspapers and other investments were bringing him an annual income of $200,000; one writer described his personal fortune as in "the early millions." *The Outlook* described him as "of medium height, medium weight, medium color, of negative personality, and with nothing external to reveal that he possessed an intelligence of singular clarity and a will of instant decision." It was Cox's focus that caught the most comment. One former McAdoo supporter said: "He makes me think of those twelve-cylinder cars that can turn around in its own length; no lost motion."

Cox was not a politician of passions; he did not invest in lost causes, if only because lost causes associated with losers. His proudest accomplishment as governor was his workmen's compensation legislation. On its behalf, Cox said it more fairly identified injured workers, more rapidly brought them appropriate compensation and, by reducing legal costs, saved money as well. Workmen's compensation was needed and humane; still, the case Cox makes for it is largely that of an efficient administrator. Whatever progressive blood ran in Cox's veins when he took over state government in 1912 had thinned by the time of his nomination for President. In his second and third terms as governor, he had brought Ohio efficiency and a strong executive hand, but aimed at no higher sites. All the more surprising, then, that in the 1920 campaign he found in the League of Nations the love and lost cause of his political life. The League was the subject of Cox's second major decision: he announced he would make America's entry the central issue of his campaign. Cox and his running mate dramatized this when, soon after accepting the nomination, they called on President Wilson to pledge their wholehearted support for the League. The President, gaunt-faced and wrapped in a shawl to conceal his paralyzed arm, received them on the White House portico. Wilson's only recorded comment was: "I am very grateful."

PEACE ~ PROGRESS ~ PROSPERITY

FOR PRESIDENT
DEMOCRATIC NOMINEE
JAMES M. COX

FOR VICE PRESIDENT
DEMOCRATIC NOMINEE
FRANKLIN D. ROOSEVELT

Cox kept that pledge. His support for the League in his 1920 campaign was clear and continuing: "The house of civilization is to be put in order. The supreme issue of the century is before us and the nation that halts and delays is playing with fire. The finest impulses of humanity, rising above national lines, merely seek to make another war impossible." He returned and returned to this issue, varying his arguments but never changing his conclusion: the League was needed to keep faith with those who had died in the trenches; the League was needed to keep Bolshevism out of Europe; the League was needed to bequeath a peaceful world to the nation's children. On the question of the League, the line between Cox and his opponent was as clear as Harding's muddled prose would permit. In his own speech of acceptance, the Republican nominee stated: "I would hopefully approach the nations of Europe and of the earth, proposing that understanding which makes us a willing participant in the consecration of nations to a new relationship, to commit the moral forces of the world, America included, to peace and international justice, still leaving America free, independent and self-reliant, but offering friendship to all the world."

Still, if Cox was clear on the League, he was forthright about little else. The Democratic platform on which he ran was, like the candidate, tepid on all other subjects. It favored a strong merchant marine. It endorsed collective bargaining. It advocated development of inland waterways. It urged attention be paid to rural schools. One independent newspaper called it "about as conservative as the Republican platform." The liberal *New Republic* commented: "It is a program including much that is sound, little that is fundamental, and nothing that a mild progressive would have thought too daring in 1896." Attempting to move to the attack, Cox leveled the charge — neither new nor necessarily false — that the Republicans were attempting to buy the election. He claimed that "a campaign fund sufficient in size to stagger the sensibilities of the nation is now being formed." The charge misfired. Whatever Republican intentions, no sensibility-staggering sums had as yet been raised, and Cox could not back his broad charge with evidence of specific misdoing. In the end, he lost twice: the public regarded his accusation as unproved, and the Republicans, by final reckoning, outspent his own campaign by better than three-to-one. Cox conducted an energetic campaign; outwardly, at least, his confidence did not waver. His running mate was less sanguine. Public sentiment was running strongly against Wilson and the League. Asked whether he had any illusions that the Democrats would emerge victorious, Franklin Roosevelt replied, "Nary an illusion."

In his autobiography, Cox stated flatly, "Election day brought an overwhelming Democratic defeat." That is understatement. Cox lost just about everything there was to lose. Nationally, Cox drew just thirty-four percent of the vote. He lost New York, his running mate's home state, by better than two-to-one; he lost his own home state of Ohio by 400,000 votes; he lost even Montgomery County, which he had represented in Congress, where he published the largest newspaper and where he lived. It was the cleanest of Republican sweeps. For the only time ever, Republicans elected 300 congressmen; setting aside a South still largely solid for the Democrats, voters in 1920 sent to Congress 293 Republicans and, of Democrats, the appalling total of thirty-five. Were it any consolation, the nation's press suggested Cox not take the defeat too personally. *The Outlook* commented: "The mind of the people was early made up and was not subject to persuasion by words. ... [Its] purpose was to bring to an end with the administration of Woodrow Wilson the policies and practices with which he and his party had become identified."

History's verdict on the 1920 election has been that the better man lost. Harding proved inept in office and, if not corrupt, then oblivious to corruption. Historian Allan Nevins takes the general view when he calls Cox "a candidate for the presidency who, as everyone will now grant, should have won." Not everyone granted it then; among them, H. L. Mencken, then the font of all scorn in American journalism, who covered the campaign on the ground.

Warren Gamaliel Harding was the kind of political gladhander H. L. Mencken loathed. The Baltimore journalist variously termed him "a second-rate provincial," "a third-rate political wheel-horse" and "flat-headed." Of Harding's policy statements, Mencken wrote: "Even a professor of English seldom writes worse English." Perhaps, then, even Mencken was surprised when a month before the election he issued his endorsement: "After meditation and prayer of excessive virulence for many days and consultation with all the chief political dowsers of the Republic, I conclude with melancholy that God lays upon me the revolting duty of voting for the numskull, [Warren] Gamaliel [Harding], on the first Tuesday in November."

What had happened?

Mencken was a man with no short list of prejudices. Indeed, he introduced his dismissal of Cox by naming a sprinkling of those he could not stand: Prohibitionists, authors, YMCA secretaries, stockbrokers, Southerners, osteopaths, uplifters, clarinetists, Armenians, bishops, commuters, children and several dozen others. With those few exceptions, Mencken writes, the thing he detests most is "the fellow who is fundamentally a fraud." This, H. L. Mencken declared James Cox to be. "His opinions are always fluent, but they strike me as being 95% dishonest. I believe he would change all of the them overnight if he thought that it would make votes for him." Cox was, Mencken wrote, an ordinary job-seeker: "resilient, sneaking, limber, oleaginous, hollow and disingenuous." Not only a fraud, Mencken wrote, but — and perhaps more woundingly — an inept one. The Democratic candidate "attempted two grand gestures... Neither gesture, of course, was honest, but that was no objection to the them.

What ailed them was that neither was wise." First, Cox hedged on Prohibition. "As it is," Mencken wrote, "the genuine wets show little active interest in him... and meanwhile the drys are suspicious of him, knowing him to be a turncoat." Next, Cox tied himself to Wilson, even though to Mencken the only campaign issue "of any actual force and weight is the issue of poor Woodrow's astounding unpopularity." Mencken endorsed Harding because the Republican,

James Cox reviews the election return, with flowers providing a funereal note. Cox lost even his home city of Dayton in the Republican landslide.

though without obvious qualification, was also without obvious guile — a charge of which Mencken could not clear Cox.

Cox's own view of the 1920 election, expressed at length in his autobiography, has all the virtue of simplicity: he was robbed. "The fact is amazing, as viewed from the present day, that almost from the beginning a conspiracy was in the making to defeat this human hope" — that is, the League. In Cox's telling, Republicans opposed the League through nothing but low partisanship:

had Wilson added the diplomatic triumph of world government to the military triumph of the war itself, Republicans would have spent the next generation in the political wilderness. Their tactics, Cox argued, were low and mean — turning Irish voters against the Democrats because the Versailles Treaty did not create an independent Ireland; turning Italian voters against the Democrats because the postwar territorial settlement brought Italy less than it had hoped; turning German voters against the Democrats for having stigmatized their beloved fatherland with responsibility for the war. Cox's account of the election was written a third of a century after the event, yet the anger still rises from the page. And it doesn't wash. When Cox lost his gubernatorial re-election bid in 1914, he petulantly stated, "Most of those in opposition were not moved by principle. With them it was grievance." His argument for 1920 is similar. Indeed, rarely if ever in his career does Cox suggest than anyone could have any honorable reason for opposing his policies, or himself.

There is more here. American politics is less ideological than tribal; we choose leaders as much for the image of ourselves they seem to present as for the policies they promise to pursue. We say we want leaders of integrity and independence, beholden to firm principles; at the same time, the softer angels of our nature suspect that anyone who demands a great deal of him or herself is likely to demand of us more than we can long endure. Such was Wilson, by whose highmindedness the nation was by turns galvanized, wearied and resentfully bored. So we look in candidates for evidence of a protecting humanity and find in FDR's patrician ease or Ike's easy Kansas grin a needed likability and reassurance.

James Cox was an American type — the self-made man. In a passage previously quoted, *The Outlook* wrote of Cox: "His story is that of an agile, energetic, intuitive, brilliant, and hard-hitting man who has forged his way from the bottom to the top by sheer force of indomitable will, who seeks the limelight, and who never hesitates to make enemies." He was the boy reporter who jammed the only telegraph line to Cincinnati to get his story in first. He never hesitated to make enemies. He never much bothered to make friends; that same article commented on "the curious lack of personal devotion [to Cox] among his Dayton associates." This, it attributed to Cox's standing apart from Dayton men and institutions, both of which he flailed with his newspaper as circumstance justified or whim provoked. The self-made man does not make allies. His drama is an act of continual rebellion, a battle of one against all: the individual as actor; all the rest is stage, backdrop, obstacle and cheering throng. Interestingly, if Cox suggests any other American politician, it is Richard Nixon. Like Cox, Nixon was born in modest circumstances, rose through native intelligence, hard work and a hard-edged contest spirit; like Cox, he had an instinct for power and a facility in its use, and, for all of that, neither man was ever much able to convince Americans that he liked them, perhaps because neither did.

In his bid for the White House, James Cox presented the public with one of its very own images — the self-made man. The public did not greatly care for what it saw. By 1920, Americans had fought the war to make the world safe for democracy; they had seen that crusade give way to the low squabbling at Versailles by people with narrow agendas and difficult to pronounce names. Americans had been "over there," they were pleased to be back and had had all the "destiny" they needed for a while. In rejecting Cox, they chose another, more comforting American type: the booster, the joiner, big, smiling, confident and syntactically outnumbered Warren Harding, who added the word "normalcy" to the English language by misreading his inaugural address and who as President is said to have hidden his mistress in a White House closet moments before the cabinet trooped in.

By the end of the First World War, Charles Kettering was an aviation junkie.

He had been taught to fly by Bernard Whelan, one of the first pilots trained by the Wrights; soon, the inventor was taking to the skies on almost any pretext. In December 1918, Kettering and Wright test pilot Howard Rinehart flew non-stop from Dayton to New York, then a distance record for cross country flying; six months later, they bested that trip with one from Dayton to Wichita. As a flyer, Kettering offered two pieces of advice to the less daring: first, he advised, never fly on days when the birds aren't flying, as they have more experience in the matter; and, second, if you're lost in fog bank, "throw out a monkey wrench. If it goes up, you are flying upside down." Nonchalance may have run in the family. Kettering's mother, Martha Hunter Kettering, once beseeched one of her son's associates: flying is so dangerous, she said; isn't there something you can do to make Charley stop? The associate said no, flying was part of Kettering's work with Dayton-Wright. Kettering researcher and biographer T. A. Boyd gives the final word to the inventor's mother: "Mrs. Kettering paused, smiled and said: 'Do you suppose Charley would take me up in his airplane?'"

Kettering took to the skies perhaps to escape the chaos he created on the ground. By late 1918, his affairs bordered on the incoherent. As a final pre-war project, he had developed the Delco-Light, a freestanding system that combined a one-cylinder engine, a generator and a bank of storage batteries to provide houselighting to rural homes and farmhouses. The first system was installed at the Loudonville, Ohio home of Kettering's parents, with the inventor personally running the wiring. The venture was incorporated as the Domestic Engineering Company, with Deeds as president and Kettering as vice president. Demand proved strong; by 1918, the company had 2,000 employees producing 60,000 units a year. Along with Domestic Engineering, Kettering was vice president of Dayton-Wright Company and vice president of Delco, and pursued a variety of research interests through another organization, the Dayton Metal Products Company. The inventor needed protection from the centrifugal force of his own inventiveness. He needed grounding. He needed, in fact, a job. Whatever Kettering's interest in aviation, the automobile remained his first love. The question, then, was how to disentangle himself from the administrative tasks he could barely tolerate and get back to the under-the-hood work at which he excelled.

Kettering and Deeds had already spun off ownership of one enterprise — in 1915, they sold Delco to William Crapo Durant, when Durant, the then ousted founder of General Motors, was organizing United Motors, a consortium of auto parts manufacturers. In 1919, Durant came calling again. He had regained control of General Motors, merged United Motors with it, and was now buying up half of everything that moved in the auto industry. Deeds and Kettering accepted offers totaling nearly 100,000 shares of GM stock for Dayton Wright Company, Domestic Engineering and Dayton Metal Products. While General Motors was prepared to pay for the body of Kettering's work, it was really only interested in his mind. The auto industry had passed the point where its technological problems were surmountable by gifted tinkerers, trial and error and the hefty swing of a mallet. Pushed by company vice president Alfred P. Sloan, GM was expanding its research activities; a company memo on who should direct that operation stated: "Mr. Kettering is by far the most valuable man known to this corporation for the position."

Kettering knew what he wanted. He wrote later: "I told Mr. Sloan that I would take it on three conditions; that I would have no responsibility and no authority, and that I would never be held accountable for the money I spent." This was the same line Kettering had pushed since his days at NCR: research work conducted in association with manufacturing must avoid bogging down in the immediate worries of management and sales; rather, it must focus on larger, longer-term tasks that build a company's intellectual capital. Sloan assented. On June 12, 1920, Kettering became manager of the General Motors Research Corporation. Sloan agreed to one further Kettering condition: namely, that all GM research be carried out in Dayton. So long as that condition held, Dayton, Ohio, was the research center of the automotive world.

At this juncture, Kettering and Deeds — partners for a dozen years in half a dozen enterprises — parted professional company. Edward Deeds took his share of the settlement with GM and launched himself on a financier's career;

eventually, he wheeled and dealed his way to a personal fortune set at $30 million. In money matters, Kettering liked to suggest he was a farm boy in continuing hazard of being fleeced by the city slickers into whose fast company he had unaccountably fallen. While Deeds diversified his holdings, Kettering sat on most of the GM stock he received. Durant, in his acquisitions, was throwing a lot of GM stock around; its long-term value depended on the success of General Motors, which under Durant's erratic leadership was no certain thing. Eventually, through stock splits and new acquisitions, Kettering held 450,000 shares, which made him the largest individual stockholder in the world's largest corporation with a personal fortune touching $200 million. The irony, if there is one, is that it was Kettering's success as research chief that put much of the backbone into the General Motors stock that enriched him.

Kettering spent twenty-seven years as head of General Motors research, from that post directing development of the high compression engine, high octane gasoline, the lightweight diesel locomotive, modern refrigeration and air conditioning, balloon tires, safety glass and more. Kettering was called the Wizard of General Motors; the products of his work, however, were less the result of sorcery than of Kettering's method — the ability to define problems, assume them to be solvable and avoid the preconceptions that might prevent solution. No single instance shows off those methods better than Kettering's long-term effort to eliminate knock.

Knock first appeared before the First World War: it is a shuddering that palsies an engine as it nears full power; in higher performance aviation engines, knock could be strong enough to crack cylinder heads. Kettering's first contribution, said Kettering researcher Carroll Hochwalt, was that "he recognized the problem." As the head of a research division, Kettering had to make choices as to where its resources would be directed. Almost unerringly, he directed attention at the problems whose resolution brought the greatest advantage to the auto industry. As one associate put it, Kettering could "visualize how things ought to go and push them that way."

With knock, Kettering made the right choice. The phenomenon was little understood, being variously attributed to problems in engine design, in fuel composition or in the spark that ignited the fuel. One thing known was that the higher the compression ratio of an engine, the worse it knocked. This, as it happened, made knock the ceiling to all efforts to raise fuel economy. The amount of usable energy released when the fuel/air mix in a cylinder is ignited is a function of the extent to which that mix is compressed prior to ignition; in short, higher compression releases more energy from the same quantity of fuel. What gave urgency to the problem was that the world was experiencing its first fuel crunch — the vast oil fields of the Middle East were yet to be discovered and demand for gasoline was pushing up against the available supplies.

In 1920, a Kettering associate wrote to an official at du Pont: "This year will see the maximum production of petroleum that this country will ever know." A search for alternative fuels was on. Du Pont looked into producing alcohol-based fuels from plant material, but concluded it would take over half the country's combined sugar and grain crops to make sufficient fuel. The best short-term answer — to stretch existing gasoline supplies by use of higher-compression engines — was ruled out by knock. Kettering stayed with knock, even after early research established that knock was a fuel problem. Strictly speaking, this placed the matter outside Kettering's expertise and concern — he was an automotive engineer, not a fuel chemist, and his employer, General Motors, produced no gasoline. Kettering pursued knock, however, because it was the problem the auto industry needed to have solved.

With the problem identified, Kettering regarded preconception as the major roadblock to success. He was suspicious of experts — "the slide rule boys," he called them — who, Kettering said, could make two quick calculations and announce that a thing was impossible. Experts, he argued, were often more the captive than the master of what they knew and consequently unable to learn much of anything new. Though Kettering hired many specialists, the research virtue he prized most was what he termed "intelligent ignorance" — a sense of things in general and a lack of preconception about the problem at hand. Thus, Kettering assigned the problem of engine knock to Thomas Midgley, a twenty-seven-year-old mechanical engineer. Trying to beg off of the assignment, Midgley told Kettering that he knew nothing of fuel chemistry. All to the good, Kettering replied: a professional chemist would "come in with a pack on his back" — that is, the weight of preconception. "We're going to make a very steep climb here and it may be that that very pack is going to keep us from getting up."

Ignorance stood Midgley in good stead. The severity of knock varied from fuel to fuel; kerosene, for example, knocked worse than gasoline. Pondering this, Midgley suggested to Kettering that it may be because kerosene is lighter in color, a speculation prompted by the pair's observation of the reddish leaves of some trailing arbutus poking through the snow near their lab. If dark leaves absorbed more heat, Midgley speculated, then perhaps dark fuels did too — which might account for differing knock characteristics. Any trained chemist would have regarded Midgley's hypothesis as nonsense. Unknowingly, Midgley decided to dye some kerosene dark to see if this would change its knock characteristics. The supply room was in its usual chaos and Midgley was unable to locate any oil soluble dye; a co-worker informed him that iodine was oil-soluble, so Midgley poured some of it into his kerosene. Iodine didn't reduce knock. Iodine eliminated it. Further experiment showed that, indeed, color had nothing to do with it: other dyes failed to stop knock, while colorless iodine did. While iodine was too expensive to use as a fuel additive, Midgley's experiment inadvertently established that some sort of chemical "pill" would eliminate knock. That conclusion launched what Kettering termed "a scientific fox hunt" for the right additive.

The first likely candidate was aniline: it was cheap, about half as effective as iodine, and it stank — in the fuel and in the exhaust. Researchers laced it with camphor, pennyroyal and citronella in fruitless attempts to mask its odor. Midgley reported: "I doubt if humanity, even to doubling their fuel economy, will put up with this smell." A second compound, selenium oxychloride, was more effective than aniline, but it dissolved spark plugs. The search continued. Hundreds of compounds were identified, synthesized and tested, without success. In all, researchers identified 143 antiknock agents — all too weak, too expensive, too foul-smelling or too destructive of engine parts to be of practical use.

Still, there was clear evidence that the payoff on an effective antiknock compound would be huge. When a Chevy engine rebuilt for higher compression was fed gasoline spiked with diethyl telluride, it roared: miles per gallon jumped by over fifty percent; acceleration time dropped by nearly a third. By some odd law, however, the better the performance of an antiknock compound, the worse its odor. Of the odor of diethyl telluride, Midgley said, "There was no getting rid of it. It was so powerful that a change of clothes and a bath at the end of the day did not reduce your ability as a tellurium broadcasting station. Nor did the odor grow much weaker when several days were passed in absence from the laboratory." One visitor to the lab wrote back: "This is to let you know that I reached home safely and that every one is greeting me with gas masks on."

Kettering kept them at their tasks — in part because of the potential payoff, in part because it was for him a simple article of faith that every problem had a solution. For Kettering, a problem in research was, by definition, a misperception on the part of the researcher. As he liked to tell later audiences, "A careful analysis will show, that nine times out of ten a difficult problem is one we do not know how to solve, so we are blaming the problem instead of our ignorance." A problem is not solved, Kettering believed, by being changed; what changes is the researcher's understanding of the problem. The purpose of all the apparatus in the lab, he added, is not to force a change in the problem, but to force a change in the researcher's understanding. Throughout the antiknock work, Kettering kept on his desk a sign that read: "The problem once solved will be simple."

As researchers proceeded on the antiknock work, they charted each compound's performance relative to its position on the periodic table of the elements, then recast this data as a three-dimensional graph they hoped would point to where the best antiknock compound should reside. The data pointed to a little used compound, tetraethyllead, first synthesized in 1859. Working through the night of December 8, 1921, Carroll Hochwalt dropped zinc ethyl onto lead chloride to produce a few teaspoonsful of the liquid. The following morning, he and other researchers used the laboratory's one-cylinder engine to test its antiknock qualities. They began with tetraethyllead in gasoline at 1 part

per 100; then diluted it to 1 part per 200; then 1 per 400. Soon, they established that tetraethyllead was an effective knock-suppressant at 1 part in 1,260 — fifty times as powerful as aniline; moreover, tetraethyllead was inexpensive, oil soluble, stable and its odor was, if anything, mildly pleasant. "Hell," Hochwalt said later, "It was 'Eureka.'"

Not quite. Tetraethyllead suppressed knock, but its combustion deposited lead oxide on spark plugs. The addition of chlorobenzene protected spark plugs, but the damage surfaced on the exhaust valves. Adding bromine prevented that damage, but bromine was scarce and prohibitively expensive: the amount required to treat the nation's gasoline supply was, according to bromine's major supplier, Dow Chemical, ten to twenty times the world's annual supply. Kettering set his researchers to finding an alternative to bromine; meanwhile, a bromine additive was used when the new fuel went on limited public sale.

Kettering orchestrated the product's introduction — he wrote the first advertisements for the new fuel and coined its name: Ethyl. The world's first antiknock gasoline was offered to motorists in February 1923 at the Refiners gas station at the corner of Sixth and Main in Dayton, with a pump price of 24 cents a gallon, a four-cent premium over regular. Two five-foot long signs announced the product — "ETHYL Gas Antiknock Gasoline, Product of the General Motors Research Corporation" — while a laboratory representative was on hand to record the response of the buying public. At first, there was none. The laboratory representative reported:

> At 10 the first morning not a single sale of the new product had been made. Then the research laboratory representative on duty at the station began to approach customers as they came into the station telling them about the new product, without exaggerating its merits. In that way 70 gallons were disposed of during the succeeding three hours. The first customer bought only two gallons, saying he would take a chance on that much.

That first customer — who took a chance on two gallons — was back for more twice again that week. Another bought a tankful. By an observer's account: "His Model T had knocked like the seven furies driving down Main Street, but the noise vanished when he drove away on 'Ethyl' gasoline." That second customer was the garage superintendent of the Dayton Power and Light Company; soon, its sixty-five vehicles were running on Kettering's high-powered fuel. Others followed. In a publicity coup promoted by Kettering, seven of the twenty cars entered in the 1924 Indianapolis 500 ran on Ethyl — with the high-octane entrants claiming first, second and third.

Demand was growing, but unless Kettering could find a corrective for the engine damage tetraethyllead caused, that demand could not be met. For once, he was stymied. A lab summary stated: "By June of 1924 it became apparent from the long series of tests... that not only was bromine the best corrective agent found, but also that there was apparently no other material which could take its place." If bromine was required, then Kettering would find it. He sent a chemist to the Dead Sea to see if bromine could be extracted from its salt; he traveled to French Tunisia to investigate bromine mining operations there; he shipped twenty-five barrels of the Atlantic back to his lab to determine if the oceans might provide a source. In the lab, seawater proved to contain 65 parts of bromine per million. That, Midgley suggested, made the task easy; bromine could be obtained simply by "pumping the Pacific Ocean over the Rocky Mountains and letting it dry out." Dow Chemical held that the task was impossible: "without first concentrating sea water — a thing that would be far too costly to think of — they [Dow] could not possibly extract bromine from it, any more than blood can be got out of a turnip."

Kettering squeezed the turnip. In cooperation with du Pont, he leased a 254-foot cargo ship, fitted it out with a prototype bromine-extraction plant, re-christened it the *S. S. Ethyl* and sent it sailing off east of the Virginia capes. There, its task was to draw bromine out of seawater; in theory, 200 pounds of bromine an hour. From the standpoint of those on board, the voyage of the *S. S. Ethyl* was a mixed success, as "many of the chemists and engineers aboard were too seasick to properly attend their duties." But the voyage demonstrated Kettering's point: bromine could be obtained from seawater. And Kettering's nautical end-run of Dow caught that corporation's attention. Concerned about losing its hold on the bromine market, Dow announced it had refigured its calculations and could assure Kettering of all the bromine his fuel needed, at a price Kettering judged reasonable.

Just as Kettering was gaining his final ingredient, health officials across the nation ordered Ethyl out of the nation's gasoline pumps. On October 25, 1924, workers at the Standard Oil plant in New Jersey where tetraethyllead was blended were rushed to the Reconstruction Hospital in New York, desperately ill. One employee, *The New York Times* reported, "died in a strait-jacket vio-lently insane," a victim of "deadly tetraethyllead fumes." Five men died at the site; ten others who worked directly with the fuel at other sites died that sum-mer and fall. Headlines nationally described Kettering's creation as "Looney Gas." More staid, *The Times* termed it "Insanity Gas" and quoted a warning from Dr. Yendell Henderson of Yale University: "If an automobile using that gas should have engine trouble along Fifth Avenue and release a quantity of gas with the lead mixture, it would be likely to cause gas poisoning and mania to persons along the Avenue."

The sale of leaded gas was halted nationwide while a commission appointed by the U.S. Surgeon General reviewed the additive's safety. It was an extremely blue ribbon group — the dean of Harvard's medical school, a physiologist from Johns Hopkins, a public health professor from Yale and others — charged with investigating the additive's effect on motorists and pedestrians. It looked for evidence of lead poisoning among those with greatest exposure, the drivers at the Dayton utility that had been using Ethyl gas and the garage workers em-ployed where the fuel had been sold the longest. No such evidence was found. The committee reported that "no definite cases have been discovered of recog-nizable lead poisoning or other disease resulting from the use of ethyl gaso-line." The workers' deaths it attributed to prolonged exposure to undiluted tetraethyllead; the committee urged — and the Surgeon General issued — regu-lations for its production and handling. On the main point, Kettering's fuel got a clean bill of health: "Your committee begs to report that in their opinion there are at present no good grounds for prohibiting the use of ethyl gasoline of the composition specified as a motor fuel."

There were grounds for using it. Tetraethyllead created high octane fuels — that is, knock resistant gasolines that permitted use of higher compression engines. The greater efficiency of such engines allowed them to take from two gallons of gasoline as much usable energy as had previously come from three. An analogous discovery today would save American motorists more than $30 billion a year in fuel costs and reduce by half or more the nation's dependence on foreign sources of oil. For decades, the development of tetraethyllead was hailed as a major example of better living through chemistry. The blending of tetraethyllead with gasoline, however, brought a mix of ironies. By the time tetraethyllead was cleared for public use, the fuel shortage it had been targeted to solve no longer existed — oil in vast quantities had been discovered in the Middle East. In practice, then, the extra energy tetraethyllead extracted from gasoline went less to improved fuel economy than to increased acceleration, giving American cars their characteristic zip.

Two years after leaded gasoline went on general sale in America, its safety was challenged in England; there, a Parliamentary review commission reported that its findings "fully confirm the [American] view" that use of leaded gasolines was safe to the public. That commission, like the U.S. Surgeon General's committee, addressed the question of whether Ethyl gasoline was hazardous to drivers and pedestrians; both concluded it was not. Neither, however, investigated whether leaded gas might, over time, be hazardous as an atmospheric pollutant. When the additive was assessed in the 1926, air pollution was nobody's great concern. In any case, not all that much of the fuel was being burned: only 300 million gallons of leaded gasoline had been sold in the three years since the first driver in Dayton "took a chance" on two gallons. By 1970 — when the hazards of leaded gasoline caught public attention — American automobiles were burning that much every two days.

For nearly a half a century, the safety of leaded fuels was largely unquestioned. The broader issue that prompted the antiknock work — the need to extend fuel supplies by drawing more power from each barrel of oil pumped from the ground — was also widely ignored, as finds of new oil fields ran consistently ahead of rates of use. Ignored by most, but not by Kettering, whose tetraethyllead had helped put to rest the concerns of almost all others. In 1925, Kettering delivered a speech to the American Chemical Society, saying in part:

> Every gallon of petroleum taken out of the ground leaves one gallon less to be taken out in the future, and some day — no one knows just when — our petroleum reserves will have diminished to the point where we can no longer supply our motorists with a sufficient quantity of cheap, volatile motor fuel from this source.

Two things followed from this fact, Kettering believed. First, he said, the "car of the future" would have to conserve fuel through lighter weight, a more streamlined design and an overdrive for better highway mileage. Second, he added, alternatives to petroleum-based fuels must be found. Kettering proceeded on this search. In 1929, he launched at his own expense a research effort into photosynthesis, the process by which green plants convert sunlight to energy. All fossil fuels — indeed, all food — is at some remove the product of photosynthesis; if its workings could be unlocked, Kettering believed, then all the food and fuel the planet might wish could be made readily available. Simplifying the question, Kettering said it was an effort to learn why grass is green: why, that is, is it a defining characteristic of plants capable of photosynthesis that they are green? A national magazine picked up on the study, passing Kettering's question along to its readers. Replies came in; Kettering's favorite was from the manager of a golf course in Arizona, who wrote: "I don't know if this is what you are looking for, but out here about the only thing that makes grass green is water." Kettering sustained the research — by direct support during his life; through a Kettering-established foundation after his death — for fifty-six years. It was called to a halt without ever finding the breakthrough Kettering sought. Doubtless, he never lost the belief that the problem had a solution.

In Dayton one morning in 1919, an acquaintance remarked to Arthur Morgan that the morning paper reported Morgan's appointment as a trustee of Antioch College. "This," Morgan later wrote, "was news to me." Indeed, Morgan — who for six years had lived within thirty miles of the school — apparently knew nothing of the place, which stands as fair comment on the low fortunes to which the institution had fallen. Antioch had been founded nobly enough. Its initial promoters in Yellow Springs, Ohio, had snared the interest of one of America's leading educators, Horace Mann of Massachusetts. Mann was "the father of the public school" — as a state legislator he led that commonwealth to establishment of the nation's first system of universal free education, financed through general taxation. In 1853, Mann forsook the comforts of New England to plant the seeds of enlightenment in the recently cultivated soil of southwestern Ohio. That seed fell on stony ground. Like most of those in Massachusetts who supported his effort, Mann was a Unitarian; local backers were Fundamentalist. The doctrinal infighting that ensued threatened the college's finances and exhausted Mann personally. He died not long after his ringing 1859 commencement address, in which he enjoined the school's graduates to be "ashamed to die until you have won some victory for humanity."

High institutional ambition did not die with Mann. In May 1862, Mann's successor, Thomas Hill, wrote a Massachusetts supporter of the college, "I told my people at Waltham [Massachusetts] some nine years ago, that the history of America began with the establishment of Antioch College, and if I had $100,000 I'd prove that the statement was not extravagant." Mr. Hill did not raise those funds; soon thereafter, he left Ohio to accept the presidency of Harvard. His single sentence, however, summarizes what some have characterized as the driving themes of Antioch's history: megalomania complicated by insolvency.

The new Antioch trustee, Arthur Morgan, would not so much resolve this conflict as raise it to national attention. He started when the institution was at a low ebb. Following Mann and Hill, Antioch continued as a largely local institution, with more downs than ups. In 1919, the sharp recession that followed the First World War pushed the college near the end of its resources. By one report, the school's enrollment dropped to sixty-four; its annual budget fell to $17,750. At this juncture, trustees welcomed a takeover offer from the national YMCA, which apparently intended to use the college as a training center. When that offer fell through, liquidation threatened. By one story, Morgan's appointment to Antioch's board was the work of persons hoping he would protect the Unitarian interest in the college's dwindling assets.

The newly appointed trustee drove out with his wife, Lucy, for a first-hand assessment. Yellow Springs was then a farming town of 1,200, with no paved streets and few sidewalks; its most notable attraction was an extraordinary natural area immediately east of town, which contained the springs from which the town drew its name and which had been the site of a popular turn-of-the-century spa. Morgan later set down his first impressions of the village: "It so completely educated and exported its intelligent young people that there was left a friendly, dull, conservative community, with scarcely a flicker of adventure or inquiry." Hardly a complimentary view of a place whose residents included seven of Morgan's fellow trustees. At the campus itself, both the work of Mann and the works of man were in deplorable condition. Plumbing was nonexistent, the few electric lights drew current from wires tacked to the surfaces of walls, much dormitory space was in states of disrepair or abandonment. Rainwater cisterns and household pumps substituted for a water system; many wells were polluted. Morgan considered the situation excellent. "I believe it is near enough dead," he told Lucy Morgan, "to start over in the form I dream of."

That dream sprang from Morgan's experience and his utopian dreaming. In his professional life, he wrote, he had worked with hundreds of engineers and attorneys. The typical engineer, he said, "had very little background or curiosity outside his field." The typical lawyer, Morgan added, "after discussing the morning paper, the sports news and the weather, lapses into interminable personal reminiscences of cases." The fault, Morgan held, lay in the narrowness of contemporary education. "We are becoming a nation of specialists," he wrote in an *Atlantic Monthly* article, "each man an authority in his own little corner, and ignorant of the relations of life as a whole." So long as narrow specialists ruled, "so long will fine men be absent, and so long will society be in chaos."

Morgan was also a utopian. Utopian yearnings, he held, were not dreams, but practical necessities: "Utopias are as essential to human societies as plans are essential for building bridges." Utopians fathered the future by imagining it today. Morgan's work at Antioch was driven by a vision he had himself experienced: walking in the woods, he was suddenly overwhelmed by the image of a small community in which families and teachers and students lived together, entrepreneurially independent, intellectually open, collectively self-sufficient. As Morgan described it, "It would be a community of explorers and inventors and teachers and students.... I remember just being so taken up with that picture that I stood there on the footpath in the hazelbrush for possibly an hour." At the Moraine Park School, he had put his ideas on elementary and secondary education into effect. Now, with the Conservancy task moving toward completion, a college was there for the taking — lock, stock and cistern. And Morgan took it. Six weeks after being appointed to the board, Morgan presented his fellow trustees with a curricular design entitled, "Plan for Practical Industrial Education."

Morgan's plan changed significantly from description to execution. Three aspects emerged as central. First, students were to be grounded in the broader culture through a general education program far more extensive than that then common at American colleges. Second, students were to gain practical experience of life by alternating periods of on-campus study with periods of off-campus employment. And third, students were to clarify their personal values and goals through required classes and papers with titles like "college aims" and "life aims." Initially, Morgan hoped the college would serve as the organizing nexus for a surrounding ring of small industries. These undertakings would be sites for industrial and business innovation; they would provide students with gainful employment and useful experience; and they would provide the economic basis necessary to community. Additionally, Morgan hoped the profits from these enterprises would in the financial scheme of things compensate for the school's absence of an endowment.

Morgan's purpose in all of this was human wholeness; his aim, a later Antioch president wrote, "was to train entrepreneurs who would know how to start enterprises, rather than to become employees of a large corporation; to help give economic vitality to a small community, rather than just to make money; to become a creative leader in a community, rather than a parasite in a large one." Antioch, Morgan told its board, could turn out such graduates; by doing so, it would be "a significant factor in our civilization." Perhaps a bit overwhelmed, the trustees of the tottering college directed Morgan to proceed.

With startling speed, Morgan took virtual control of the institution. He restocked its board of trustees. When Morgan was appointed, twelve of the remaining eighteen trustees lived within a dozen miles of the school; only one came from out-of-state. Barely a year later, "Morgan men" held a solid majority. As trustees, Morgan enlisted men he respected from Dayton — Charles Kettering; William Chryst, Delco's chief engineer; and Frank Slutz, head of the Moraine Park School. To these he added others of national reputation and influence, some of whom signed on at the urging of ex-Harvard president Charles Eliot, a strong supporter (there was an institutional tie: Thomas Hill, Mann's successor at Antioch, was Eliot's immediate predecessor at Harvard). Pulling such strings, Morgan added to his board Ellery Sedgwick, editor of the *Atlantic Monthly*; Joseph P. Cotton, law partner of William Gibbs McAdoo; William Mayo, the chief engineer at Ford; and Edward Gay, president of *The Saturday Evening Post* and former dean of Harvard's School of Business Administration.

As with Moraine Park, Morgan intended to set direction, then cede daily control of the institution to an appointed president. When, however, he found no one to meet the criteria he had in mind, Morgan asked to be named to the post himself. The trustees complied. Morgan was pulling the college from its local grounding into his own orbit: the meeting at which he was named Antioch president, for example, was held at the Dayton Engineers' Club. Soon thereafter, the trustees authorized Morgan to raise $900,000 — a figure fifty times Antioch's most recent annual budget — to finance physical renovation and curricular reorganization. Morgan's Dayton ties drew in funds: Charles Kettering, who was to become Antioch's single most important benefactor, contributed $30,000; John H. Patterson, writing that he was "heartily in favor of the Antioch idea," added $10,000 more. As money came in, Morgan's engineers began scurrying about campus, planning its physical renovation —

Antioch College, 1926.

wiring, heating, plumbing, new flooring, new window and door frames and roof repair.

Morgan was a skilled promoter. Even before the "new Antioch" admitted its first student, leading magazines were praising Morgan's plans for the school: in 1921, favorable stories appeared in *The Nation, The New Republic, School and Society, World's Work, Scientific American* and *Leslie's* — the last by Arthur Ruhl, who came to Dayton to laud Patterson's 1913 rescue work. And Morgan networked. In 1920, he was elected as first president of the Progressive Education Association — John Dewey and H. G. Wells were among the vice presidents. The post brought Morgan dozens of contacts for seeking funds, faculty and students. This publicity and these connections helped prompt 800 applications to Morgan's first class, one-fourth of whom — each reviewed by the college president — were admitted in the fall of 1921.

Morgan was less successful in attracting faculty. The academic luminaries he sought — philosopher John Dewey, historian Arthur Schlesinger, Sr. and others — begged off. The range of Morgan's requirements is suggested in a letter he sent to one prospect, who is asked to consider teaching "a single general course, lasting through two or more years, and covering the entire field beginning with anthropology, giving a bird's eye view of history, and ending with a general treatment of economics, sociology and probably psychology." The prospect declined. One student of the institution, Burton Clark, observed: "The ideal man was one who, forceful in personality, broad in interest, matured by practical experience and reflection, would also commit himself totally to the adventure of working out a new education and a new philosophy of life at Antioch. Morgan quickly found such men to be in short supply." The men Morgan wanted from academia simply didn't exist; the men he wanted from business commanded salaries he could not afford. He ended with an odd mix: one-third of the faculty he chose lacked any college degree, and were picked for their practical experience and personal qualities; an equal number were bright young Ph.D.s from Harvard, Yale and other prestigious schools. Morgan trusted to his own messianic abilities to lead them to his New Jerusalem.

Thus, a young mathematics instructor from Ohio State University came down for the afternoon to interview as a possible short-term replacement. "I thought he'd ask me a lot of questions," J. D. Dawson recalled. "He didn't. He sat back and started to talk about his dreams for the college. I was enthralled." Dawson came for a term and stayed with Antioch and Morgan for four decades. Similarly, Morgan persuaded Algo Henderson, a promising Harvard graduate student who planned a career in accounting and law, to come to Ohio to visit the school. "We got off the train," Henderson recalled, "and the dean met us and took us to stay in a house with no indoor plumbing and a pump near the street." Henderson went to discuss with Morgan what courses he might teach. Morgan didn't want to talk about courses. He wanted to talk about a bronze foundry. Should he start one in an abandoned barn near campus? What did Henderson think? Why didn't Henderson look into the matter and make a report? Henderson did, urged the foundry be established, and stayed at Antioch as faculty member, dean of the college and Morgan's successor.

Under its new president, Antioch became an entrepreneurial college. College-run and student-run enterprises circled the campus: Antioch Press, Antioch Foundry, Antioch Landscaping and for a time in the 1920s — when Morgan discovered a man who believed that health worked its way up from the feet — Antioch Shoe. Students sold the shoes through four states at a commission of $1 a pair; sales reached a third of a million dollars. With one hand, Morgan kept a finger in every pie; with the other, he baked more pies.

Morgan's plan for small industries faltered; the college lacked the managerial resources to make it work, but much else succeeded, and the alternating work-study plan was a triumph. "I couldn't imagine how it would work," said J. D. Dawson. "Five-week shifts, then go away? How in heck could students learn mathematics that way? I was wrong. I realized you don't learn anything the first time you think about it. If you go away and return, the residue is greater." Originally, the plan placed students largely with Dayton-area employers; soon, it expanded geographically, with Antioch students working in business, industry and social services across the country. One Morgan-era student recalls: "The most pervasive feeling was that students were having an experience in education that was exceptional, even unique — focusing on liberal arts and having work experience as part of liberal arts. We took pride in the fact that we could go out and be on our own."

By the sixth year of Morgan's presidency, Antioch had grown from sixty-four to 674 students, from a faculty of twelve to one of fifty-seven, and from a budget of $17,750 to one of $403,000. The campus expanded physically, as well. Morgan gained control over the 1,000 acre nature preserve, Glen Helen, immediately adjacent to campus. As makers of a much-talked about educational experiment, the campus community developed a high esprit d'corps. Henderson recalled, "There was a complete new spirit of adventure." J. D. Dawson upped Henderson's estimate, saying: "I felt I'd reached utopia." Morgan never stopped pressing his view of what the college should be.

Finances remained shaky: in 1924, the college carried $300,000 in short-term debts — one-third consisted of loans from Charles Kettering, with the total nearly equaling the school's annual operating budget. Consequently, Morgan was frequently absent from campus, seeking the contributions that kept his experiment afloat. On campus, he was an austere figure; someone, one student recalls, "you didn't speak to except on a very elevated plane." Tall, somewhat gaunt, bordering on handsome, Morgan always wore white shirts with long

The importance
of being earnest.

The rising
professional class,
Robert Wiebe
wrote, was
characterized by
"an earnest desire
to remake the
world upon their
private models."

The Morgans
were more than
earnest —they
were skilled and
unswerving.

sleeves firmly buttoned and often the red ties favored by his wife, Lucy, whose own highmindedness set much of the social tone of the college. She was not, says one who knew her then, "tolerant of laziness or of unhealthy habits, or of a tendency to maybe want to have a drink." She believed in simple living, whole wheat flour and banana flakes, and could be as high-handed as high-minded. Two faculty members had names spelled differently, but pronounced alike; Lucy Morgan informed them they must either agree upon a common spelling or adopt differing pronunciations. She believed in hard work. She hosted teas for faculty wives on Friday afternoons, events to which the women were expected to bring their knitting or handwork so they wouldn't simply sit there, idle.

Her husband's views were similar. He didn't understand sports and games; if people needed exercise, why didn't they do something productive, like chop wood, like he did? Morgan had no "timewasters" in his life. When a faculty member made reference to an article in *Saturday Evening Post*, Morgan was genuinely startled: where had he found the time to read something so inessential? He could be petty, personally raiding dormitories to search out liquor. And he would lecture the faculty on the responsibility the more fit had to multiply, lest the offspring of their inferiors come to dominate the future. After one such

urging, Dean Henderson surveyed the faculty, determined that the average number of their progeny exceeded Morgan's own three, and suggested to the college president that he address his genetic responsibilities closer to home. Morgan, Henderson recalls, made no further comment on the subject.

Morgan, Henderson said, "was not really authoritarian. He expected conformance." Morgan believed that all questions — not simply the technical ones involved in hydraulic engineering, but questions in life and ethics — gave themselves to a single right answer, provided one thought them through with rigor and honesty. As he in his own view had thought through Antioch more thoroughly than anyone, he regarded his answers as best, and expected others to agree. Early on, Edward Deeds offered to take a place on Antioch's board. Morgan turned him down, later commenting that Deeds was so strong a personality he might have dominated the board; meaning, perhaps, that Morgan might not have dominated him.

Whatever the tensions, the Antioch experiment increasingly looked good, even to more orthodox eyes. In 1927, an accrediting team described Antioch as a school "of a very high type... a self-critical institution inspired by a scientific spirit and working with modern techniques in education." Later test data supported the school's claims to high academic achievement. Such rankings were, of course, relative to traditional measures of success for liberal arts colleges: measures — and colleges — that Antioch's own president often scorned. When in the mid-1920s the "new Antioch" began producing graduates, they confirmed the school's success and suggested Morgan's failure. Fully one-fourth of those graduating, an extremely high proportion at the time, headed off for further study at graduate school The others were far more likely to begin careers with corporations or in government than to strike out on their own, as Morgan had intended, as socially conscious entrepreneurs and agents of small-scale revitalization. Morgan's curricular model proved at odds with his ambitions. Work-study worked; students given experience in the world were often more grounded, more mature, more able to bring a critical perspective to their studies. However, for a bright undergraduate engaged by first-rate teaching, an academic career was a logical next step; likewise, for a student exposed through co-op jobs to the resources of a large organization, a corporate career might be more inviting than one spent organizing rural purchasing co-operatives in eastern Nebraska.

To J. D. Dawson, Antioch was a "utopia." Morgan, however, set fairly high standards where utopias were concerned. In 1924, he wrote: "Being a good college is not the end; the fact that we have achieved high standards is no cause for contentment. We dream of a college such as never has existed." In the late 1920s, the gap between Morgan's intentions and the school's results appeared bridgeable; it would remain so, just as long as what struck J. D. Dawson as utopian struck Arthur Morgan as sufficient.

Orville Wright was unusual, not least in that he appears to have been a genuinely happy person. He was also principled. When, in 1939, a list was compiled of flyers trained by the Wrights at Huffman Prairie, an effort was made to exclude one flyer who had later been a draft dodger. Orville wrote Edward Deeds demanding the name be included: draft dodging wasn't the issue; accuracy was.

Departures

On May 7, 1922, John H. Patterson boarded the late train east from Dayton, intending to rest at Atlantic City. Back at NCR, his executives took the usual precautions. They checked with Patterson's Far Hills estate to see if the chauffeur was off duty. Often, the NCR president bid his executives adieu, boarded an eastbound train, then disembarked at the first stop to return to headquarters to see what his staff, guard down, was up to. As one future NCR chief executive, Stanley Allyn, wrote, "If the chauffeur was relaxing at Far Hills, then we knew that John H. Patterson was relaxing on the Pennsylvania Railroad, and that we, too, could risk a breathing spell." West of Philadelphia, the seventy-eight-year-old company president grabbed his throat; he died soon thereafter, apparently of a heart attack. Fifteen hundred Dayton schoolchildren strewed blossoms along the path Patterson's hearse took to Woodland Cemetery, the same burial place as Milton, Susan and Wilbur Wright.

The year before his death, Patterson stepped down from direct management of NCR, assuming the then little used title of chairman of the board. He anticipated an active retirement. Through his working life he had kept in his office a chart, "Things To Do In The Next Five Years By Mr. Patterson," listing the woes of the world as he saw them and identifying himself as the source of their solution. Among the tasks he took into retirement with him were Help Other Nations Get Off Their Feet, Stop Social Disease, Better Laws and Lower Taxes, Eliminate Canal, Stop Bolshevism, Less Snobbery. These tasks, and others, Patterson bequeathed to his successor.

His successor, as it happened, was Patterson's son, Frederick. When Stanley Allyn first joined NCR, he spotted a poster listing reasons why NCR was a good place to work. One was: "No relatives employed in the business." By the time John H. retired, that rule was bent just enough to allow the appointment of his son. Frederick Patterson liked going on safari; during his absence, company affairs were ably managed by his father's former second-in-command,

John Barringer. NCR thrived with the boom years of the 1920s: sales, $29 million in John H.'s last year, reached $45 million by 1925; profits more than doubled. With the onset of the Depression, however, the company was taking on red ink faster than it could bail.

The crisis came in May 1931. NCR officials, desperate to place company affairs in the hands of someone reassuring to Wall Street, traveled secretly to New York City to offer the posts of chairman and chief executive to Edward Deeds. Deeds had not set foot at NCR since 1915, when Patterson had canned him following the overturn of his antitrust conviction. In the meanwhile, Deeds had become a notable figure in finance — president of General Sugar and a director of twenty-eight corporations. Deeds considered the matter for two weeks, then accepted; returning to NCR, he discovered waiting for him the same desk in the same office he had vacated sixteen years previously. In command, Deeds directed the reorganization that made NCR a publicly-held company; his administrative surehandedness then managed NCR through the Depression. Deeds expanded NCR's holdings overseas: in Germany, he acquired the cash register interests of Krupp; in Japan, he gained a controlling interest in the Fujiyama cash register concern. Perhaps the Depression had driven the prices of these operations down to tempting levels; perhaps Krupp, if not Fujiyama, wanted some ready American cash to put into the booming armaments sector.

Deeds was a full generation younger than Patterson, corporate where John H. was sputtering. John H. Patterson was a transitional figure in the history of American business. In his manners — the paternalistic tyrant who decreed that shredded wheat must be consumed by all — he reflected the personalized rule possible when owners managed and managers owned. In his methods — systematized training, systematized production, systematized sales — he pointed the way to the modern corporation, where ownership is dispersed among stockholders, power diffused through committees and personality reduced to a logo.

By the time Patterson died, personalized rule was passing from the American business scene. While such newer leaders as Deeds were more 'business-like' than Patterson, they became so by surrendering the power Patterson had prized most, the freedom to be arbitrary. In a life of many arbitrary acts, perhaps the most outlandish was when, his antitrust conviction overturned, Patterson discharged all two dozen of his co-defendants. Those discharged included one who, as a central figure in mid-twentieth century American business, was a bridge between Patterson's world and our own. At NCR, he had almost been Patterson's surrogate son. He had directed Patterson's "knockout" organization, then rose to become sales manager. From NCR's New York office, he organized the relief trains speeded to Dayton at the time of the 1913 flood, then quashed his chief's first vituperative telegram — the one in which Patterson threatened to jail the judge who had sentenced him to prison. This subordinate lived in the house and drove the Pierce-Arrow Patterson had bestowed. Fired, he left NCR vowing "to build a bigger business than John H. Patterson ever has." Which, at IBM — the very model of the modern corporation — is exactly what Thomas J. Watson did.

By the common report of his newspaper employees, James Cox never referred to the 1920 election, or to his defeat in that contest. One reporter observed, "When he missed becoming President, it took a lot of the starch out of him." Defeat of his life's ambition by so paltry a figure as Warren Gamaliel Harding might do that. Cox's autobiography puts a brave face on defeat: "I had this great advantage: I was still in public life. I had my newspapers." Soon, he had more of them. In 1923, Cox visited Miami and "fell completely in love with the place." Miami, he told columnist Arthur Krock, was going to be the next Los Angeles; he gave an Horatio Algerish explanation in a letter: "The place is filled with ambitious young men who are here to shape their destinies. You cannot find a pessimist anymore, because those who come here either for employment or health have found the joy of success and improvement of physical condition." Cox decided he needed something to do in Miami, so he purchased the *Miami Metropolis*, renamed it the *Daily News*, and deposited its operations in a freshly-built 279-foot skyscraper.

Cox never again sought or accepted public office — in 1930, he ignored urgings that he seek an Ohio Senate seat; after the 1932 election, Franklin Roosevelt offered him the chairmanship of the Federal Reserve Board or the ambassadorship to Germany. Cox declined both, leaving one to wonder what he and Adolf Hitler, two short men with an instinct for power, would have made of each other. Instead, he built his empire. Cox had an eye for the coming city — first Miami, then Atlanta, where in 1939 he bought two newspapers and combined them into the *Journal*. In 1949, he created a monopoly in Dayton, buying out his two rivals and merging them into the *Journal Herald*. Working parallel lines, Cox's son, James Cox, Jr., backed Cox-owned newspapers with Cox-owned radio and television stations. By 1950, the former farm boy was worth an estimated $40 million. Today, Cox Enterprises is one of the nation's dozen largest media corporations.

Cox was no absentee publisher. One Dayton reporter completed a series on Ohio's prisons; pleased with his work, he sent copies to Cox. They came back within forty-eight hours with the curt note: "I read every line of the paper every day." He ran a tight ship. Once, attempting small talk, a *Daily News* employee asked Cox how he had spent his morning. Cox replied: "I called up every goddamn editor of every newspaper I've got and gave them all hell." Having so pronounced, chances are he spit: Cox smoked cigars and chewed tobacco; often, he smoked and chewed simultaneously, and spat on the carpet as he motored through the building. The habit made him an easy man to trace. "You could tell he'd been in the city room," one reporter recalls, "because sometimes he missed the spittoon." Cox's reporters addressed him as "Governor" and held him in a respect that sagged at times toward dread; one sportswriter insisted on standing whenever he talked with Cox — even if they were speaking by phone. Cox grilled new employees, posing questions faster than they could be answered. When one new hire answered a query by saying she had attended Oberlin, Cox paused long enough to comment, "Bunch of Republicans."

Cox was a Democrat. He was canny politically; that and the power of his presses brought a steady stream of state and national figures to his office in

Dayton, to seek advice or to pay homage. One day in Washington, Cox's Capitol Hill reporter bumped into Speaker of the House Sam Rayburn. The speaker eyed the reporter, said — "Cox. Solid as a nut. Solid as a nut"—and strode on. Cox was solid, though skeptical of the direction his party was taking. While he remained personally fond of Franklin Roosevelt, Cox was no great fan of the New Deal. He preferred Ohio conservatives, Democratic Governor Frank Lausche, and even Republican Senator Robert Taft. The New Deal had encroached on what Cox considered the prerogatives and rewards of business. Dayton columnist Roz Young recalls, "One day, I was walking through the office and Cox came along muttering to himself. Muttering about taxes. He stopped me and said, 'Do you realize I had to pay over one million dollars in income taxes this year?' I thought: If you're making enough money to owe that much in taxes, you don't have anything to complain about." Antipathy ran deeper than Cox's wallet. The New Deal had undermined the game as Cox played it. Cox had been a business progressive — government should level the playing field, not give undue aid and comfort to the downtrodden. Let them strive and rise as he had done.

But if Cox was a type, then he was at least true to his type. The self-made man recognizes no obstacles in circumstance, no limits other than personality. In 1920, a calculating and competent politician named James Cox embraced the cause of world government, of nations leagued against war, and fully expected to achieve it. As the election neared, his advocacy of the League, one magazine reported, "took on a kind of Billy Sunday fervor, an emotional and evangelical quality rather foreign to Cox's normal personality of cautious conservatism." Campaigning in Pueblo, Colorado, Cox quoted these fevered words from a visitor to the graves of American soldiers in France:

> I wish some men in public life who are now opposing the settlement for which these men died could visit such a spot as that. I wish that the thought that comes out of these graves could penetrate their consciousness. I wish they could feel the moral obligation that rests upon us not to go back on those boys, but to see them through, to see it through to the end of making good their redemption of the world. For nothing less depends upon this decision, nothing less than the liberation and salvation of the world.

Maybe James Middleton Cox simply overestimated what the self-made man could accomplish. In Horatio Alger's *Paul Prescott's Charge*, a young man rushes out into the middle of street, full in the path of furious horses and cries "Whoa!" at the top of his voice. The horses stop. In the 1920 election, Cox placed himself in the path of an electorate in full galloping retreat from the demands of world leadership. Singly, he bade it stop. And he got trampled.

Most defeated presidential candidates fall back on good works and golf; James Cox pursued his second career. A fine newsman, a fine businessman, he built a major media empire. He was a paternalistic employer: in Dayton, he didn't pay well, but he supplied the lunchroom with vegetables from his farm.

Like James Cox, Arthur Morgan was a type; a harder one to place, perhaps, but equally unyielding. In 1920,

Morgan took over a college that was on its last legs and by force of idea and personality transformed it within a decade into one widely regarded as in the front rank of American education. Morgan pushed himself; he was incapable of not doing so. Between fund raising trips on behalf of the college, he consulted on engineering projects, spoke widely and wrote on every subject under the sun; by 1930, he was exhausted. In a memoir, he writes of how he would squeeze his fingertips on the underside of tables to remain awake at meetings.

Morgan, stated Algo Henderson, then dean of the college, had the almost complete faith of the school's faculty; such faith was not entirely reciprocated. Morgan wanted an institution that would dive off the dock of all previous experience; he doubted his faculty was making the leap. As the Depression began drying up sources for the private funds that kept the college afloat, Morgan neared despair. It grated on him. Here he was, going hat in hand, selling a slightly used dream in a continuing effort to raise the monies needed to pay faculty salaries, while the faculty that gained from such labors sat comfortably home in Yellow Springs and, he had reason to believe, played bridge.

In June 1931, Arthur and Lucy Griscom Morgan sailed to Europe; their travels ended in Portugal. Lucy returned home; Arthur remained in the small town of Cintra, where after considerable brooding he concluded that it was time to denounce the entire enterprise. He wrote what melodramatically came to be known as the "Epistle from Portugal." He mailed it to his wife, asking Lucy if she thought it too strong; she didn't, and passed it to the Morgan's son Ernest for reproduction and distribution on campus. Dean Henderson got wind of the matter, secured the letter, convened a campus assembly and read its contents to an increasingly stricken college community.

Morgan began with characteristic bluntness: "Such as they are," he wrote, "there are too many colleges in America." A college should exist, he wrote, only if it offered something distinctively valuable. Antioch, he acknowledged, had made progress in teaching methods and "to a considerable degree" deserved its reputation:

> Yet, when I compare Antioch as it is with what I believe to be reasonable expectations for such an institution, and what were certainly my hopes for Antioch, I feel a very keen and deep-seated disappointment. I am disappointed by the infrequent occurrence of great expectations. I am disappointed in that commonsense judgment of our faithful, experienced people that really we have done very well, that all human changes come by slow degrees, and that we must not expect too much. I am disappointed that we do not break through the current ways of life with greater creative discontent.

He added:

> I have had certain hopes and purposes for Antioch and I have talked of these in trying to raise money. For short periods I can present my hopes as in process of fulfillment, but unless such statements become more and more nearly true in fact, they become closer and closer to hypocrisy. In the long run the facts and the story must not conflict.

Either the facts must conform to my statements, or I must tell a different story, or I must become silent.

Henderson considered Morgan's statements "entirely unjustified," but added, "I excused it a bit on his part. He had been under a great deal of stress." The faculty "was quite despondent," said math teacher Dawson, who added a softening note: "Morgan felt tremendous responsibility in the Depression. He was physically and emotionally worn down." Anxious rounds of self-study and conferences between faculty delegations and the wounded president ensued, but little better than uneasy truce existed between the college and its chief when, in 1933, Franklin Roosevelt invited Arthur Morgan to the White House.

Roosevelt was looking for an engineer; James Cox, his former running mate, recommended Morgan. To Morgan, FDR spoke of the Tennessee River — potentially the strongest asset of its region, it each spring pulled topsoil from the denuded hillsides, rutting the fields, turning creeks into gullies and forcing the farmers progressively higher up the progressively less fertile slopes. Roosevelt spoke of the need to recreate the life of the region, where many farmers received a cash income of less than $100 a year and where only one farmhouse in twenty-five had electricity. The President was assigning this task to a newly-created federal agency, the Tennessee Valley Authority, with broad responsibilities throughout the 40,000-square-mile watershed. Did Arthur Morgan wish to be its first chairman?

"Morgan," J. D. Dawson said, "was in the seventh heaven."

The TVA is now best known for the great dams built by Morgan's engineers to control flooding, permit navigation and generate electricity. Morgan, however, had wanted much more. Small-scale industries to build regional independence. Model rural schools. Purchasing co-operatives. Efforts to eradicate malaria. Reform of local government. Possibly a special local currency to keep purchasing power in the region. TVA was to be Morgan's great opportunity to show what concerted planning and civic highmindedness could accomplish. A vast forestry program. The story of Morgan's successes and failure at TVA in many ways parallels his Antioch experience — high hope, strong vision and an inability to deal with those whose motives were different from his own. Early, Morgan lost the support of the two junior members of the TVA board, who had little liking for their chairman's more visionary schemes. One scoffed at Morgan's plans for rural self-sufficiency, calling it no more likely than "the Second Coming of Daniel Boone." More substantially, Morgan lost the battle over the nature of the TVA: he wanted it to be a showpiece of nonpartisan public enterprise; in the politically contentious 1930s, his rivals saw it as a card to be played in the conflict with the New Deal's enemies.

FDR tried to reconcile his squabbling subordinates. At one point, he wrote Morgan to suggest that everyone get together for a chat, as he had always believed, he said, there was no problem gentlemen could not solve if they sat down with a snifter of brandy and a good cigar. Somewhat awkwardly, the President added that he knew Morgan neither drank nor smoked. Which in some ways was the point. Morgan wasn't simply non-political, he was anti-political: both outside of and opposed to the entire world in which gentlemen and brandy rubbed elbows and made decisions. In the end, Morgan lost the support of the one man who mattered. In March 1938, Franklin Roosevelt dismissed Morgan for what he termed the temperamental inability to exercise shared authority, which, whatever the ins and outs of the matter, was certainly a Morgan trait.

Ousted from the TVA, he returned to Yellow Springs, to brood, to rest, to recover. He founded an organization to promote his ideas about the small community; he wrote a biography of utopian writer Edward Bellamy, a second book attempting to prove that Thomas More's Utopia was based on actual reports of the Inca empire, and a practical guide to entrepreneurship, *A Business of My Own*. And in 1956, he received a telephone call from the president of the Seneca Nation in New York State. The Army Corps of Engineers was planning to dam a river that ran through the heart of its reservation; the dam would drive the Senecas off land guaranteed them by George Washington in a 1794 treaty that was to last "so long as the sun rises and the river runs." Morgan told his caller that he had never taken an interest in Native Americans, had never heard of the Senecas, and that if there was no other reasonable way to protect Pittsburgh from floods, the Senecas should not oppose the Army Corps plan. Still, he agreed to look into it.

When he looked, he discovered the Conewango Basin. This natural glacial depression, Morgan calculated, could store far more water at less cost than the Army plan, provided Morgan could find a route to drain the water to Lake Erie. At eighteen, Morgan had despaired of his frail constitution. Now, at eighty, he walked the periphery of the Conewango: "I tramped on foot through the woods and gullies, following up each hint of a prospect.... I located the men who had drilled for water and oil in the area and went over the ground with them personally." He found what he was looking for: a path by which the Conewango could drain into Lake Erie. It would save the Seneca land. It would save taxpayers $100 million. Morgan drafted his proposal and turned the plans over the Army Corps for review. The Army Corps was not interested in having its prerogatives challenged by an old man and a bunch of Indians. Arthur Morgan might know how to build dams, but the Army Corps knew how to sandbag. Three years of dreary wrangling ensued. Morgan kept at it. His appearance at age eighty-two on *The Today Show* to argue the case sparked over

1,000 letters, a significant number, but nothing like enough. In the end, Morgan lost; Native Americans and the environment were not yet causes sufficiently popular to counter the Corps' skill at bureaucratic infighting. It was, in effect, the story of Morgan's life: being right wasn't enough.

As a storyteller, Charles Kettering did not let fact interfere with truth.

A story Kettering loved to tell gives the inventor's version of how, early in his days at General Motors, he persuaded GM's production divisions to adopt fast-drying automotive paints. Cars were then still painted by hand; the coats were many, the drying was slow and the whole task took as long as thirty-seven days. Simply to maintain the space required to store all those drying vehicles was a major headache and expense. Kettering's story opens with his hauling the paint manufacturers into his office and telling them they have to do better. Some while later, they return bearing the good news that they think they can cut the painting cycle to thirty days. Is that quickly enough?

Kettering snapped: "An hour would be more like it."

Soon after his session with the paint makers, Kettering was browsing along New York's Fifth Avenue. There, in a jewelry store window, he spotted a wooden pin tray finished with a lacquer he'd never seen. He bought the tray, tracked the maker of the lacquer to a backyard shed in New Jersey and bought some of the liquid. By homogenizing that lacquer with existing paints, he produced a liquid that was thin enough to spray and that dried glossy and weather-resistant in a few minutes.

The GM production people were skeptical. Kettering invited one doubter to lunch, listened while he claimed it was impossible to paint a car in a hour, then walked his visitor to the parking lot. There, the production man confessed himself unable to find his car. Kettering pointed to a particular vehicle and asked: "Isn't that your car?"

"It looks like my car," the man replied, "but my car isn't that color."

Kettering said: "It is now."

In truth, the development of fast-drying lacquer-based automotive paints involved more than just a little messing around in a backyard shed in New Jersey; it was a multi-year effort of Kettering researchers and chemists from du Pont. Kettering's broader point, though, was this: inventing something is only half the battle, you still have to get someone to use it.

In transferring the fruits of research to the facts of production, Kettering enjoyed the wholehearted support of General Motors' chief executive, Alfred P. Sloan. In his autobiography, Sloan — the most buttoned-down of men — wrote of his research chief, "The story of General Motors research under Mr. Kettering by itself is a romance." The modern corporation that Sloan and others were building is not, by its nature, a very romantic being. Perhaps more than anything, a large corporation is an entity that proceeds by the making and carrying out of plans. As the size and complexity of the organization grows, the process by which targets are set and the resources for achieving those targets assigned grows in importance. It becomes a central corporate task to coordinate around its planning all its disparate functions — personnel, finance, training, marketing, purchasing, production, service and others — to reach results unobtainable unless everyone is reading from the same memo. Nothing so disrupts this rationalized, incremental and at times glacial progression as when a tall, gangly, nearsighted chief of research bursts from his laboratory and yells out, "Eureka."

The falling out between research and production came with a project known as "the copper-cooled engine." It was aimed at solving a problem inherent in the internal combustion engine: namely, how to get rid of the waste heat produced when gasoline is burned. Kettering's was a simplifying mind. In his thinking, the whole clunky system of radiators, fans, hoses, belts and circulating fluids could be replaced by a series of copper fins mounted on the engine itself. The fins would radiate out the engine's heat, requiring no moving parts, no circulating fluids, nothing to maintain and nothing to boil over. Never wholly modest about the value of his ideas, Kettering pronounced the copper-cooled engine as "the greatest thing that has ever been produced in the automobile world."

Except GM never produced it; at least, not in any large numbers. The idea posed technical challenges: the copper of the fins and the alloys of the engine had different coefficients of expansion. When heated, the fins swelled more than the engine; consequently, it was a tricky metallurgical task to affix the fins to the engine. That, Kettering maintained, was resolvable. To his mind, the real problem was foot-dragging within GM: the copper-cooled engine wasn't built because no division was prepared to let the research department call its production shots. The project ended in a multimillion-dollar writeoff, the major failure of Kettering's General Motors career. To improve coordination between research and production, Sloan in 1925 decreed that Kettering and his research operation must move from Dayton to Detroit. Kettering gave in halfway. The research division moved; Kettering commuted, returning each weekend to Dayton and Ridgeleigh Terrace. Kettering joked of his traveling. "I live in Dayton," he said frequently, "but since I can't get a job there, I have to work in Detroit." He offered this as an amusing comment, but the underlying truth was that Dayton no longer had work to offer large enough to hold a man of Kettering's abilities.

For two decades after the creation of high octane fuel, Charles Kettering remained chief of General Motors research. During those years, Kettering followed the tug of his curiosity, and GM followed Kettering's lead. He pulled the corporation beyond the automotive world — into modern refrigerants, making a household name and a major GM division of Frigidaire; into the two-cycle lightweight diesel locomotive engine. When Kettering got interested in the diesel, he sought $500,000 from Sloan for development work. Would that be enough, Sloan asked. No, Kettering replied affably, but if you give me that much now then you'll certainly give me the rest when I need it. In 1934, a Kettering prototype diesel locomotive made the 1,071-mile run from Denver to Chicago, the trip marking the opening of the second season of the Century of Progress exposition. At the time, steam locomotives generally took twenty-four hours to make the trip; Kettering's diesel arrived in thirteen hours, fifteen minutes, snapping a tape pulled across Chicago's Halsted Street before an early morning crowd of 100,000. Within several years, diesel locomotives were outselling steam-powered ones, and General Motors was outselling all others combined. As ever, Kettering had his eye on market: asked what the draw-pull of his locomotive was, he replied, "Strong enough to pull thirty railroads out of the hands of receivers."

By that time, Kettering was the nation's best-known engineer. In 1933, *Time* put him on its cover and *The Saturday Evening Post* ran a series about him. Fame permitted foible. Kettering dressed simply, loved flying, fell asleep at the cultural events favored by his wife and never carried any cash. He would invite people to lunch; when the check came, he would calmly explain that they would have to pay. Once, in Dayton's Union Station, his guest remonstrated, "Tell me, Ket. Two blocks up the street you own the Moraine Hotel. Why didn't we just eat there?" Said Kettering: "It's simpler this way." Wealth broadened Kettering's pursuits. Though politically conservative, he remained the major benefactor of liberal Antioch College, donating its library, its student union and its science building. When college president Algo Henderson offered to name the science building for Kettering, Kettering refused. His presence in the building is limited to a small framed portrait photograph, hung in the lobby over the statement: "This is not a monument to anyone. This is a place to work."

Charles Kettering retired from General Motors in 1947, age seventy-one; the

Science and technology was the day's grandest show, Kettering believed, and could be made clear to anyone provided scientists spoke clearly. All Newton's Second Law meant, he told audiences, is that "you can't push something that is moving faster than you are."

previous year, Olive Kettering died of cancer. Aware of her disease and unable to do anything else, Charles Kettering joined with Alfred P. Sloan to create the Memorial Sloan-Kettering Institute in Manhattan. After Olive's death, an associate recalls walking into the Miami Valley Country Club, seeing Kettering sitting with the pilots assigned him by General Motors and realizing that this great, gregarious, generous man — with a sculptor's hands and very weak eyes — was lonely. In retirement, Kettering became the nation's acknowledged spokesmen on research. By one estimate, he gave over 4,000 talks on the subject — or, more accurately, he gave pretty much the same talk that many times. Gathering himself at the podium, he would peer out over his gold-rimmed spectacles and, like some old-fashioned professor who warmed to his audience as much as to his text, tell tall stories in a twangy voice. He spoke as though his audience of the moment was his needed ally against everyone who thought they knew more than they did and, hence, was unwilling to try anything new. He'd tell the story about painting a car to prove a point. He'd talk about his photosynthesis work. And he'd tell about commuting for years from home in Dayton to work in Detroit.

Kettering traveled between Dayton and Detroit along old U.S. Route 25. Typically, he made the trip in under four hours, a time no other GM executive who made the journey could match. Asked how he accomplished it, Kettering's cryptic reply was: "The whole world lies either to the left or to the right of Route 25." Finally, a company executive asked to ride along to see how it was Kettering made the trip. In those pre-Interstate days, major highways were also the Main Streets of every city and town along their way. Driving, Kettering skipped the traffic-clogged city centers, bypassing them on the lesser roads and the country lanes he had scouted out to save time. Of course you save time, his passenger complained, you aren't taking the normal route. And that, Kettering replied, was precisely the point: "You never get anywhere going the obvious way," said the Boss. "If you want to get anything done in this world, you've got to get off Route 25."

Orville Wright was not sentimental about things. For a time, the gliders he and Wilbur had flown at Kitty Hawk were stored in a Dayton-Wright hangar at South Field. Near the end of the First World War, Orville directed that the gliders be taken out and burned. The task fell to a workman named Ernest Dubel. "They were light and thin," Dubel recalled. "They didn't make much fire." Orville nearly ordered the destruction of the Kitty Hawk plane, the first in flight. In this, he may have been motivated less by the absence of sentiment than by a building frustration. The aircraft had been lent out on display; when it was returned, the crankshaft and engine flywheel were missing. To Orville, that was about the final indignity.

When in 1908 the Wrights presented flight in Europe and America, no one of consequence doubted their mastery or their achievement. Soon, however, the Wrights were enmeshed in the oddest controversy in aviation history, one that pitted them against an unlikely antagonist, the Smithsonian Institution. The dispute turned on how much of the credit for the conquest of flight should go the Smithsonian's former director, Samuel Langley, whose Aerodrome crashed nose first into the Potomac on both of its launch attempts. When Langley died in 1906, Wilbur wrote of him: "The knowledge that the head of the most prominent scientific institution of America believed in the possibility of human flight was one of the influences that led us to undertake the preliminary investigation that preceded our active work." Further, Wilbur noted, Langley's supplying the brothers with the reading list from which they began their investigation of flight constituted "a helping hand at a critical time and we shall always be grateful." It was a fair tribute, one that graciously ignored the failure of Langley's work.

Soon, though, friends of Langley and antagonists of the Wrights were arguing that its was Langley's Aerodrome and not the Wright Flyer that was the world's first "flyable" craft. They nimbly sidestepped the Aerodrome's sad performance by claiming it could have flown, had it only been properly launched. The Smithsonian welcomed the Wrights' 1903 plane, but planned to display it side-by-side with the Aerodrome — Langley's to be described as embodying the theoretical solution to flight; the Wrights' as flight's first practical application, in short, a Solomonic willingness to give the Wrights half the credit due solely to them. Remarkably, in 1914 the Smithsonian moved from misrepresentation to what Orville regarded as complicity in fraud. The museum released the extant pieces of the Aerodrome to Wright rival Glenn Curtiss, who took them to a lake at Hammondsport, New York. There, he rebuilt the craft with a different wing area, different wing curvature and different carburetor; he added hydroplane floats, replaced a small vane rudder with a large one and reinforced the wing spars, which had collapsed during the craft's earlier launchings. On May 28, 1914, Curtiss taxied down the lake and got airborne for fifty yards. To some, this proved the Aerodrome had been a flyable craft; the claim gained in plausibility when a second Wright opponent "independently" attested that the craft had flown "entirely unmodified" from its original design.

Orville was infuriated, all the more so as Wilbur was no longer alive to defend his stake in the matter. This, along with the disappearance of the crankshaft and flywheel while the Kitty Hawk plane was out on loan, prompted him to consider destroying the aircraft. Dayton-Wright employee Louis Christman stated, "See, Orville Wright was much incensed over the fact that the United States did not recognize them as being the first to fly." A relative of a Wright associate added, "I think it was Roy Knabenshue — who was the great aeronaut and balloonist in his early days, and finally managed the Wright Brothers flyer team... — [who] finally convinced Orville he ought not burn it up, that it had historic value."

Orville had no doubt where the first Wright Flyer ought to reside. In 1923, he wrote to Griffith Brewer, a British aviation figure, "Of course the machine ought to be in the National Museum at Washington." He had little optimism that this would occur. In 1925, he announced he was offering the aircraft on long-term loan to the Science Museum, London. "In making my offer," he wrote, "I did reserve the right, after a term of years, of bringing it back to America, if I found a suitable home for it here. However, the likelihood of this seemed so remote that I did not expect its return." Orville Wright, his secretary Mabel Beck and James Jacobs worked at Orville's laboratory on Broadway in Dayton to ready the rather moth-eaten craft for delivery to England. Ruth Jacobs, Jim's widow, recalled:

> They had to recover most of [the wings] with that linen, you know. They called the linen "The Pride of the West," not linen, muslin.... The first muslin that they had used on the plane, they had gotten from Rike-Kumler company [a Dayton department store], but the Rike-Kumler company wasn't able to get it at this time.... They had to send away to the mill company to get this, and they had a hundred and twenty-five yards of this muslin. Orville cut the muslin out to fit the wings and Miss Beck sewed the muslin and my husband applied it.

Jacobs' son added: "When they had it all together, I remember my father, who was quite a camera fan at the time, getting his flash out and taking a series of flash pictures of the Wright airplane just sitting in the laboratory. Orville was there, and I always had a feeling that Orville had a sense of, in his own mind, a sense of admiration for this airplane, and a sense of feeling that this was part of his life. But he never openly expressed this in any way." The plane was shipped to England. With it, the most important artifact of man's attempts to fly and the signal physical treasure in Dayton, left the city. Neither Dayton, nor Orville, ever saw it again.

The fact that the most important aircraft in the world — American-designed and American-flown over the American sands of Kitty Hawk — was sitting in a museum in London was a source of some discomfort to the Smithsonian. The museum sought to have the original Wright Flyer brought to Washington, but hoped to do so in a way that would limit the institution's embarrassment over its involvement in the bogus trials of the rebuilt Langley Aerodrome. Orville had no interest in saving anyone any embarrassment. He wanted pretty close to a flat-out admission that the Smithsonian had been a party to fraud. In 1934, Charles Lindbergh, the only name in aviation on a par with Orville's, attempted mediation. The greater fault, Lindbergh concluded, lay with the museum, "but Orville Wright is not an easy man to deal with in the matter." He was not. In 1937, Orville wrote a will directing that the Kitty Hawk plane was to remain permanently in England, unless he, Orville, left written instructions to the contrary.

For his final two decades Orville lived the life of a semi-retired gentleman of ample means, avoiding the spotlight, never trading on his fame. He was private. Orville agreed to allow writer Fred Kelly to prepare an authorized biography of the Wright Brothers. When the drafts were presented to Orville, "he just wrote red pencil all the way through it," striking out all the personal notes and anecdotes he claimed would be of no interest to the general public.

Orville liked quiet and the out-of-doors and to gain both acquired a three-room cottage in Ontario's Georgian Bay. Family members were frequent guests at Georgian Bay, where they fished for the black bass that Orville cooked in deep lard or were served a dish their host called lobscouse, which began by cooking up a large piece of beef, to which Orville added whatever was within reach. Like Hawthorn Hill, the Georgian Bay cottage profited by Orville's inventiveness. After much experimenting, he devised a system that produced perfect toast; he devised a record changer that let him load hours of music at a time, then sit and listen without having to get up from his chair. Getting up was often painful. He had suffered from sciatica ever since his 1908 crash at Fort Myer, Virginia; often, the pain was incapacitating. He would sit in his cottage when his sciatica was bad and listen to spirituals, the only music he found soothing. The cottage sat on a rocky point; family members expressed concern that a good strong wind might some day blow it off the cliff. Speaking as the co-inventor of the first wind tunnel designed for aeronautical research, Orville assured them that it would take a 100-mile-an-hour wind to move the cottage. "And the funny thing is," Orville's nephew Horace said, "after he died, we had a hundred mile an hour wind and [the cottage] moved."

In their
seventies,
Arthur
Morgan and
Charles
Kettering
stroll the
Antioch
College
campus, still
sorting it out.

Last words

His life, John H. Patterson was inclined to assert, was guided by three simple precepts: "Do justly, love mercy, and walk humbly" — three traits, some critics observed, not notably a part of Patterson's character. Patterson had the last word, however, those words being carved in stone on the base of the statue the people of Dayton raised to the man who calmly considered himself their leading citizen. Appropriately, the statue presents Patterson on horseback, thirteen bronze feet from the forehead of the rider to the fetlocks of his horse. Most man-and-horse statuary is a parade ground thing: stiff, straight, frozen in a time that has passed. This rider looks like he leapt from the mold without waiting to cool; he stands ready now to do battle, or business, with anyone approaching. The inscription chiseled at its base says the statue was dedicated "by a grateful citizenry of Dayton to the memory of an apostle of progress and a creative idealist who made good things come true." It lauds Patterson as a Promoter of Good Citizenship. A Practical Educator. A Pioneer in Industrial Welfare and Co-operation. The Originator of School and Municipal Gardens in America. As Benefactor During the Flood of 1913. A Lover of Dayton. A Friend of Children. And, not least, as a Promoter of Health and Hygiene, who "taught and practiced the virtues of abstinence, sobriety and self-control." It closes with some words from the horseman: "My best investments are in humanity." Patterson, doubtless, could not have said it much better himself.

James Cox died of heart failure at his home, Trailsend, in 1957, aged eighty-seven. Cox once entertained as a house guest at Trailsend the historian Allan Nevins; at dinner, Nevins wrote, Cox spoke of his rural boyhood, his rise in publishing, his years as Ohio's first three-term governor. Conversation finished, Cox retired for the evening to his library. His host, Nevins wrote, had a lively, muscular and self-improving mind; he read "chiefly history and biography," trying to gain in his later years the education he had earlier been either too poor or too busy to obtain. To a certain extent Cox had made history, Nevins wrote, as "governor of Ohio at a critical time." Nevins' judgment was that Cox should have made more of it: he was, the historian wrote, "a candidate for the presidency who, as everyone will now grant, should have won." Cox, who succeeded in everything except his central ambition in life, likely agreed.

Defeated over Conewango by the Army Corps of Engineers, Arthur Morgan got the last word with a scathing book about the Corps' methods and motives. A few years later, his final book gave his version of the creation of the Tennessee Valley Authority. Near the close of that book, Morgan restated his central theme: personal character, or its absence, makes or breaks a society. "We may desire to create a bridge of greater span than ever has been built," he wrote, "yet, if the only steel available is of very low strength, no amount of fine design and no abundance of finance can overcome that limitation." Morgan continued: "If personal character is on a low level, then there comes a time when no refinement of social planning and no expenditures of public wealth, however great, will create a good social order. Additional complexities of planning and additional expenses for supervision, inspection, investigation and enforcement finally begin to break down of their own weight." Morgan's book on the TVA was published the year before he died. As a young man, Morgan concluded that as he would not live long, he could at least live with purpose; that, he continued to do, up until his death in 1975, aged ninety-seven.

Until shortly before his death in 1958 at age eighty-two, Charles Kettering remained active, conducting experiments of interest to himself and speaking on research and technology. Towards the end of his life, Kettering spoke increasingly of failure. He was for it. "I think it was the Brookings Institute," he told one audience, "that made a study that said the more education you had the less likely you were to become an inventor. The reason why is: from the time a kid starts kindergarten to the time he graduates from college, he will be examined two or three times a year, and if he flunks once, he's out. Now, an inventor fails 999 times, and if he succeeds once, he's in.... It therefore seems that the factor which needs to be corrected is to teach the educated person that it is not a disgrace to fail, and that he must analyze each failure to find its cause.

We paraphrase this by saying, 'You must learn how to fail intelligently.' Failing is one of the greatest arts in the world. One fails forward toward success."

However unbudging Orville Wright was with the Smithsonian, he was immediately forthcoming when, after the Second World War, NCR chairman Edward Deeds announced plans to create in Dayton a park around the theme of the city's contributions to transportation. Orville immediately offered to donate the second most important aircraft in the history of flight — the first practical airplane, the 1905 Huffman Prairie machine that Wilbur flew for twenty-four miles in a single October afternoon. In late 1947, Orville headed to NCR headquarters for a meeting; uncharacteristically tardy, the seventy-six-year-old inventor was hurrying up the steps to the building when he suffered a heart attack. It was a mild one. Three months later, a second attack killed him. At his death, Orville Wright's last public pronouncement on the 1903 Kitty Hawk plane was that it was to remain in England; his will confirmed that, absent written instructions to the contrary, that stipulation remained in effect. In his papers, Wright's executors found the letter presenting the world's first heavier-than-air flying machine, which Orville had flown for 120 feet on a blustery December day near the Atlantic coast, to the Smithsonian Institution, where it remains on display.

Always leave
yourself a
way out.
Company
demonstator
shows how,
bungee-style,
*Dayton Daily
News*
employees
were to exit
the building
in an
emergency.
Attach
yourself to a
wire; leap out
the window;
rotate feet
down and
release. In
theory, the
method was
suitable for
everyone.
Even sports-
writers.
The idea never
caught on.

Introduction

1 Characterization of America as a society of "island communities" is drawn from Robert H. Wiebe,
  The Search for Order: 1877-1920, Hill-Wang, 1967, page xiii.
  Example of differing times is from Derek Howse, *Greenwich Time and the Discovery of the Longitude*, Oxford University Press, 1981, page 120.
3 Brooks Atkinson comment on Ibsen. Reported by Paul Treichler, professor of theatre, Antioch College, 1932-1970.
  "They acted like they were..." Author's interview with Marie Aull.

Chapter 1: Four Sketches

5 Orville and the cows anecdote. Wright Brothers/Kettering Oral History Project, University of Dayton Archives, interview with William Sanders, page 3. Hereafter, UD oral history/interviewee's name.
  "If he is an honest man..."Fred C. Kelly, Miracle at Kitty Hawk, Farrar, Straus & Young, 1951, page 7. Hereafter, Kelly/Miracle.
  Orville's truancy anecdote. Fred C. Kelly, *The Wright Brothers*, Harcourt, Brace & Company, 1943, page 5-6. Hereafter, Kelly/Brothers.
6 "It's a funny thing..." UD oral history/Ivonette Wright Miller, page 16.
  "They had financed the world's first airplane..." UD oral history/Bernard Whelan, pages 6-7.
  "They first started flying..." UD oral history/Ruth Jacobs, page 16.
7 Library service anecdote. UD oral history/Max Kohnop, pages 9, 23.
  "There was a little awe whenever..." Ibid., page 2.
  "A nice sort of blowup..." UD oral history/William Sanders, page 3.
  Pole digging anecdote. T. A. Boyd, *Professional Amateur*, E. P. Dutton and Co., 1957, pages 35-36. Hereafter Boyd/Professional.
8 Working through annual shutdown anecdote: Stuart W. Leslie.
  Boss Kettering: Wizard of General Motors, Columbia University Press, 1983, page 27. Hereafter, Leslie/Kettering.
  $1.6 million life insurance. Ibid., 121.
  "I lost my job and..." Charles F. Kettering, *Prophet of Progress*, edited by T. E. Boyd, P. Dutton and Company, 1961, page 159. Hereafter, Kettering/Prophet.
  "I don't want to be conspicuous." Author's interview with Dr. Perino Wingfield.
  Kettering's storytelling. Accounts are legion; reference here is from author's interview with W. Walker Lewis.
  "I know glass is transparent..." Kettering/Prophet, pages 206-207.
9 Kettering's eyesight. Numerous, including Leslie/Kettering, pages 3, 7, 10; Boyd/Professional, page 29.
  "I never read, so I thought a lot." Robert Chollar, interviewed for Kettering Oral History project. Series of interviews conducted 1957 and 1959; tapes in file at the Kettering Foundation, Dayton, Oh. Hereafter, Kettering tapes/interviewees' name.
  "Yes, the auto mechanic..." Leslie/Kettering, page 327.

"With scarcely a moment's hesitation ..." From Horatio Alger's *Paul Prescott's Charge* quoted in Edwin P. Hoyt, *Horatio's Boys: The Life and Works of Horatio Alger, Jr.*, Chilton Book Company, 1974, page 56. Hereafter Hoyt/Horatio.

10 "It is always pleasant to see..." Quoted from Horatio Alger's *Ragged Dick*, in Hoyt/Horatio, page 81.
Railway wreck anecdote. *The Outlook*, September 22, 1920, page 142.

11 "That of an agile, energetic, intuitive,..." Ibid.
"Never anybody I was taught to be proud ..." Author's interview with Timothy Patterson.

12 "He would never cheat..." Ibid.
Robert Patterson's departure from Kentucky. Patterson family anecdote, told by Timothy Patterson and Mollie Chesire.
"Right is right..." Samuel Crowther, *John H, Patterson—Pioneer in Industrial Welfare*, Doubleday, Page & Company, 1924, page 19. Hereafter, Crowther/Pioneer.
"A tousled but well-tailored..." William Rodgers, *Think! A Biography of the Watsons and IBM*, Stein and Day, 1969, page 47. Hereafter, Rodgers/Think.
Cigar pitching anecdote. Stanley C. Allyn, *My Half Century With NCR*, McGraw-Hill, 1967, page 40. Hereafter, Allyn/Half Century.

13 Bicycle riding anecdote. Lena Harvey Tracy, *How My Heart Sang*, Richard R. Smith, 1950, page 116. Hereafter, Tracy/Heart.
"What do we live for..." Charlotte Reeve Conover, *Builders in New Field*, G. P. Putnam's Sons, 1939, page 161. Hereafter, Conover/Builders.

Chapter 2: The Setting

15 "An extraordinary rise in the river." *The Great Flood*, supplement marking the 75th anniversary of the Dayton flood, *The Dayton Daily News*, March 25, 1988. page 9. Hereafter, Daily News/Anniversary.
"Deep enough to swim a horse." Ibid., page 9.

16 "Some of us can remember how..." Mary Davies Steele, quoted in Daily News/Anniversary, page 9.
"Mr. Lincoln is a very seductive reasoner..." Quoted in Lloyd Ostendorf, *Mr. Lincoln Comes to Dayton*, Otterbein Press, 1959, page 27.
Notes on Al Shartle. Charlotte Reeve Conover, *Dayton, Ohio, An Intimate History*, Lewis Publishing Co., 1932, page 131. Hereafter, Conover/Intimate.

17 Dunbar as elevator operator. Charlotte Reeve Conover, *Some Dayton Saints & Prophets*, United Brethren Publishing House, 1907, page 179. Hereafter, Conover/Saints.
"We kept it going as long as..." Orville Wright to Edward Johnson, January 2, 1934, published in *The Papers of Wilbur and Orville Wright*, edited by Marvin W. McFarland, McGraw-Hill Book Company, 1953, page 1162. Hereafter, Wright/Papers.
"The first instance of an American negro..." William Dean Howell's review, published as introduction to Paul Laurence Dunbar, *Lyrics of Lowly Life*, Citadel Press, 1991., xvi.

18 Irwin Feller, "the Urban Location of United States Invention, 1860-1910," *Explorations in Economic History*, spring 1971 [volume 8], page 292, from "1900: Annual Report of the Commissioner of Patents for the Year 1900," Washington, D.C., Government Printing Office, 1901.
List of Dayton products from *Speeches*, Dayton Board of Trade Centennial Dinner, April 1, 1896, on file at the Dayton and Montgomert County Public Library.
"The city of a thousand factories." Multiple references, including James H. Perkins, *Dayton During World War I*, thesis, Miami University, 1959, page 15.

Chapter 3: The Businessman

21 John H. Patterson as coal dealer, including merchandising innovations.
Crowther/Pioneer, pages 36-48.

22 "Mr. Patterson shipped coal as though..." Ibid., page 42.
"It is not your coal..." Ibid., page 47.
"We were doing a business of..." pages 58-59.
Diamond-owning clerk anecdote. NCR centennial publication, *1884-1922 The Cash Register Era*, published by NCR, 1984, page 11. Hereafter, NCR/Centennial.

23 James Ritty's invention of the cash register. Numerous sources, including Gerald Carson, "The Machine that Made them Honest," *American Heritage*, August 1966, page 52.
"I would not have it back as a gift." Isaac Marcosson, Wherever Men Trade, Dodd, Mead & Company, 1948, page 28. Hereafter, Marcosson/Wherever.
"We teach through the eye." Crowther/Pioneer, page 238.
"Eighty-seven percent of all we know..."/"The optic nerve is..." *Welfare Work*,

National Cash Register, undated and unpagenated; c. 1915.
Workers rolling ball anecdote. Conover/Builders, page 167.
24 "No ad is large enough..." NCR/Centennial, page 13.
 Early company finances. Crowther/Pioneer, pages 98-105.
 Patterson organizing direct mail. Ibid., page 90.
 "For Heaven's sake let up..." Conover/Builders, page 154.
 "I don't want to see the bank..." "Patterson's Marvelous Money Machine,"
 by Charles Wertenbaker, *Saturday Evening Post*, September 1953.
25 "We are now working on a new plan..." NCR/Centennial, page 14.
26 "Providing orders push..." Ibid., page 15.
 Origin of canned sales speech. Crowther/Pioneer, page 111.
27 "The man who is seldom turned down..." NCR publication,
 Instructions to NCR Salesmen, 1910, page 8. Hereafter, NCR/Instructions.
 "Get the hayseed off them..." Crowther/Pioneer, page 129-130.
 "There is nothing that denotes..." NCR/Instructions, page 8.
 "The object of your visit..." Ibid., page 18.
 "Give your [PP] to understand..." Ibid., page 22.
 "When Mr. Westinhouse first took." NCR/Selling Points, Page 113.
 "Can't spare the money..." *Selling Points,*' published by NCR, 1910, page 15.
 Hereafter, NCR/Selling Points.
 "When you pay your employees..." NCR/Instructions, page 46.
28 "Well, Mr. Blank, you seem to trust..." NCR/Selling Points, page 93.
 "And can even carry a likeness..." NCR/Instructions, page 35.
 "Do not let [the prospect] sidetrack..." Ibid., page 18.
 The "cast-iron rule." Crowther/Pioneer, page 77.
29 "I have found nothing but excuses..." Ibid., page 139.
 First sales school. Ibid., page 154.
 "Patterson developed the dynamics..." Rodgers/Think, page 16.
30 "Serve simple well-cooked food..." Conover/Builders, page 187-188.
 Removal of building. Conover/Builders, page 238.

Chapter 4: The Brothers

33 "been made painfully acquainted with the fact..." Wilbur E. Landis, *Minutes Book,* The Annual
 Club of the Ten Dayton Boys, on file at the Dayton and Montgomery County Public
 Library, entry for October 21, 1887. Hereafter, Dayton club minutes/year of meeting.
34 "As successful as could reasonably be..." Frank Gilbert entry, Dayton club minutes, 1886.
 Ice skating accidents and aftermath. Kelly/Wright, page 26.
 Orville's chewing gum business. Ibid., pages 14-15.
 Orville and the red pepper anecdote. Orville Wright to W. R. Jacks
 July 19, 1917, Wright/Papers, page 1107.
35 "The interests of the people and business..." *West Side News,* March 1, 1889, page 2.
 "Yesterday Eugene Staley..." *West Side News,* April 13, 1889, page 2.
 "Dan High is building..." *West Side News,* March 30, 1889, page 2.
 "An exciting ball game..." *West Side News,* May 5, 1889, page 2.
 "Give them all the trade..." *West Side News,* April 20, 1889, page 2.
 Anecdote about visiting printer. Kelly/Wright, page 35.
36 "Base ball is on the decline at Vincennes..." *Evening Item,* June 7, 1890, page 2.
 "The reasons can be stated..." *Evening Item,* July 30, 1890. page 2.
 "Amid the cheers and groans..." Dayton club minutes, 1890.
37 "Wilbur Wright, who came as usual without his wife." Dayton club minutes, 1901.
 "Still selling groceries..." Report of William Andrews, Dayton club minutes, 1893.
 "I am the happy father of a bouncing..." Report of Wilbur Landis,
 Dayton club minutes, 189.
 "There is so little prospect of an increase..." Report of Wilbur Wright,
 Dayton club minutes, 1893.
 The Wrights at the Columbian Exposition. Ibid., 1893.

Chapter 5: The Philanthropist

39 Girl fainting; visit to NCR. Tracy/Heart, pages 97-98.
40 "From the children... dropping metal caps..." Daniel T. Rodgers, *The Work Ethic in*
 Industrial America, University of Chicago Press, 1974; page 67. Hereafter, Rodgers/Ethic.
 "Has a grievance beyond being overworked..." Jane Addams, *Democracy and*

Social Ethics, Harvard University Press, 1964, page 211. Hereafter, Addams/Democracy.
"A smoldering apathy toward work..." Randolph Bourne,
  quoted in Rodgers/Ethic, page 92.
  Sabotaged cash registers. Tracy/Heart, pages 138-140, and Conover/Builders, page 164.
  "Had no heart in their jobs..." Crowther/Pioneer, page 196.
41 "All men should have the same kind..." Crowther/Pioneer, page 197.
  Umbrellas anecdote. Conover/Fields, page 170.
  Malted milk anecdote Conover/Builders, page 204.
  "The first step toward self-respect is..." Crowther/Pioneer, page 201.
42 Rosa Stuckey anecdote and quotation. A.A. Thomas, Suggestions from Employes,
  NCR, 1905, pages 11-12. Hereafter, NCR/Suggestions.
  "I think the best thing about..." NCR/Suggestions, introduction.
  "I can't see that you people are..." Allyn/Half Century, page 35.
  "At least for the moment..." Addams/Democracy, page 218.
  "It pays." Crowther/Pioneer, page 206
43 Patterson-sponsored boys' club. Tracy/Heart, page 123.
  Boy gardeners. Ibid., page 117.
45 "Upon those rules for a garden..." Tracy/Heart, page 113.
  List of NCR programs. Ibid., pages 148-149.
  "It was an inspiring and really beautiful sight..." Ibid., page 134.
46 Strike and Patterson's reaction. Tracy/Heart, page 164.

Chapter 6: The Farmboy

49 Loss of population in rural Ohio. Arthur Meier Schlesinger, Sr., The Rise of the City: 1878-1898,
  The Macmillan Company, 1933, pages 61-67. Hereafter, Schlesinger/Rise.
  "In the middle of the forenoon..." James Cox, Journey Through My Years,
  Simon & Schuster, 1946, page 14. Hereafter, Cox/Journey.
  "Will probably add to the medical literature..." Middletown [Ohio]
  Daily Signal, February 27, 1891, page 1.
50 "The first thing council should have done..." Middletown [Ohio] Daily Signal,
  October 24, 1891, page 3.
  Account of fatal abortion, including all quotations. Middletown [Ohio] Daily Signal,
  November 27, 1891, page 3.
  Cox dismissal at Cincinnati Enquirer. James E. Cebula, James M. Cox:
  Journalist and Politician, Garland Publishing, 1985, page 16. Hereafter, Cebula/Cox.
51 Role of the press. Schlesinger/Rise, page 185.
  Bennett dispatching Stanley. John W. Tebbel, The Compact History of
  American Journalism, Hawthorn Books, 1963; page 177. Hereafter, Tebbel/Journalism.
  "A good man, weighing..." Ibid., page 187.
  "You go back and tell..." Ibid., page 215.
  "The fundamental principle..." Larzer Ziff, The American 1890s, Viking Press, 1966,
  page 147. Hereafter, Ziff/American.
52 "The bookkeeper was once asked..." Cox/Journey, page 39.
  Lowes' role in Dayton politics. Hoyt Landon Warner, Progressivism in Ohio,
  Ohio State University Press, 1964, page 14. Hereafter, Warner/Progressivism.
  Cox's campaign against Dr. J. E. Lowes ran from October 14 to November 7, 1898.
  Editorial cartoons cited are from October 15, 18, 19 and November 4, 1898.
  "The bootlicking organ of the vulgar..." Dayton Daily News, November 3, 1898, page 4.
54 "It is the rights..." Dayton Daily News, November 4, 1898, page 4.
  Claims no personal abuse. Dayton Daily News, October 20, 1898, page 4.
  "A thirsty leech." Dayton Daily News, November 4, 1898, page 4.
  Election eve coverage, including "the abuses imposed..."
  Dayton Daily News, November 7, 1898, page 1.
  "Following its constant policy..." Dayton Daily News, December 12, 1898.
55 News' shutdown anecdote, Cox/Journey, page 43.
  "Coxsure... for hair-trigger certain..." The Outlook, September 22, 1920, page 143.
56 "Following it's constant policy..." Dayton Daily News, December 10, 1907.

Chapter 7: The Businessman Abroad

57 "How this great business enterprise..." John H. Patterson's Letters from Europe,
  published by NCR, 1902, on file at the Dayton and Montgomery County Public Library,
  pages 24-25. Hereafter, Patterson/Letters.

"The principles of open spaces..." Patterson/Letters, page 33.
"I believe that our factory ought to be..." Ibid., page 18.
"I entered the building..." Ibid., page 24.
"Has been for centuries..." Ibid., page 69.
58 "The chief duty they have..." Patterson/Letters, page 65.
Patterson at Kremlin anecdote. Ibid., page 56.
"A warning to other people..." Ibid., page 57.
"Let us not forget that..." Ibid., page 36.
59 Norwegian salesman anecdote. NCR/Centennial, page 21.
Quotes from award winners in Berlin. Patterson/Letters, pages 100-104.
"Quota Song" and "The character of the singing..." Ibid., page 117.

Chapter 8: The Miracle

61 "For some years I have been afflicted..." Wilbur Wright to Octave Chanute,
May 13, 1900, Wright/Papers, pages 15-19.
Background on Chanute. Wright/Papers, page 15-16; Crouch/Bishop's, pages 146-156.
"Chauffeurs" vs. "bird." Charles H. Gibbs-Smith, *The Invention of the Aeroplane*,
1799-1909, Taplinger Publishing Co., 1966, p. xiv. Hereafter, Gibbs-Smith/Invention.
62 "As he had not solved..." Alfred W. Marshall and Henry Greenly, *Flying Machines: Past, Present,*
and Future, Percival Marshall & Co., London, 1907, page 104.
"I have not the smallest molecule..." Lord Kelvin, December 8, 1896,
quoted in Gibbs-Smith/Invention, page 22.
"Probably before 1950." H. G. Wells, quoted in Walter Lord, *The Good Years*,
Harper & Row, 1960, page 6. Hereafter, Lord/Good Years.
"It will not settle steadily down..." From Wilbur Wright's address to the Western Society
of Engineers, Chicago, Illinois, September 18, 1901, Wright/Papers, page 100.
63 Helicopter anecdote. Kelly/Brothers, page 8.
"I entirely agree that the boys..." Wilbur Wright, quoted in Crouch/Bishop's, page 130.
"Almost the only great problem..." Wilbur Wright to Bishop Wright, September 3, 1900,
Kelly/Miracle, page 27.
"I make no secret of my plans..." Wilbur Wright to Octave Chanute, May 13, 1900,
Wright/Papers, page 17.
64 Wilbur and Orville sewing. Katharine Wright to Milton Wright, August 20,1902.
Wright/Papers, page 244.
"The thrust depends upon the speed..." Kelly/Wright, page 88.
"I like Orville..." Author's interview with Ivonette Wright Miller.
65 "An enthusiast, but not a crank." Wilbur Wright to Smithsonian Institution, May 30, 1899,
Wright/Papers, page 4.
"Even the simplest intellectual..." Wilbur Wright to Octave Chanute, May 13, 1900,
Wright/Papers, page 16.
Lilienthal's tactics inadequate. Ibid., page 16-17.
66 "My observation of the flight of buzzards..." Wright/Papers, page 18.
Bike shop torsioning anecdote. Kelly/Wright, pages 49-50.
"Lateral equilibrium is gained..." Crouch/Bishop's, page 172.
67 Wrights' approach. Peter Jakab, *Visions of a Flying Machine*, Smithsonian Institution Press,
1990, pages 1-5. Hereafter, Jakab/Visions.
"In a good God..." Ibid., page 80.
68 "A stretch of sandy land one mile..." Crouch/Bishop's, page 183.
For account of Wilbur's crossing to Kitty Hawk,
see Wright/Papers for report of c. September 13, 1900, pages 23-25.
Mrs. Tate turning wing covering into dresses. Kelly/Wrights, page 66.
Katharine Wright's comments on her brothers' departure. Katharine Wright to Bishop
Wright, September 26, 1900, Wright/Papers, page 27.
Conditions at Kitty Hawk and "The sand is..." Orville Wright to Katharine Wright,
October 14, 1900, Wright/Papers, pages 28-34.
69 Tates' assistance to Wrights. Jakab/Visions, pages 97-100 and 104.
"We tried it with tail in front..." Orville Wright to Katharine Wright, October 18, 1900,
Wright/Papers, page 38.
"A motion was made..." Dayton club minutes, 1900.
"Setting out as we did..." Jakab/Visions, page 100.
70 "They chewed us clear through..." Orville Wright to Katharine Wright, July 28, 1901.
Wright/Papers, page 73-74.
Assessment of deficient lift, 1900 glider. Kelly/Wrights, page 64.

Deficient lift, 1901 glider. Wright/Papers, page 77; Orville Wright, *How We Invented the Airplane*, David McKay Company, Inc., 1953, page 35. Hereafter, Wright/How.
Poor handling of 1901 glider. Kelly/Wrights, page 69.
"Five minutes practice..." Wright/Papers, page 77.

71 Spratt's "blues." Wilbur Wright to George Spratt, January 23, 1902, Wright/Papers, pages 205-206.
"You make a great mistake..." Wilbur Wright to George A. Spratt, April 20, 1903, Wright/Papers, page 306.
Separating wings of glider for testing. Kelly/Wrights, page 71; Jakab/Visions, page 110.

72 Glider's reversal during wing warping. Wright/How, pages 36-38.
"When we looked at the time..." Crouch/Bishop's, page 213.
"Not within a thousand years..." From Wilbur's summary of the experiments of 1901, quoted in Crouch/Bishop's Boys, page 213.
"If... some rich man should give..." Octave Chanute to Wilbur Wright, December 1, 1901, Wright/Papers, page 183.
"As to your suggestion..." Wilbur Wright to Octave Chanute, December 23, 1901, Wright/Papers, page 187.
"Having set out with absolute faith..." Gibbs-Smith/Invention, page 41.
Note: An excellent description of the Wrights' wind tunnel and the problems it was designed to solve is given in Jakab/Visions, Chapter 6.

73 "We spent nearly a month..." Jakab/Visions, page 127.
"Wilbur and I could hardly..." Crouch/Bishop's, page 228.
"The boys have finished..." Katharine Wright to Milton Wright, December 7, 1901, Wright/Papers, page 171.
"I believe we possessed in 1902..." Jakab/Visions, page 156.
Note: 1901 glider had a wingspan of 22 feet with the wings measuring seven feet front-to-back (known as the chord) The 1902 glider had wings measuring 32 feet, with a chord of five feet. The 1901 craft had, therefore, a wingspan to chord relationship (known as the aspect ratio) of 3:1; in the 1902 craft, this ratio was 6:1. Additionally, the 1-in-20 camber of the 1902 glider was significantly flatter than the 1-in-12 camber originally used in 1901, and the high point of the 1902 wing was closer to the front. In wing surface area, the two craft were little different: 315 square feet in 1901; 305 square feet in 1902. Figures from Crouch/Bishop's, pages 203 and 235.

74 Addition of fixed rear rudder. Jakab/Visions, page 159.
"All she needs is a coat of feathers..." Kelly/Wrights, page 80.
"Well digging." Jakab/Visions, page 173; Kelly/Wright, page 81.
Solution to "well digging." Kelly/Wright, pages 81-82.

76 "Everything is so much more satisfactory..." Jakab/Visions, page 172.
"The question of equilibrium... " Crouch/Bishop's, page 167.
Wrights' visit to Dayton Public Library. Kelly/Wrights, page 87.
"What at first seemed a simple problem..." Jakab/Visions, page 194.
"Both boys had tempers." Crouch/Bishop's Boys, page 68.

77 "It was apparent that a propeller..." Jakab/Visions, page 194.
Description of propellers. Ibid., page 197.
"We worked out a theory of our own..." Orville Wright to George Spratt, June 7, 1903, Wright/Papers, page 313.
"As with so many aspects of their..." Jakabs/Visions, page 195.
Charlie Taylor background. Author's interview with and review of materials assembled by Howard duFour, New Carlisle, Ohio, long-time student of Charlie Taylor and his work; Crouch/Bishop's, pages 204-205.
Charlie Taylor v. Katharine Wright. Crouch/Bishop's, page 121.

78 "One of us would sketch..." Jakab/Visions, page 190.
Description of engine. Jakab/Visions, page 191, with the assistance of Howard duFour.
"The rain has descended in such torrents..." Orville Wright to Katharine Wright, September 9, 1903, Wright/Papers, pages 356-357.
"4 a.m. effort to repair roof of cabin..." Wilbur Wright to Katharine Wright, October 18, 1903, Wright/Papers, page 367.
October 7, 1903 launch of Aerodrome. Crouch/Bishop's, page 258.

79 "How can he [an aviator] reach the ground..." *The Independent*, October 22, 1903, quoted in Lord/Good Years, page 94.
Departures: Dan Tate, Wright/Papers, page 375; Spratt and Chanute, Crouch/Bishop's, page 259.
"As to absent Will Wright..." Dayton club minutes, 1903.

80 "On arising found ponds around camp frozen ..." Orville Wright's diary,

November 11, 1903, Wright/Papers, page 383.

"In addition to the classification..." Wilbur Wright to Milton and Katharine Wright, November 23, 1903, Wright/Papers, page 383n.

"After six or seven runs of from..." Orville Wright's diary, November 28, 1903, Wright/Papers, page 388.

"An article from a German paper..." Wilbur Wright to Milton and Katharine Wright, November 15, 1903, Wright/Papers, page 382.

Second launch of Langley's Aerodrome. Ibid., page 390n.

"Success assured." Telegram from Wilbur Wright to Bishop Wright, December 12, 1903, Wright/Papers, page 391.

Circumstances of first flight. Jakab/Visions, pages 209-211.

81 "Dayton Boys Emulate..." *Dayton Daily News*, quoted in Kelly/Wright, page 107.

"P.S. Wilbur is 36... " Bishop Milton Wright to Carl Dienstbach, December 22, 1903, Wright/Papers, page 400.

Chapter 9: Mr. Wizard

83 Alfred Sloan car purchase. Alfred P. Sloan (with Boyden Sparkes), *Adventures of a White-Collar Man*, Doubleday, Doran & Company, Inc., 1941, pages 34-35. Hereafter, Sloan/Adventures.

"Humanity never wanted any machine..." Ibid., page 53.

"Experts all agree..." Quoted in James J. Flink, *America Adopts the Automobile*, MIT Press, 1970, page 89. Hereafter, Flink/America.

84 "It is hardly possible to conceive..." Quoted in Lord/Good Years, pages 5-6.

"The man who owns a motorcar..." Quoted in Flink/America, page 64.

"Every factory here... " Ibid., page 294-295.

Durant's new Oldsmobile anecdote. Sloan/Adventures, page 84.

Henry Ford's entry. Flink/America, page 295.

"A race to produce cars..." Sloan/Adventures, page 31.

Henry Leland's engine improvements. Flink/America, page 262, and Maurice C. Hendry, *Cadillac: Standard of the World*, Automobile Quarterly Publication, 1973, page 22. Hereafter, Hendry/Cadillac.

85 Charles Kettering's childhood. Leslie/Kettering, pages 1-6.

X-ray anecdote. Boyd/Professional, pages 24-25.

Kettering's work in Ashland. Boyd/Professional, pages 25-37; Leslie/Kettering, pages 10-15.

Kettering's college years. Boyd/Professional, pages 41-47.

Kettering urged to visit NCR. Isaac F. Marcosson, *Colonel Deeds: Industrial Builder*, Dodd, Mead and Company, 1947, page 87. Hereafter, Marcosson/Deeds.

86 Deeds' ascent of the smokestack. Marcosson/Deeds, pages 72-73.

Invention of OK Credit System. Leslie/Kettering, page 19.

Invention of electric cash register. Ibid., page 22.

"I didn't hang around much..." Boyd/Professional, page 53.

"I think that Ket was worshiped..." UD history/Carl Beust, page 13.

87 "He would come in with an idea..." UD history/Carl Beust, page 9.

Fixing the disabled vehicle. Boyd/Professional, pages 54-55.

Chapter 10: The Apiarist

88 References from *Gleanings in Bee Culture* are from issues of January 1, 1905, and September 15, 1910, reprinted by the A. I. Root Company, Medina, Ohio. Hereafter, Root/Gleanings.

"We want a machine..." Root/Gleanings, October 15, 1904.

"We are told it is hard for women..." Root/Gleanings, January 1, 1905.

"For 32 years, I have been ransacking..." Ibid.

90 "A fool and his money..." and subsequent quotes in same paragraph, Root/Gleanings, January 1, 1904.

"Was just to prove..." UD oral history/Bernard Whelan, page 10.

"In addition to the cattle..." Wilbur Wright to Octave Chanute, June 21, 1904, Kelly/Miracle, pages 130-131.

Accounts of Wright flights. Test flights October 15-November 3, 1904, reported in Wright/Papers, pages 461-463.

91 Presenting aircraft to reporters: Crouch/Bishop's, pages 281-282.

"Plowed along the prairie sod." *Dayton Daily News*, May 27, 1904.

"Was to have made a circle..." Ibid.
"An unqualified success." *Dayton Press*, May 27, 1904.
"'Learned to fly'" Root/Gleanings, January 1, 1905.
"At first we did not know just..." Wright/Papers, page 469.
92 "When it turned that circle..." Root/Gleanings, January 1, 1905.
"Dear Friends..." and all quotes to bottom of page 92. Root/Gleanings, January 1, 1905.
93 "They did not say the passenger..." Root/Gleanings, April 1, 1905.
"When turning a very small circle..." Wilbur to George A. Spratt, September 17, 1905,
Kelly/Miracle, page 147.
Orville and honey locust. Kelly/Wright, pages 131-132.
"When we had discovered..." Wright/Papers, page 520-521.
Flight of October 5: Ibid., page 514.
94 Roosevelt victory flight. Lord/Years, pages 102-103.
Orville would have sold. Wright/Kelly, page 112.
Flight as a colloquialism for impossibility. Kelly/Wright, page 119.
"As many requests have been made..." Major General J. C. Bates to Wilbur Wright,
October 16, 1905, Kelly/Miracle, page 148-149.
"We have no thought of asking..." Wilbur and Orville Wright to President,
Board of Ordnance and Fortification, War Department,
October 19, 1905, Wright/Papers, page 518.
Government "does not care to formulate..." Board of Ordnance to Wilbur and Orville
Wright, October 24, 1905, Kelly/Miracle, page 151-152.
95 "We have no intention of forgetting..." Wilbur Wright to Octave Chanute, June 18, 1905,
Kelly/Miracle, page 144.
"The idea of selling to a single government..." Wilbur Wright to Octave Chanute,
December 27, 1905, Kelly/Miracle, page 162.
"But what we must have..." *The Criterion*, March 1905, page 6.
"Amplified in several very interesting directions." Ibid.
"I enclose a letter..." Octave Chanute to Wilbur Wright, May 23, 1905,
Wright/Papers, page 492.
"Reports would come in to our office..." Cox/Journey, page 83.
"Unfortunately, the Wright brothers..." *Scientific American*, January 13, 1906.

Chapter 11: The Feud

97 "Published in the interests..." Subhead of *NCR Weekly*. $50,000 compensation.
Allyn/Half Century, page 46.
Firing stories. Allyn/Half Century, page 22; Thomas and Marva Belden,
The Life of Thomas J. Watson: The Lengthening Shadow, Little Brown and Co., 1962,
page 83. Hereafter, Belden/Lengthening.
"When a man gets indispensable..." Allyn/Half Century, page 25.
98 One-sixth, hired and fired. Allyn/Half Century, page 26.
"There are just two things..." Crowther/Pioneer, page 76.
"No, I won't explain." Ibid., page 16
"That young man has the most efficient..." Marcosson/Trade, page 88.
"To start clean..." Allyn/Half Century, page 23.
99 "When I began the work..." Tracy/Heart, page 125.
Patterson diet schemes. Crowther/Pioneers, pages 215-216;
Conover/Builders, pages 197-200.
100 Rejection of park land. *Dayton Daily News*, March 4, 1907, page 1.
Railway spur. Conover/Builders, pages 243-244.
"Mr. Patterson stepped lightly..." *Dayton Daily News*, March 4, 1907, page 1.
"Dayton is known..." Ibid., page 1;
"This is a malarious climate..." Ibid., page 10;
"Every man here is a miser..." Ibid., page 1;
"Mr. Patterson at this point..." Ibid., page 10;
"Where people have a higher ambition..." Ibid., page 1;
Patterson's threatened departure. Ibid., page 1.
NCR's departure "a lesson..." *Dayton Journal*, March 8, 1907, page 1.
101 Visits to NCR complex. *Dayton Daily News*, March 5, 1907, page 1.
"And all this money is gathered..." *Dayton Journal*, March 6, 1907.
"It is especially desired..." *Dayton Daily News*, March 5, 1907.
"The object of the N.C.R...." *Dayton Daily News*, March 8, 1907, page 2.
"For eleven years I have appealed to you..." *Dayton Journal*, March 9, 1907.

"If the ministers will preach..." *Dayton Daily News*, March 8, 1907.

"Higher class visitors." *Dayton Journal*, March 9, 1907, page 1.

"Will be the best thing..." *Dayton Daily News*, March 8, 1907, page 1.

102 "IF THE NATIONAL..." *Dayton Daily News*, March 8, 1907, page 1.

"Criticisms, While Apparently..." *Dayton Journal*, March 9, 1907, page 1.

"Mr. Patterson's entire address will convince..." Ibid., page 1.

"Grand Meeting at the Glue Factory." Advertisement, *Dayton Daily News*, March 11, 1907, page 5.

COWARDLY ATTACK... *Dayton Journal*, March 13, 1907, page 1.

103 "As a unit..." Ibid.

James Cox's financial success. Cox/Journey, page 52.

"A man of insignificant personality..." Ibid., page 44.

"Mr. Palmer and I congratulate you." Ibid., page 46.

104 NCR Roughriders. Crowther/Pioneer, page 221.

"Probably nothing like this..." Ibid., page 221.

"We ought not to have a man like that... " Marcosson/Deeds, page 90.

Palmer v. Chalmers. Rodgers/Think, page 49.

"Behind the resignation of Hugh Chalmers..." Cox/Journey, page 46.

Closure of NCR, rallies against Cox. Rodgers/Think, pages 49-50.

"The simple rules of health and exercise..." Ibid., page 50.

Cox and his banker. Cox/Journey, page 45.

105 Patterson and riflemen. Cox/Journey, page 44.

Depositions and Patterson's disappearance. Ibid., pages 48-49

"This was a surprise to Patterson's attorneys..." Ibid., page 49.

"If his attack... " Ibid.

"I will not be even with the old man..." Belden/Lengthening, page 69.

"About the most amusing thing..." Wilbur Wright to Katharine Wright, October 13, 1907, Kelly/Miracle, page 239.

106 "Although we are not now..." Wilbur Wright to Barnum & Bailey, March 1, 1907, Kelly/Miracle, page 196.

"If it were indeed true that others..." Wilbur Wright to Octave Chanute, October 10, 1906, Kelly/Miracle, pages 180-181.

107 Chanute spilling beans. Gibbs-Smith/Invention, pages 54-55.

"There was not one pioneer..." Ibid., page 59.

"The famous Wright brothers may today claim..." Crouch/Bishop's, 345.

Ferman wins Prix Deutsch-Archdeacon. Gibbs-Smith/Invention, page 86.

Chapter 12: The Summer of 1908

109 Kettering: 99 percent of automobiles. Kettering/Prophet, page 158.

Patterson's cleaning crews. W. H. Tolman, *Temple of Hygiene*, International Congress of Hygiene and Demography, Washington, D.C., page 21.

110 "There is one reason for this..." From *Harper's Weekly*, 1907, quoted in Flink/America, page 50.

"Extravagance is reckless... " quoted in *Horseless Age*, Flink/America, page 103.

"There is a river of gold..." Marcosson/Deeds, page 114.

Deeds' barn description. Author's visit.

Work on ignition system Leslie/Boss Kettering, pages 39-50

111 Deeds' approach to Cadillac. Leslie/Boss Kettering, page 41.

Leland's first Dewar's Cup. Hendry/Cadillac, page 49-51.

Subcontracting of ignition system. Ibid., page 83.

Incorporation of Delco. Boyd/Professional, page 64.

"Advertisement and Specification..." Crouch/Bishop's page 347.

112 "In the excitement of this first flight..." Byron Newton, *Aeronautics*, June 1908, quoted in Crouch/Bishop's, page 357.

Wilbur's flying in France. Crouch/Bishop's, pages 366-370; Gibbs-Smith/Invention, pages 147-150.

Wilbur Wright to Orville Wright, "Last Sunday I took the machine..." Wilbur to Orville, August 15, 1908, Kelly/Miracle, page 292.

"We are as children compared with..." Gibbs-Smith/Wright, page 18.

"All accounts... " From *The Times*, London, August 10, 1908, quoted in Gibbs-Smith/Invention, page 147.

114 "Queen Margherita of Italy was in the crowd..." Wilbur Wright to Orville, October 9, 1908, Kelly/Miracle, page 323.

"I advise you most earnestly..." Wilbur Wright to Orville Wright, August 25, 1908,

Kelly/Miracle, page 297.
"Air of perfect confidence." Orville Wright to Katharine Wright, August 31, 1908,
Kelly/Miracle, page 301.
Orville's flying at Fort Myer. Crouch/Bishop's, pages 373-375;
Gibbs-Smith/Invention, pages 153-154.
Orville's crash, Selfridge's death. Kelly/Miracle, pages 315-317;
Crouch/Bishop's, page 347.
Cox, on Hanley's influence. Cox/Journey, page 57.

115 *Daily News* bank-like building. Cox/Journey, page 52.
William Jennings Bryan. Cebula/Cox, page 30.
Cox and pension bills. *The Independent*, September 18, 1920, page 327.
"It's the high cost of living..." Cox/Journey, pages 60-61.
116 New Dayton post office. Cox/Journey, page 66.
Cox's general record in Congress. Cebula/Cox, pages 34-36.
"And by Gad, you know they all stood up." Cox/Journey, page 65.
"As the House, in its usual..." Cox/Journey, page 82.
117 "Seconds grew into minutes..." Cox/Journey, page 83.
Wilbur's smile. Crouch/Bishop's, page 398.

Chapter 13: Before the Flood

119 Samaritan at Belle Island bridge. Cited in Hendry/Cadillac, page 84;
Marcosson/Deeds, page 125-126; and Boyd/Professional, page 68.
"Required the strength of Sampson..." Marcosson/Deeds, page 125.
"The Cadillac car will kill no more men..." Hendry/Cadillac, page 84.
"No woman is physically fit..." Lord/Good Years, page 275.
Background on starting. Hendry/Cadillac, pages 84-87; Leslie/Kettering, page 46.
120 Kettering's work on self-starter, including Hendry/Cadillac, pages 80-90;
History of Starting, Lighting & Ignition System, no author given,
on file at the Kettering-Moraine Museum, Kettering, Ohio.
"I made some calculations..." A. E. Roach, *Ket: America's Best-Loved Inventor*,
unpublished and unpagenated manuscript on file with Montgomery County
Historical Society. Hereafter, Roach/Ket.
Mechanical advantage of 18:1. Given in Robert B. Habingreither, *A Case Study of the First
Commercially Successful Electric Self-Starting System*, Ph.D. dissertation,
West Virginia University, 1978, as 18.6:1. Hendry/Cadillac reports a Cadillac engineer's
recollection that mechanical advantage was 20:1 or 25:1.
Switching mechanism. Leslie/Kettering, page 47.
Voltage regulation. Hendry/Cadillac, page 89.
121 "We didn't know anything about 5 p.m...." Boyd/Professional, page 70.
"'When You and I Were Young, Maggie'." Ibid..
Rebuild of self-starter. Leslie/Kettering, page 49;
Kettering testing automobile. Boyd/Professional, page 72.
122 First production plant/first salesman. Leslie/Kettering, page 51.
"Mr. Ford, that is something..." Boyd/Professional, page 134.
Employment at Delco. Leslie/Kettering, page 60.
"Very plain notice." Root/Gleanings, September 15, 1910, page 602.
"Ice cream wagon came..." Ibid., page 602.
123 "One of the students took a seat..." Root/Gleaning., page 602.
"And Mr. Wright was plainly visible..." UD oral history/Bernard Whelan, page 1.
"It was the only thing..." Ibid., page 2-3.
'Hap' Arnold's flight training. Crouch/Bishop's, page 437.
"I heard him say..." UD oral history/Bernard Whelan, pages 4-5.
124 "I might mention that there has been some criticism..." Root/Gleanings,
September 15, 1910, page 603.
"Asked me my experience..." UD oral history/Fred Kreusch, pages 1-2.
"I always addressed them as Mr. Wright..." UD oral history/Fred Kreusch, page 16.
125 "About a pound box of chocolates..." UD oral history/Tom Russell, page 31.
"Orville wasn't as sober as... " Ibid., page 68.
"I used to say he could see through..." Ibid., page 39.
"Orville was there..." UD oral history/William Conover, page 2.
Patent wars. See Crouch/Bishop's, pages 411-423 and 456-467.
Exhibitions of Claude Grahame-White. Crouch/Bishop's, page 414.
"Personally, I do not think..." Ibid., page 419.

"It is our view that morally..." Ibid., page 419.
Accounts of Curtiss' flights. Ibid., page 425.
126 "There wasn't anyone there..." Crouch/Bishop's, page 429.
"I says, 'I understand...'" UD oral history/Tom Russell, page 6.
Hoxsey and Johnstone on Long Island. Ibid., page 51. For information on their deaths,
see Crouch/Bishop's, pages 433-434.
Results from Reims. Ibid., pages 403-404.
127 "During the past three months..." Crouch/Bishop's, page 440.
"When we think what we might..." Ibid., page 447.
"Thus freshly alerted and inspired..." Gibbs-Smith/Invention, page xv.
Wilbur's final illness. Crouch/Bishop's, pages 447-449.
128 "A short life,..." Crouch/Bishop's, page 449.
Coverage of Wilbur Wright's funeral. *Dayton Daily News*, June 1, 1912, page 1;
Dayton Journal, June 2, 1912, page 1.
"One of [!] the foremost men..." Hiram Maxim, *Dayton Daily News*, June 1, 1912.
Philip Parmalee's death. *Dayton Journal*, June 2, 1912, page 1.
Dayton cash registers; street cars. *Dayton Daily News*, June 1, 1912, page 4.
"If there be a domineering..." *Dayton Daily News*, May 30, 1912, page 1.
"The only organization of which the decedent..." *Dayton Journal*, June 1, 1912, page 1
129 "The youngest member of our club is gone..." Dayton club minutes, special meeting,
May 31, 1912.
Cox as pallbearer. Cox/Journey, page 86.
Cox 1910 re-election. Cebula/Cox, page 35.
Johnson and Jones mayoralties. Warner/Progressivism, pages 24-32 and pages 71-72;
George W. Knepper, *Ohio and Its People*, Kent State University Press, 1989, pages 328-332.
Hereafter, Knepper/Ohio.
"I am elected in spite of..." Warner/Progressivism, page 26.
130 "His chances of re-election were determined..." Cox/Journey, page 159.
McMahon background. Cox/Journey, pages 74-75.
Patterson and McMahon. Cebula/Cox, page 79. McMahon placed Cox's name in
nomination at the 1912 state Democratic convention; for his remarks, see Cox/Journey,
page 127.
"It had been the dream of McMahon's..." *The Outlook*, September 29, 1920, page 193.
1911 constitutional convention. Warner/Progressivism, pages 326-338;
Knepper/Ohio, pages 333-335.
131 Thirty-four of forty amendments approved. Warner/Progessivism, pages 341-342.
Cox's election as governor. Vote: Cox (D) 439,323; Brown (R) 272,500; Garford [P] 217,903;
Ruthenberg [S] 87,709; *Ohio Almanac*, edited by Damaine Vonada,
Orange Frazer Press, 1992, page 119. Hereafter, Vonada/Almanac.
Post-election dinner in Dayton. *Dayton Daily News*, November 26, 1912, page 1.
"The business men..." *The Outlook*, September 29, 1920, page 193.
"Why you are only a boy..." Rev. W. A. Hale, *Dayton Daily News*,
November 26, 1912, page 11.
"I have no false notions..." Ibid., page 11.
Cox's reform package. James Cox, "Inaugural Address to Ohio Legislature,"
January 13, 1913; published in James K. Mercer, *Ohio Legislative History*;
Cox legislative proposals summarized in Warner/Progressivism, page 391.
132 Legislative composition. Warner/Progressivism, page 387.
"To the logical exactness..." *The Outlook*, September 29, 1920, page 195.
"The governor has the rare..." Warner/Progressivism, page 428.
"Subject to the hazards of business." Cox/Inaugural, page 37.
Cox tax measures. Warner/Progressivism, pages 429-430; Cox/Inaugural, pages 33-34.
Cox and workmen's compensation. Cox/Journey, page 138-140;
and Cox/Inaugural, pages 35-37.
Workman killed in vat. Cox/Journey, page 140.
133 Workman dragging himself across state line. Cox/Journey, page 142.
"When he told the inmates..." Warner/Progressivism, page 432.
Cox and organized labor. Cebula/Cox, page 48.
McMahon defending Patterson. *Dayton Journal Herald*, November 11, 1912.
134 "Divinely inspired..." Conover/Builders, page 225.
"The best way to kill a dog..." Belden/Lengthening, page 30.
Patterson's knocker organization... Rodgers/Think, pages 36, 40-45.
"Men especially trained in persuasion..." Ibid., page 35.
List of failed cash register concerns. Ibid., page 57.

135 "If a patent is granted to the Lamson..." Rodgers/Think, page 44.
    "In case we desire to re-enter..." Ibid., page 58
    Indictment. Belden/Lengthening, page 66; Marcosson/Wherever, page 102.
    Accounts of trial. From Rodgers/Think, pages 53, 57 and 60; Lengthening/pages 69-70;
    Dayton Journal Herald, November 19, 21, 22, 23, 28, December 1, 3, 4, 11, 13, 18 and 21,
    1912; January 8, 16, 18, 24.
    Former sales agent for American Cash Register. *Dayton Journal Herald*,
    December 13, 1912.
136 "Committed no greater wrong..." *Dayton Daily News*, February 15, 1913, page 4.
    Verdict. *Dayton Daily News*, Friday, February 14, 1913, page 1.
    Judge Hollister's comments. *Cincinnati Enquirer*, February 18, page 10.
137 McMahon: "astounding." *Cincinnati Enquirer*, February 18, 1913, page 10.
    "The self-possession and coolness... " *Cincinnati Enquirer*, February 18, 1913, page 10.

Chapter 14: Flood

139 "It seemed as if the windows..." Quoted in Morgan/Conservancy, page 13.
    "I apprehended a flood." Diary of Bishop Milton Wright, March 24, 1913.
    Wright/Papers, page 1060.
    River configuration. Arthur Ruhl, *The Outlook*, April 12, 1913, page 806.
    Hereafter, Ruhl/Outlook.
140 Patterson visit to river. Allan W. Eckert, A Time of Terror, Little, Brown and Co., 1965, page 35.
    Hereafter, Eckert/Terror.
    Emergency meeting at NCR. Ibid., pages 61-63.
141 "Suddenly... the levee fifty feet..." Quoted from *New York Tribute*, April 6, 1913,
    in Morgan/Conservancy, pages 16-17.
    Flooding of Delco. *Being a story of the great flood as seen from Delco factory*,
    no author listed, Delco, 1913, page 13. Hereafter, Delco/Flood.
    "I had a buck-board..." Quoted in Leslie/Kettering, pages 53-54.
    Cox hears news; telephone service ends. Cox/Journey, page 166.
142 "Unbelievable was the rapidity..." and "It seemed to me that..."
    Quoted from *Dayton Daily News*, April 5, 1913 in Morgan/Conservancy, page 21.
    "Before noon on Tuesday..." Quoted from *Troy [Ohio] Democrat*, April 3, 1913,
    in Morgan/Conservancy, page 18.
    1,400 horses died. *Dayton Daily News* 'The Great Flood' supplement, March 25, 1988, page
    3. Hereafter, News/supplement.
    Rescue by telegraph line. From accounts of flood, Morgan/Conservancy, page 32.
    Man chops way out of attic. Ibid., page 23.
143 Adams family escape. Presentation by Charles Adams, Dayton Engineers' Club, March 25, 1993.
    Hereafter, Adams/Talk.
    Wrights' departure. Crouch/Bishop's Boys, page 452; Orville Wright to Griffith Brewer,
    April 22, 1913, Wright/Papers, pages 397-398. Bishop Wright's rescue by neighbor,
    reported in his diary for March 25, 1913, Wright/Papers, 1060.
    Women battle blaze at candy factory. From accounts of flood,
    Morgan/Conservancy, page 46.
    "My Sunday school teacher always talked..." Dayton resident Kathryn Blakesly,
    quoted in News/supplement, page 3.
    Orville's fears of loss. Orville Wright to Andrew Freedman, April 11,1913,
    Wright/Papers, page 1061.
    "Mother called to us, 'Boys,...'" Dayton resident Rodney Miller,
    quoted in *Daily News*/Anniversary, page 23.
144 "Dayton, O., Engulfed..." *New York Times*, March 26, 1913, page 1.
    "There is duplicated in varying degrees..." *Albany Times-Union*, March 26, 1913,
    reprinted in *Daily News*/Anniversary, page 11.
    NCR rowboats; relief efforts. Eckert/Terror, page 169; Morgan/Conservancy, page 31.
    Relief efforts. Morgan/Conservancy, pages 62-73; Delco/Flood, page 7-11.
145 "To step from the silent sodden..." Ruhl/Overlook, page 808.
    Childbirths. Eckert/Terror, page 207.
    Escape from Beckel Hotel. Quoted from *Troy [Ohio] Democrat* in Morgan/Conservancy,
    pages 19-20.
    Delco supply line. Delco/Flood, pages 13-14.
146 Mr. Adams clings to tree. Adams/Talk.
    "Our children advertise for me." Bishop Wright's diary for March 26, 1913,
    Wright/Papers, page 1060.

"DAYTON CUT OFF FROM WORLD." Headline of *NCR Weekly*, March 26, 1913.
"The worst calamity that has ever befallen..." James Cox telegram to *New York Times*, March 27, 1913, page 1.
"Full authority to act for..." Eckert/Terror, page 221.
"All orders signed by Mr. Patterson..." Morgan/Conservancy, page 76.
Patterson's guests at Far Hills. Conover/Builders, page 296

147 "Situation here is desperate." Patterson to *New York Times*, telegram dated March 27, 1913; reprinted in Morgan/Conservancy, page 25.
NCR relief trains. Morgan/Conservancy, page 64.
Relief effort, northwest. Ibid., pages 64-67.
"W. G. Sloan, the well-known colored..." *Dayton Journal*, April 7, 1913, quoted in Morgan/Conservancy, page 39.
"A relief train from Detroit..." Quoted in Morgan/Conservancy, page 64.

148 Patterson's guests at Far Hills. Conover/Builders, pages 262-263.
"Newspaper reporters, shot off..." Ruhl/Outlook, page 809.
Ben Hecht in Dayton. Ben Hecht, *Child of the Century*, Donald I. Fien, Inc., 1954, pages 192-197.
NCR center of press coverage. Morgan/Conservancy, page 75-76.

149 "What Dayton might have done..." Ruhl/Outlook, page 808.
"The wreckage in some cases reached..." Conover/Builders, page 263.
"I have calculated..." Quoted in Morgan/Conservancy, page 61.
Cleanup efforts. Morgan/Conservancy, page 139.
Largest number of people formally engaged in clean-up work was 4,565.
Dayton Bicycle Club. Morgan/Conservancy, page 89.

150 "Dad worked outside..." Adams/Talk.
Disappearing sugar. Ruhl/Outlook, page 806.
232 cities sent aid; Pennsylvania RR. Morgan/Conservancy, page 87.
Offer from Bartenders' League. Morgan/Conservancy, page 71.
"So thickly covered with slimy mud..." Delco/Flood, page 15.
Kettering to Ahrens-Fox. Delco/Flood, page 15.

151 Press delivered to *Daily News*. Cox/Journey, page 170; *The Outlook*, September 22, 1920, page 144.
"The remarkable capacity of the human..." Cox/Journey, page 166.
"My personal losses have been slight..." Orville Wright to Andrew Freedman, April 11, 1913, Wright/Papers, page 1061.
"I walked home after dinner." Diary of Milton Wright, April 5, 1913, Wright/Papers, page 1060.
Cox appointment of Patterson. Eckert/Terror, page 221.
Telegram sent Wednesday, March 26, 10:55 a.m.
"I do not suppose there has ever been..." Orville Wright to Andrew Freedman, April 11, 1913, Wright/Papers, page 1061.
Cox appoints Patterson colonel. Morgan/Conservancy, page 102.

152 "Mr. Patterson may technically be a convict..." *Chattanooga Times*, March 30, 1913.
"I make haste to assure you..." Belden/Lengthening, page 81.
Telegram destroyed in New York. Rodgers/Think, page 63.

Chapter 15: The Seed Man

155 "No work that could have been constructed..." Delco/Flood, page 3.
Morgan: insurgent v. incumbent. Author's interview with Lee Morgan.

156 Arthur Morgan's childhood. Talbert/Utopian, pages 8-11; author's interviews with Ernest Morgan, Lee Morgan.
Morgan's trip to Minneapolis. Arthur Morgan, *The Making of the TVA*, Prometheus Books, page 43. Hereafter, Morgan/TVA.
"My friends and Sunday School teachers..." Arthur Morgan to Ernest Morgan, December 25, 1907. Antioch archives.
Adolescent reading. Reading list on file, Antioch archives.
"Gave us our minds to use..." Arthur Morgan to Ernest Morgan, December 25, 1907. Antioch archives.

157 "Whittling their lives away..." 1898 Morgan letter to home, on file with Morgan letters, Antiochiana, Antioch College. Hereafter, Antioch archives.
"In its essential character..." Morgan/Standard, 13.
Morgan quits lumbering job. Morgan/TVA, page 44.
"John Morgan taught his son..." Roy Talbert Jr., *FDR's Utopian*,

University Press of Mississippi, 1987, page 22. Hereafter, Talbert/Utopian.
Morgan joins Dept. of Agriculture. Talbert/Utopian, page 25.
158 "Your duty is not..." Arthur Morgan to Ernest Morgan, December 25, 1907,
Antioch archives.
"The long climb of the race..." Arthur Morgan essay,
"A New Moral Standard for American Business," 1912, page 13, Antioch archives.
The Seed Man. Arthur Morgan, *Antioch Press*, 1934.
Refuses to leave position. Morgan/TVA, page 46.
Everglades; congressional investigation. Talbert/Utopian, pages 33-34.
159 Morgan's second marriage. Talbert/Utopian, page 27.

Chapter 16: The Conservancy

161 Morgan's summons to Dayton. Morgan/Conservancy, page 151.
"To an engineer who usually found..." Ibid., page 141.
Hanley's recommendation to hire a professional. Ibid., page 152.
162 "A peculiar combination..." Morgan/Conservancy, page 75.
Final fundraising event. Conover/Builders, pages 266-267;
Morgan/Conservancy, pages 138-139;
163 "We want, we want,...?" *Dayton Daily News*, May 26, 1913, page 1.
"When the head of the parade..." *Dayton Journal*, March 27, 1913.
"There can be found no finer..." Cecelia Tichi, *Shifting Gears*,
University of North Carolina Press, 1987, page 121. Hereafter, Tichi/Shifting.
"There are more and more people..." Ibid., page 67.
164 "Every day you hear people say..." August 13, 1913 letter to *Dayton Journal*,
quoted in Morgan/Conservancy, page 155.
"Is the mechanical result..." *Scientific American*, January 1915,
quoted in Morgan/Conservancy, page 215.
Great Miami v. Seine. Morgan/Conservancy, page 164.
Storm Rainfall in the Eastern United States, 352-page report,
described in Morgan/Conservancy, 356-358; Marcosson/Industrial, page 186.
Recruitment for Conservancy. Morgan/Conservancy, page 277.
165 Flood flow of Danube and Tiber. Ibid., pages 357-358.
"Every possibility for solution..." Morgan/Conservancy, page 284.
Explanation of dry dams. Ibid., page 171.
"The rare combination of great need..." Morgan/Conservancy, page 165.
166 Ohio Conservancy Act. Marcosson/Deeds, 156; Morgan/Conservancy, page 176-183.
"Drown Us First." Marcosson/Industrial, page 171.
"More despotic and drastic..." Quoted in Morgan/Conservancy, page 195.
"Who called Mr. Morgan into the deal?" *Troy Daily News*, January 22, 1914,
reprinted in Morgan/Conservancy, page 196.
Alternate proposals. Ibid., pages 210-211.
Deeds on behalf of the Conservancy Act. Marcosson/Deeds, pages 162-169;
Morgan/Conservancy, page 143.
167 "Oh Jimmy Cox, my Joe Jim." Marcosson/Industrial, page 172.
"I shall carry Ohio this fall..." James Cox to William Jennings Bryan, April 7, 1914,
page 2, Wright State University archives.
"Four thousand unworthy characters..." Ibid., page 2.
"Had been turned over to Socialism..." Ibid., page 1.
168 Bryan's visit; newspaper support. Warner/Progressivism, pages 474-475.
"A jovial fellow, big in heart..." Cox/Journey, page 180.
"It's a time of unrest...?" James Cox' speech of acceptance, *Dayton Daily News*,
June 7, 1912, page 1.
"Efficient business organization..." Cebula/Cox, page 64.
Cox rejects endorsement of women's suffrage and the eight-hour day,
Cebula/Cox, page 154.
"Think of it — 300 bills enacted..." *Ohio State Journal*,
quoted in Warner/Progressivism, page 411.
"Every saloon in Ohio..." James Cox to William Jennings Bryan,
September 27, 1914, page 1, Wright State University archives.
"They double-crossed you..." William Jennings Bryan to James Cox,
November 13, 1914. Archives, Wright State University.
1914 Election results: Willis (R) 523,074; Cox (D) 493,804; Garfield (P) 60,904;
Wilkins (S) 51,441. Vonada/Almanac, page 119.

"Most of those in opposition..." Cox/Journey, page 185.
Deeds' defense of Conservancy Act. Marcosson/Deeds, page 179;
Morgan/Conservancy, pages 198-200 and 216-220.
169 Legislature sustains Conservancy Act. Morgan/Conservancy, page 220.
Cox's aide credits Deeds. Marcosson/Builder, page 179.
Constitutionality of Conservancy Act. Morgan/Conservancy, page 223.
Deeds' gift of headquarters. Marcosson/Builder, page 180.
Hydraulic jump at Deeds' farm. Marcosson/Industrial, pages 196-197; Carl Becker and
Patrick Nolan, *Keeping the Promise*, Miami Conservancy District, 1988, pages 123-124.
170 "Before it was apparent to everyone..." Morgan/Conservancy, page 239.
"During the five days..." Ibid., page 239.
"Morgan Admits Dams May Fail." Ibid., page 247.
Cox candidacy to aid Wilson. Cebula/Cox, page 102.
1916 election results: Cox (D) 568,218; Willis (R) 561,602; Clifford (S) 36,908.
Vonada/Almanac, page 119.
Donations to Cox campaign fund. Sharts/Biography, page 121.
"In explanation it was stated..." Morgan/Conservancy, page 413.
Overturn of Patterson's acquittal. 'Patterson et al v. United States,'
Circuit Court of Appeals, Sixth Circuit, March 13, 1915.
171 *Saturday Evening Post* ad. Conover/Builders, page 218.
"If business was not good..." Ibid., 218.
"One of them got me into this mess." Allyn/Half Century, page 41.

Chapter 17: At Home

173 The Wright's patent suits. An involved subject; see Crouch/Bishop's, pages 411-423
and, for Curtiss decision, pages 460-461.
Sale of Wright company. Ibid., pages 465-466.
174 Description of Hawthorn Hill. Crouch/Bishop's, pages 476-478;
author's inspection, November 23, 1992.
"It's a beautiful home inside". UD history/James Wilbur Jacobs, page 29.
Suffragettes march. UD history/Ivonette Wright Miller, page 9.
Relationship of Orville and Katharine. Ibid., page 9.
Death of Bishop Wright, Crouch/Bishop, pages 479-480
Description of Ridgeleigh Terrace. Leslie/Kettering, pages 65-66; and brochures
published by the home's current owner, Kettering Memorial Hospital, Dayton, Ohio.
175 Kettering's trick shooting. Leslie/Kettering, page 29.
"Practically wear his partner out." Author's interview Dr. Sam Gould.
"Don't think he ever..." Author's interview with Dr. Algo Henderson.
"Now, Ginny..." Author's interview with Virginia Kettering.
Description of Trailsend. Cox/Journey, page 227; and Allan Nevins,
"Not Capulets, Not Montagus," *American Historical Review*, January 1960.
176 Cox's first wife. Author's interviews with *Daily News* staff members; Cebula/Cox, page 67.
Cox's second wife. Cebula/Cox, page 67; author's interview with Fred Robbins.
"He didn't pay well." Author's interview with Fred Robbins, August 18, 1993.
Reston as Cox's caddy. Cox/Journey, page 443.
Founding of Dayton Engineers' Club. Leslie/Kettering pages 66-67. Description of inside
of club from author's interview with early employee, Charles Hoffman. Author's visit.
Monthly speakers, including Herman Schneider. John H. Paul,
A History of the [Dayton] Engineers' Club, 1943, pages 6-8.
Early members. Paul/Engineers, page 43.
Dedication of Engineers' Club. Paul/Engineers, page 9 and 11-12; and event program,
"Opening of the New Building," February 2, 1918, printed by the Dayton Engineers' Club.
Non-washing of tablecloths. Author's interview with Jim Custer.
177 "The schoolhouse has received..." Arthur Morgan, "Education: The Mastery of the Arts of Life,"
Atlantic Monthly, May 1922, page 340. Hereafter, Morgan/Atlantic.
Comments on the Morgans. Author's interviews with Xarifa Bean, Otto Matthieson,
Joan Horn, Lee Morgan, Ernest Morgan.
"People in Englewood thought the Conservancy..." Author's interview with Ernest
Morgan.
Founding of Moraine Park School. Leslie/Kettering, page 62; Directors. Moraine Park
School annual, 1918, page 3. On file in Morgan Papers, Antiochiana, Antioch College.
Hereafter, Moraine/Annual.
178 "My first impression as he entered the room..." All comments are from Arthur Morgan's trip

notes, December 1916, Antioch archives.
"The object of education is not primarily..." Arthur Morgan,
An Experiment in Educational Engineering, 1917, page 1,
Morgan Archives, Antiochiana, Antioch College. Hereafter, Morgan/Experiment.
Curriculum notes. Moraine/Annual, pages 14-15; Morgan/Atlantic, page 344.
"A coach, his assistants, and the physically favored few... "
Report of student Anthony Haswell, Moraine/Annual, page 30.
179 "We loved it. Later, with college,..."
Author's interview with Virginia Kettering, October 21, 1988.
"As tools to live and work with..." Morgan/Experiment, page 2.
"I feel we are neglecting the fundamentals..." Charles Kettering to Frank D. Slutz, quoted
in Leslie/Kettering, page 65; additional similar comments, Boyd/Professional, page 90.
Pre-wedding encounter. Author's interview with Virginia Kettering.

Chapter 18: The Innocents

181 "A great loss..." Dayton club minutes, 1913.
"Presumably on account of the fact..." Dayton club minutes, 1915.
182 "Or otherwise tied up by..." Dayton club minutes, 1917.
"Don't shout for war unless..." James H. Perkins, *Dayton During World War I*,
Miami University thesis, 1959, page 32. Hereafter, Perkins/WWI.
Gross-Daytoner Zeitung sold German war bonds. Ibid., page 29.
"Nor is a victory by Germany..." *Dayton Daily News*, November 7, 1915,
quoted in *The Outlook*, July 28, 1920, page 560.
"The crime of all the ages..." Ibid..
First conscription. Perkins/WWI, page 59.
Draftees, departure from Dayton. Ibid., page 60.
Morgan and Wright scout airfield. Morgan/Conservancy, page 353-354.
184 "The army spirit is cynical... " Arthur Morgan, notes titled 'For and Against Peace,' page 5,
Antioch archives.
League to Enforce the Peace. A. Lawrence Lowell, *A League to Enforce Peace*,
World Peace Foundation, 1915.
"There have been several criticisms..." Edward Deeds to Arthur Morgan
February 27, 1918, Antioch archives.
Sales of Conservancy bonds. Marcosson/Deeds, page 203;
Morgan/Conservancy, page 344.
Wartime involvements of Dayton Ten. Dayton club minutes, 1917 & 1918.
185 Patterson sits out the war. Allyn/Half Century, page 46.
"These men are extraordinarily good businessmen..."
Orville Wright to Glenn L. Martin, May 19, 1917, Wright/Papers, pages 1101-1102.
"When my brother and I built and flew..." Orville Wright to C. M. Hitchcock,
June 21, 1917, Wright/papers, pages 1104-1105.
"Are apparently nearly equal in aerial equipment ..." Ibid., 1005.
"If the Allies' armies are equipped..." Orville Wright to C. M. Hitchcock, June 21, 1917,
Wright/Papers, page 1105.
186 U.S pre-war aviation. Marcosson/Industrial, page 225.
Deeds as chief of aircraft procurement. Marcosson/Industrial, page 221.
"It was much easier than at first..." Leslie/Kettering, page 73.
"Was to prevent more changes being made." Orville Wright's testimony,
Hughes Aircraft Investigation, October 3, 1918, Wright/Papers, page 1118.
"It was built completely by hand..." UD oral history/Ernest Dubel, page 29-30.
187 Winter of 1917-1918. Perkins/WWI, page 73-74.
Seizure of coal at Lake Erie. Cebula/Cox, page 75.
Fort Sherman construction. Ibid., page 74.
"How the red clay flew..." Ibid., page 80.
Conservancy construction. Summary in Morgan/Conservancy, 364-365;
188 "The nearest railroad line..." Becker/Promises, page 7.
"All right, get you a blanket..." Morgan/TVA, page 119.
"This human wreckage was part..." Morgan/Conservancy, page 387.
Conservancy camps. Morgan/Conservancy, pages 386-387;
Becker/Promises, pages 131-132, 135; Talbert/Utopian, page 37.
189 Investigation of Deeds. Leslie/Kettering, pages 74-75; Marcosson/Deeds, pages 272-283.
Borglund's participation. Marcosson/Deeds, pages 255-266; see also,
John K. Barnes, "The Vindication of Squier and Deeds," 'World's Work,' July 1921.

Kettering and the "bug." Leslie/Kettering, pages 80-87.
"Walked out of his office..." UD oral history/John Wright, page 5.
Description of bug. Ibid., page 2.
190 "By pinching pieces..." Boyd/Professional, page 107.
"The ship went up about 500 feet..." C. H. Willis to Elmer Sperry, October 1918,
quoted in Leslie/Kettering, page 84.
191 Unfavorable Army report on "bug." Leslie/Kettering, page 86.
James Cox 1918 re-election. 1918 vote for Ohio governor: Cox (D) 486,403;
Willis (R) 474,459. Vonada/Almanac, page 119.
"The treasurer reported a balance..." Dayton club minutes, 1918.

Chapter 19: A Study in Limits

193 "We need to move to a more liberal candidate or a less expensive hotel."
Attributed to chairman of Alabama delegation at 1924 Democratic convention,
which went 103 ballots before nominating John W. Davis.
Background to 1920 Democratic convention. James McGregor Burns,
Roosevelt: The Lion and the Fox, Harcourt, Brace, Jovanovich, Inc., 1956, pages 72-73.
Hereafter, Burns/Roosevelt. Arthur M. Schlesinger, Jr., *Age of Roosevelt*, Volume 1,
Houghton Mifflin, 1957,
pages 361-362. Hereafter, Schlesinger/Roosevelt. Cox/Journey, pages 225-226.
194 "Many delegates were perfectly willing..." *The Nation*, July 17, 1920.
Literary Digest poll. A then highly regarded mail-in poll, published June 12, 1920,
with these results: William McAdoo, 102,719; Woodrow Wilson, 67,588;
Edward Edwards, 61,393; William Jennings Bryan, 46,448; James Cox, 32,343.
"Every Vote is on the Payroll." Cox/Journey, page 230.
"A quick response of a fine community..." Cox/Journey, page 234.
"Cox is literally confident..." *The Outlook*, September 29, 1920, page 193.
195 "the Marion stonehead,..." H. L. Mencken, *On Politics*, Vintage Books, 1960, page 34.
This is a collection of Mencken's columns on politics, cited here with original
publication date, July 26, 1920. Hereafter, Mencken/Politics (with original date).
"The curious imbecility..." Mencken/Politics, page 22 (September 13, 1920).
"A jovial fellow, big in heart and body..." Cox/Journey, page 180.
"I told him I had given the matter some thought..." Ibid., page 232.
196 "I don't like Roosevelt..." Burns/Roosevelt, page 73.
"No matter what happens in November..." *Literary Digest*, July 17, 1920,
page 12, in article summarizing press comments on the nominees.
"The early millions." *The Outlook*, September 22, 1920, page 143.
"Of medium height, medium weight..." *The Outlook*, September 22, 1920, page 142.
"He makes me think of those twelve-cylinder..."
The Outlook, September 29, 1920, page 195.
197 Cox visit to Wilson and "I am very grateful." Burns/Roosevelt, page 74.For Cox's version,
Cox/Journey, page 239.
"The house of civilization is to be put in order..."
Cox, quoted in *The Independent*, September 18, 1920, page 328.
"I would hopefully approach..." Harding, quoted in *The Independent*,
September 18, 1920, page 329. See also, Republican National Committee advertisement,
The Outlook, October 20, 1920: "With all sympathy for foreign lands in distress and
willingness to help our friends abroad, as the people through the Congress may direct,
these men [Harding and Coolidge] will realize that they have been elected to carry out
the people's will, not their own will or fantasy."
"About as conservative as..." ,
quoted in *Literary Digest*, July 17, 1920, page 13.
"It is a program including..." *The New Republic*, August 18, 1920, page 323.
198 "A campaign fund sufficient..." Cox/Journey, page 239;
Campaign expenditures. Cox/Journey, page 239. Mencken/Politics, page 24
[September 13, 1920]; *New Republic*, September 15, 1920, page 60.
"Nary an illusion." Schlesinger/Roosevelt, page 365.
"Election day brought an overwhelming..." Cox/Journey, page 280.
Note: Election results: Harding (R) 16,152,220; Cox (D) 9,147,553;
House of Representatives, 300 Republicans, 132 Democrats.
1923 World Almanac, Press Publishing, Inc., 193, pages 883-884.
"The mind of the people..." *The Outlook*, November 10, 1920, page 448.
"A candidate for the presidency who..." Nevins/Capulets, page 258.

"A candidate for the presidency who..." Nevins/Capulets, page 258.
"A second-rate provincial," and "a third-rate political wheel-horse" and "flat-headed."
   Mencken/Politics, pages 7 (February 9, 1920), 18 (July 26, 1920), and 27 (October 4, 1920).
"Even a professor of English..." Mencken/Politics, page 19 (July 26, 1920).
"After meditation and prayer..." Mencken/Politics, page 25 (October 4, 1920).
199 "the fellow who is fundamentally a fraud." Ibid., page 25 (October 4, 1920).
"His opinions are always fluent..." Mencken/Politics, page 27 (October 4, 1920).
"Resilient, sneaking, limber, oleaginous..." Ibid.., page 27 (October 4, 1920).
"As it is, the genuine wets..." , Mencken/Politics, page 23. (September 13, 1920)
"Of any actual force and weight..." Mencken/Politics, page 28. (October 4, 1920).
"The fact is amazing, as viewed from..." Cox/Journey, page 247.
   Cox, on Republican tactics. See Cox/Journey, chapter 23,
"The Great Conspiracy," pages 246-263.
200 "Most of those in opposition..." Cox/Journey, page 185.
"His story is that of an agile,..." The Outlook, September 22, 1920, page 142.
"the curious lack of personal devotion..." The Outlook, September 29, 1920, page 195.
201 Kettering taught to fly. Boyd/Professional, page 110.
Kettering's flight with Rinehart. Leslie/Kettering, page 87.
"Throw out a monkey wrench..." Boyd/Professional, page 112.
"Mrs. Kettering paused, smiled..." Ibid., page 10.
Development of the Delco-Light. Ibid., pages 93-95.
202 Delco-Light employees and production, 1918. Leslie/Kettering, page 60.
Sale of Kettering/Deeds assets; Delco: Leslie/Kettering, page 57;
   other holdings: Leslie/Kettering, page 96.
"Mr. Kettering is by far..." Sloan/Years, page 81.
"I told Mr. Sloan that I would take it..." Leslie/Kettering, page 96.
Deeds' career as financier. Marcosson/Industrial, pages 320-321.
203 Kettering's GM stock. Leslie/Kettering, page 207.
"He recognized the problem." Kettering oral history/Carroll Hochwalt.
"Visualize how things ought to go..." Kettering oral history/Fred Hooven.
Engine knock, generally. Major sources include T. A. Boyd,
   The Early History of Ethyl Gasoline, General Motors Corporation, 1943,
   Hereafter, Boyd/Ethyl; Joseph C. Robert, Ethyl: A History of the Corporation and the People
   Who Made It, University Press of Virginia, Hereafter, Robert/Ethyl; Boyd/Professional,
   pages 142-158; and Leslie/Kettering, pages 149-176.
Engine knock: problem defined. Ethyl Corporation 1923-1948, no author listed, pages 5-9;
   Boyd/Ethyl, pages 2-3; Charles F. Kettering, The New Necessity, Williams and Wilkins,
   1932, page 74. Note: U. S. Bureau of Mines, 7/27/1918: "Engineers have therefore believe
   knocking to be the unavoidable result of too high a compression." Boyd/Ethyl, page 25.
204 "This year will see the maximum..." Boyd/Ethyl, page 73.
"The slide rule boys." Author's interview with W. Walker Lewis.
"Intelligent ignorance." Kettering/Prophet, page 238.
"Come in with a pack on his back." Leslie/Kettering, page 150;
   Boyd/Professional, page 101.
205 Trailing arbutus. Boyd/Ethyl, pages 4-5.
Camphor, pennyroyal, citronella. Boyd/Ethyl, page 74.
"A scientific fox hunt." Boyd/Amateur, page 145.
Timeline, December 1984/January 1985, page 11.
"I doubt if humanity, even to doubling..." Boyd/Ethyl, page 76.
Summary of anti-knock work. Ethyl/Summary, page 21.
Note: Work on aniline, Boyd/Ethyl, 38; on selenium oxychloride, Boyd/Ethyl, 83;
   on diethyl telluride, Boyd/Ethyl, 83.
Test engine results. Boyd/Ethyl, page 91.
"There was no getting rid of it..." Ibid., pages 88-89.
"This is to let you know that..." Ibid., page 89.
"A careful analysis will show..." Kettering/Necessity, page 67.
206 "The problem once solved will be simple." Kettering/Prophet, page 95.
Hochwalt synthesizes tetraethyllead. Boyd/Ethyl, page 110.
"Hell, it was 'Eureka.'" Kettering Oral History/Carroll Hochwalt.
Use of bromine additive. Boyd/Ethyl, page 230.
207 First sale of leaded gas. Ibid., page 195.
"ETHYL Gas Antiknock Gasoline..." Boyd/Ethyl, page 196.
"At 10 the first morning not a single sale..." Ibid., page 196.
"His Model T had knocked..." Ethyl Corporation, page 31.

1924 Indianapolis 500. Ibid., page 32.
"By June of 1924 it became apparent..." Boyd/Ethyl, page 241.
"Pumping the Pacific Ocean over..." Leslie/Kettering, page 169.
"Without first concentrating sea water..." Boyd/Ethyl, page 242.
208 *S. S. Ethyl*. Boyd/Ethyl, pages 247-248.
"Many of the chemists and engineers..." Robert/Ethyl, page 114.
Note: to produce tetraethyllead, General Motors and Standard Oil of New Jersey
created the Ethyl Corporation, August 18, 1924, with Kettering as president
and Midgley as second vice president. Boyd/Ethyl, page 257.
"Died in a strait-jacket..." *The New York Times*, October 28, 1924.
"If an automobile using that gas..." Dr. Yandell Henderson,
quoted in *The New York Times*, October 28, 1924.
Hazards of tetraethyllead lead. Boyd/Ethyl, page 271; Robert/Ethyl, page 121-123;
Leslie/Kettering, pages 165-166.
Tests of leaded gas. Boyd/Ethyl, pages 275-278.
"No definite cases have been discovered..." Ibid., page 280.
"Your committee begs to report..." Ibid., page 281. Note: *A Bill of Health for Looney Gas*,
Literary Digest, February 6, 1926.
209 Impact of leaded gasoline. Kettering/Prophet, pages 165-166; *Ethyl Corporation*, page 23.
"Fully confirm the view..." Boyd/Ethyl, page 284
"Every gallon of petroleum taken out of the ground..." Leslie/Kettering, page 175.
210 Photosynthesis research. Leslie/Kettering, pages 322-326.
"I don't know if this is what..." Ibid., page 288.
"This was news to me." George Charles Nelson,
The Morgan Years: Politics of Innovative Change, dissertation, University of Michigan,
1978, page 69. Hereafter, Nelson/Change.
211 "Ashamed to die until you have won..." Words engraved on Horace Mann memorial,
Antioch College, Yellow Springs, Ohio.
"I told my people back at Waltham..." Dr. Thomas Hill to Dr. Henry W. Bellows,
April 17, 1862, Antioch archives.
Antioch pre-1919 history. Burton Clark, *The Distinctive College*, Aldine Publishing,
Hereafter, Clark/Distinctive. Nelson/Change, pages 24-36.
"It so completely educated and exported..." Nelson/Change, page 70.
"I believe it is near enough dead..." Nelson/Change, page 71.
212 "Had very little background or curiosity..." Arthur Morgan, "Education: The Mastery of the Arts
of Life," *Atlantic Monthly*, May 1922, pages 642-650. Hereafter, Morgan/Atlantic.
"We are becoming a nation of specialists..." Ibid.
"So long will fine men be absent..." Ibid.
"Utopias are as essential..." Clark/Distinctive, page 21.
"It would be a community of explorers..." Talbert/Utopian, page 46.
Morgan's plan. For one early version, see "The Reorganization Program for Antioch
College," July 1920, in Harvard Forrest Vallance, *A History of Antioch College*,
pages 464-472, Ph.D. dissertation, Ohio State University, 1936.
Hereafter, Vallance/Antioch.
213 "Was to train entrepreneurs..." Algo Henderson to the author.
"A significant factor..." Clark/Distinctive, page 21.
New trustees. Well detailed by Herr, pages 130, 145-146.
Fund raising. Vallance/History, pages 213-214.
214 "Heartily in favor of the Antioch idea..." Newman/Change, page 100.
Stories on Antioch *The Nation*, *The New Republic*, *School and Society*, *World's Work*, *Scientific
American*, and *Leslie's*; mentioned in Clark/Distinctive, pages 31-32.
Progressive Education Association. Talbert/Utopian, pages 43-44.
Meeting in Dayton, April 8-9, 1921 is described in Herr, pages 176-177.
"The ideal man was one who..." Clark/Distinctive, page 25.
"I thought he'd ask me..." Author's interview with J. D. Dawson.
"We got off the train..." Author's interview with Algo Henderson.
215 Bronze factory. Ibid.
Entrepreneurial activities. Author's interview with Ernest Morgan, Xarifa Bean;
Herr, page 291.
"I couldn't imagine..." Author's interview with J. D. Dawson.
"The most pervasive feeling..." Author's interview with Xarifa Bean.
Expansion under Morgan. Clark/Distinctive, pages 25, 27-30.
"There was a complete new spirit..." Author's interview with Algo Henderson.
Note: Ellery Sedgwick, in the *New York Evening Post*, October 15, 1923, wrote:

of the independence of the individual." Herr/279.
"I felt I'd reached utopia..." Author's interview with J. D. Dawson.
Antioch finances; Kettering loans. Newman/Change, pages 101-102.
216 "You didn't speak to except..." Author's interview with Xarifa Bean.
Profile of Lucy Griscom Morgan. Author's interviews with Xarifa Bean,
Algo Henderson, Otto Mathiasen.
"Tolerant of laziness..." Author's interview with Xarifa Bean.
Saturday Evening Post anecdote. Author's interview with Otto Mathiasen.
Faculty progeny story. Author's interview with Dr. Algo Henderson.
"Was not really authoritarian...." Correspondence from Dr. Algo Henderson to the author,
April 22, 1986.
Deeds offering to serve. Stephen Herr, *Connected Thoughts: A Reinterpretation of the
Reorganization of Antioch College in the 1920s*, doctoral dissertation, Teachers College,
Columbia University, 1994, page 410.
217 "Of a very high type..." 1927 review conducted for the North Central Association,
Antioch archives. See also results of standardized tests in 1932 and 1934
reported in Clark/Distinctive, 34-35.
Post-college plans of graduates. Clark/Distinctive, pages 35-36; 38.
"Being a good college..." Arthur Morgan, 1924, quoted in Newman/Change, page 213.

Chapter 20: Departures

219 Patterson's departure for Atlantic City. Tracy/Heart, pages 187-188.
"If the chauffeur was relaxing..." Allyn/Half Century, page 51.
"Things To Do..." Crowther/Pioneer, follows page 330.
"No relatives employed in the business..." Allyn/Half Century, page 8.
220 NCR sales and profits, after Patterson. Allyn/Half Century, page 54.
Crisis of 1931. Ibid., page 61.
Recruitment of Deeds. Ibid., page 61.
Foreign acquisitions. Ibid., page 67.
Dismissal of co-defendants. Ibid., page 41.
221 "To build a bigger business..." Belden/Lengthening, page 87.
"When he missed becoming President..." Author's interview with Roz Young.
"I had this great advantage..." Cox/Journey, page 285.
"Fell completely in love with the place." Ibid., page 313.
"The place is filled with ambitious..." Cebula/Cox, page 129.
Purchase of *Miami Daily News*. Cox/Journey, page 313.
Offers from FDR. Cebula/Cox, page 134.
Purchase of *Atlanta Constitution*. Cox/Journey, page 387.
222 Cox worth $40 million. Author's interview with Homer Hacker.
"I read every line..." Author's interview with Richard Cull, Jr.
"I called up every goddamn editor..." Author's interview with Roz Young.
"You could tell he'd been in..." Author's interview with Richard Cull, Jr.
Sportswriter standing. Author's interview with Ann Ferneding.
"Bunch of Republicans." Author's interview with Roz Young.
"Cox. Solid as a nut." Author's interview with Richard Cull, Jr.
"One day, I was walking..." Author's interview with Roz Young.
223 "Took on a kind of..." *World's Work*, June 6, 1923, page 286.
"I wish some men in public life..." Cox/Journey, pages 269-270.
224 Algo Henderson's assessment. Author's interview with Algo Henderson.
Morgans to Europe, 1931. Talbert/Utopian, page 64.
Henderson convenes campus community. Author's interview with Algo Henderson.
"Such as they are..." Arthur Morgan, June 18, 1931, Clark/Distinctive, page 39-40.
225 "Entirely unjustified" and "I excused it a bit on his part." Author's interview with
Algo Henderson.
"Was quite despondent..." Author's interview with J. D. Dawson.
Morgan's meeting with FDR. Talbert/Utopian, pages 81-82.
Note: Cox takes credit: "I remember well remarking to the President that Morgan would
be honest and efficient but had no patience with politics in matters such as this."
Talbert/Utopian, page 83. Conditions in the Tennessee Valley. Thomas K. McCraw,
Morgan vs. Lilienthal: *The Feud within the TVA*, Loyola University Press, 1970,
pages 14-15. Hereafter, McCraw/Feud.
"Morgan was in the seventh heaven..." Author's interview with J. D. Dawson.
"The Second Coming of Daniel Boone..." *Knoxville News-Sentinel*, March 5, 1937;

"The Second Coming of Daniel Boone..." *Knoxville News-Sentinel*, March 5, 1937;
    quoted in Morgan/TVA, page 156.
226 Morgan's dismissal. McCraw/Feud, page 102.
    Morgan's writings. Morgan's post-TVA books include *Edward Bellamy* (a biography),
    Columbia University, 1944; *Nowhere was Somewhere*, U. of North Carolina, 1946;
    and *A Business of My Own*, Community Service, 1946.
    Consultant to the Seneca. Talbert/Utopian, pages 199-200.
    "I tramped on foot through..." Arthur Morgan, *Dams and Other Disasters*,
    Porter Sargent, 1971, page 328. Hereafter, Morgan/Dams.
227 *Today Show*. Antioch archives.
    Paint story. Kettering/Prophet, pages 138-139.
228 "The story of General Motors research..." Sloan/Adventures, page 156.
    Copper-cooled engine. Sloan/Years, chapter 5.
    "The greatest thing..." Ibid., page 85.
    Problems with copper-cooled engine. Leslie/Kettering, pages 126, 131-133.
    GM research moves to Detroit. Boyd/Professional, page 131.
    "I live in Dayton..." Charles Kettering, "Running Errands for Ideas," long-playing record
    issued by the Thomas Alva Edison Foundation, 1979, excerpted on flimsy disk recording
    included in *Boss Ket*, published by the Charles K. Kettering Foundation.
    Hereafter, Kettering/Recording.
229 Kettering and the lightweight diesel. Sloan/GM, pages 398-413.
    Prototype, Denver to Chicago. Leslie/Kettering, page 269.
    "Strong enough to pull thirty railroads..." Boyd/Amateur, page 175.
    Personal habits. Author's interviews with Dr. Samuel Gould, Dr. Algo Henderson,
    W. Walker Lewis, Jr., Xarifa Bean, Lee Hennessey.
    "Tell me, Ket." Kettering Oral History/Robert G. Chollar.
    "This is not a monument to anyone." Statement posted in lobby, Antioch Science Building.
230 Sloan-Kettering. Leslie/Kettering, page 319.
    Kettering at country club. Author's interview with Sam Gould.
    "The whole world lies either..." Author's interview with W. Walker Lewis.
    "You never get anywhere..." Boyd/Professional, page 131.
231 "They were light and thin..." UD oral history/Ernest Dubel, page 27.
    Aircraft damaged. UD oral history/Lewis P. Christman, page 31.
    "The knowledge that the head..." Wilbur Wright to Octave Chanute, November 8, 1906,
    Wright/Papers, page 737.
    "A helping hand at a critical time..." Ibid.
    Conflict with Smithsonian. Statement of Orville Wright, March 1928,
    Wright/Papers, pages 1145-1146.
232 "See, Orville Wright was much incensed..." UD oral history/Lewis P. Christman, page 31.
    "I think it was Roy Knabenshue..." UD oral history/James Wilbur Jacobs, page 14.
    "Of course the machine ought to be..." Orville Wright to Griffith Brewer,
    November 13, 1923, Kelly/Miracle, page 408.
    "In making my offer..." Orville Wright to James M. Magee, May 29, 1925,
    Wright/Papers, page 1136.
    "They had to recover most..." UD oral history/Ruth Jacobs, page 6.
    "When they had it..." UD oral history/James Jacobs, page 13.
233 "But Orville Wright is not an easy man..." Crouch/Bishop's, page 495.
    "He just wrote red pencil..." UD oral history/Max Konop, page 20.
    Cottage at Georgian Bay. Crouch/Bishop's, page 478.
    Orville's cooking; record changer. UD oral history/Horace Wright, pages 19 and 24-25.
    Orville's sciatica. Ibid., page 25.
    "And the funny thing is..." Ibid., pages 10-11.

Last Words:

235 "By a grateful citizenry..." Inscription on John Patterson memorial,
    Hills and Dales Park, Dayton, Ohio.
    'Do justly, love mercy, and walk humbly.' NCR/Suggestions, page 5.
236 "Chiefly history and biography..." Allan Nevins, "Not Capulets, Not Montagus,"
    American Historical Review, January 1960, page 258.
    "We may desire to create a bridge..." Morgan/TVA, page 189.
    "I think it was the Brookings..." Kettering/Recording.
237 Orville's heart attacks. Crouch/Bishop's, page 524.
    Aircraft to Smithsonian. Crouch/Bishop's, page 256.

Source List, By Subject:

General Background: The Period

Books:
Mansel G. Blackford and K. Austin Kerr, *Business Enterprise in American History* (2nd edition), Houghton Mifflin Publishers, 1990.
Ann Cook, Marilyn Gittell and Herb Mack, eds., *City Life: 1865-1900*, Praeger Publishers, 1973.
Derek Howse, *Greenwich Time and the Discovery of the Longitude*, Oxford University Press, 1981.
Thomas P. Hughes, *American Genesis*, Viking, 1989.
George W. Knepper, *Ohio and Its People*, Kent State University Press, 1989.
Walter Lord, *The Good Years*, Harper & Row, 1960.
Allan A. Marcus and Howard P. Segal, *Technology in America: A Brief History*, Harcourt, Brace, Jovanovich, Inc., 1989
Daniel T. Rodgers, *The Work Ethic in Industrial America*, University of Chicago Press, 1974.
Kenneth M. Roemer, ed., *America as Utopia*, Burt Franklin & Company, 1981.
Arthur Meier Schlesinger, Sr., *The Rise of the City: 1878-1898*, The Macmillan Company, 1933.
Cecilia Tichi, *Shifting Gears*, University of North Carolina Press, 1987.
Hoyt Landon Warner, *Progressivism in Ohio*, Ohio State University Press, 1964.
Robert H. Wiebe, *The Search for Order, 1877-1920*, Hill and Wang, 1967.
Daniel Wren, *The Evolution of Management Thought* (3rd edition), John Wiley & Sons, 1987.
Larzer Ziff, *The American 1890s*, Viking Press, 1966.

James M. Cox:

Books:
James McGregor Burns, *Roosevelt: The Lion and the Fox*, Harcourt Brace Jovanovich, 1956.
James E. Cebula, *James M. Cox: Journalist and Politician*, Garland Publishing, 1985.
James M. Cox, *Journey Through My Years*, Simon & Schuster, 1946.
Edwin P. Hoyt, *Horatio's Boys: The Life and Works of Horatio Alger, Jr.*, The Chilton Book Company, 1974.
H. L. Mencken, *On Politics*, Vintage Books, 1960.
Charles E. Morris, *The Progressive Democracy of James M. Cox*, The Bobbs-Merrill Company, Indianapolis, 1920.
Frank Luther Mott, *American Journalism*, [3rd edition], The Macmillan Company, 1962.
Arthur M. Schlesinger, Jr., *Age of Roosevelt*, Houghton Mifflin, 1957.
Michael Schudson, *Discovering the News*, Basic Books, 1978.
John W. Tebbel, *The Compact History of the American Newspaper*, Hawthorn Books, 1963.

Other:
Special Collections and Archives; Paul Laurence Dunbar Library; Wright State University, Dayton, Ohio; including:
1912 speech of acceptance, gubernatorial nomination, *Dayton Daily News*, June 7, 1912;
1913 Commencement Address, University of Notre Dame, South Bend, Indiana;
correspondence with William Jennings Bryan, 1914-1915.

James Cox, "Inaugural Address," January 13, 1913, published in James K. Mercer,
        Ohio Legislative History.
Allan Nevins, "Not Capulets, Not Montagus," address published in *American Historical Review,*
        January 1960, pages 253-271.
The Independent— September 1, 1913; September 18, 1920.
The Literary Digest'— June 12; July 17-24, 1920.
The Nation — July 17, 1920.
The New Republic — August 18; September 8 & 15, 1920.
The Outlook — July 28; September 22-29; October 13-20; November 10, 1920.
World's Work — November 10 ,1920; June 6, 1923.
Dayton Daily News — various dates, including, for the campaign against Lowes,
        October-November 1898; for the feud with Patterson, March 1907.
Dayton Herald — various dates, including March 1907 for the feud with Patterson.
Dayton Journal — various dates, including March 1907 for the feud with Patterson.
Middletown Journal — various dates, 1892-1893.
Interviews by author.

Charles Kettering:

Books:
Thomas A. Boyd, Jr., *The Early History of Ethyl Gasoline,* General Motors Corporation, 1943.
Thomas A. Boyd, Jr., *Professional Amateur,* E. P. Dutton, 1957.
Maurice D. Hendry, *Cadillac: Standard of the World,* Automobile Quarterly Publications, 1977.
James J. Flink, *America Adopts the Automobile,* MIT Press, 1970.
Charles F. Kettering and Allan Orth, *The New Necessity,* Williams and Wilkins Company, 1932.
Charles F. Kettering; edited by Thomas A. Boyd, Jr., *Prophet of Progress,*
        E. P. Dutton and Company, 1951.
Robert Lacey, *Ford: The Men and the Machine,* Little Brown and Company, 1966.
Stuart W. Leslie, *Boss Kettering: Wizard of General Motors,* Columbia University Press, 1983.
Joseph C. Robert, *Ethyl: A History of the Corporation and the People Who Made It,*
        University Press of Virginia, 1983
Alfred P. Sloan, Jr. (with Boyden Sparkes), *Adventures of a White-Collar Man,*
        Doubleday, Doran & Company, Inc., 1941.
Alfred P. Sloan, Jr., *My Years With General Motors,* Doubleday & Company, Inc., 1972.
Gladys Zehnphennig, *Charles F. Kettering: Inventor and Idealist,* T. S. Denison and Co., 1962.

Other:
Kettering-Moraine Museum, Kettering, Ohio, including:
        Zerbe Bradford ("barn gang" member) unpublished correspondence, November 25,1965;
        [no author listed] *History of Starting, Lighting & Ignition System,*
        dated June 12, 1912, on file at the Kettering-Moraine Museum.
Paul deKruif, "Boss Kettering," *Saturday Evening Post,* July 15, August 12, 1933.
Robert B. Habingreither, *A Case Study of the First Commercially Successful Electric Self-Starting System,*
        doctoral dissertation, West Virginia University, 1978.
A. E. Roach, *Ket: America's Best-Loved Inventor,*
        unpublished manuscript on file at the Montgomery County [Ohio] Historical Society.
Kettering Digest, Reflections Press, 1982.
The Literary Digest, "A Bill of Health for 'Looney Gas'," February 6, 1926.
The Patent, Trademark and Copyright Journal of Research and Education (special issue on Charles
        Kettering), summer 1959.
Time magazine, January 9, 1933.
Charles F. Kettering Oral History, Charles F. Kettering Foundation, 1957 and 1959.
The Book of the Delco, company published viewbook, 1915.
Articles on effects of tetraethyllead, published in *Fortune,* March 1970; *New Republic,*
        November 21, 1970; *Newsweek,* March 23, 1970.
Interviews by author.

Arthur E. Morgan:

Books:
Burton C. Clark, *The Distinctive College,* Aldine Publishing, 1970.
Donald Davidson, *The Tennessee: Civil War to TVA,* Rinehart, 1946.
Thomas K. McCraw, *TVA and the Power Fight,* Lippincott, 1971.

Arthur E. Morgan, *Dams and Other Disasters*, P. Sargent, 1971.
Arthur E. Morgan, *Miami Conservancy District*, McGraw-Hill, 1951.
Arthur E. Morgan, *Nowhere Was Somewhere*, University of North Carolina, 1946.
Arthur E. Morgan, *The Seed Man*, Antioch Press, 1932.
Arthur E. Morgan, *The Making of the TVA*, Prometheus Books, 1974.
Roy Talbert, Jr., *FDR's Utopian: Arthur Morgan of the TVA*, University Press of Mississippi, 1987.

Other:
Antiochiana (college archives); Antioch College, Yellow Springs, Ohio, including:
       correspondence to family, 1898-1900;
       correspondence to Griscom Morgan, 1907-1910;
       "A New Moral Standard for American Business," an unpublished essay
       by Arthur Morgan, c. 1913;
       unpublished notes on militarism and pacifism, c. 1916;
       correspondence and notes on Moraine Park School, 1916-1918;
       materials on the League to Enforce the Peace, especially correspondence from
       Edward Deeds, February 27, 1918;
       unpublished comments on Dayton's city manager form of government, 1964.
Steven Herr, *Connected Thoughts: A Reinterpretation of the Reorganization of Antioch College in the 1920s*,
       (doctoral dissertation), Teachers College, Columbia University, 1994.
George Charles Newman, *The Morgan Years: Politics of Innovative Change —*
       Antioch College in the 1920s' (doctoral dissertation), University of Michigan, 1978.
Harvard Forrest Vallance, *A History of Antioch College* (doctoral dissertation),
       Ohio State University, 1936.
"Flood Prevention in the Miami Valley." Proposal to the Public;
       published by the Miami Conservancy District, 1913.
Interviews by author.

John H. Patterson:

Books:
Jane Addams, *Democracy and Social Ethics*, Harvard University Press, 1964.
Stanley C. Allyn, *My Half-Century with NCR*, McGraw-Hill, 1967.
Thomas and Marva Belden, *The Life of Thomas J. Watson: The Lengthening Shadow*,
       Little, Brown and Co., 1962.
Charlotte Reeve Conover, *Builders in New Fields*, G. P. Putnam's Son, 1939.
Samuel Crowther, *John H. Patterson — Pioneer in Industrial Welfare*,
       Doubleday, Page & Company, 1924.
Elbert Hubbard, *John H. Patterson: An Appreciation*, Roycrofters, 1912.
Isaac F. Marcosson, *Wherever Men Trade*, Dodd, Mead & Company, 1948.
William Rodgers, *Think! A Biography of the Watsons & IBM*, Stein & Day, 1969.
Lena Harvey Tracy, *How My Heart Sang*, Richard R. Smith, New York, 1950.

Other:
Gerald Carson, "The Machine that Kept Them Honest," *American Heritage*, August 1966.
Charlotte Reeve Conover, *A History of the Beck Family*, Dayton, privately printed, 1907.
Samuel Crowther, "The Origin of 'Register Your Money and Give a Receipt,'"
       System: The Magazine of Business, December 1922.
John H. Patterson, *What Dayton, Ohio, Should Do to Become a Model City*,
       National Cash Register, 1907.
Dr. William H. Tolman, *Temple of Hygiene: How a Manufacturing Concern Promotes Industrial Hygiene*,
       International Congress of Hygiene and Demography, Washington, D.C., 1912.
Charles Wertenbaker, "Patterson's Marvelous Money Box," *Saturday Evening Post*,
       September 19, 1953.
Edwin Wildman, "Morality in Business," *Forum*, August 1919.
"Living with 'The Cash'," *Dayton Daily News*, special supplement; February 24, 1991.
"Patterson et al v. United States," Decision of the 6th Circuit Court of Appeals, March 13, 1915.
Cincinnati Enquirer — coverage of antitrust trial/various dates; announcement of verdict, February 14,
       1918.

NCR publications:
John H. Patterson, *Letters from Europe*, National Cash Register Company, 1902.
Alfred A. Thomas, *Suggestions from Employes*, National Cash Register Company, 1905.

Alfred A. Thomas, *The Temptations of Employes Who Handle Money*,
National Cash Register Company, 1905; reprinted 1910.
Art Nature and the Factory, National Cash Register Company, 1904.
Celebrating the Future, 1984 centennial history, NCR, 1984.
Instructions to NCR Salesmen, National Cash Register Company, 1906.
The N.C.R, National Cash Register Company, January 1 & February 15, 1901; February 15, 1902.
Selling Points, National Cash Register Company, 1910.
Use of National Cash Registers in Stores Using Sales-Slips, National Cash Register, 1914.
Welfare Work, National Cash Register Company (undated; c. 1900).
Interviews by author.

Wilbur and Orville Wright:

Books:
Tom Crouch, *The Bishop's Boys*, W. W. Norton, 1989.
Sigmund Freud, *Leonardo da Vinci: A Psychosexual Study of an Infantile Reminiscence*,
Dodd, Mead & Company, 1932.
C. H. Gibbs-Smith, *The Invention of the Airplane*, Taplinger, 1966.
C. H. Gibbs-Smith, *The Wright Brothers*, Science Museum, London, 1963.
Clive Hart, *The Prehistory of Flight*, University of California Press, 1985.
J. E. Hodgson, *Aeronautics in Great Britain: From the Earliest Times to the Latter Half of the Nineteenth
Century*, Oxford University Press, 1924.
Peter L. Jakab, *Visions of a Flying Machine*, Smithsonian Institution Press, 1990.
Fred C. Kelly, editor, *Miracle at Kitty Hawk*, Farrar, Straus & Young, 1951.
Fred C. Kelly, *The Wright Brothers*, Harcourt, Brace & Company, 1943.
Alfred W. Marshall and Henry Greenly, *Flying Machines: Past, Present, and Future*,
Percival Marshall & Co., London, 1907.
Orville Wright, *How We Invented the Airplane*, David McKay Company, Inc., 1953.
Marvin W. McFarland, editor (two volumes), *The Papers of Wilbur and Orville Wright*,
McGraw-Hill, 1953.

Other:
Aviation History Collection; Paul Laurence Dunbar Library; Wright State University; Dayton, Ohio,
including:
Diaries (transcribed) of Bishop Milton Wright;
The Criterion, January 1906;
Incidental press clippings on flight, 1903-1905.
Dayton Collection; Dayton & Montgomery County [Ohio] Public Library, including:
Minutes Book, The Annual Club of Ten Dayton Boys [1886-1937];
West Side News, published by the Wrights, March 1889 - April 1890;
Evening Item, published by the Wrights, May - July 1890.
Charlotte K. and August E. Brunsman, *The Other Career of Wilbur and Orville*,
(privately published) 1988.
Arthur Ruhl, "History at Kill Devil Hill," *Colliers*, May 30, 1908.
"Official Program: The Wrights Brothers Home Celebration," Dayton, Ohio, June 17-18, 1909.
Wilbur Wright, "An Evening Tour to Miamisburg," account of bicycle trip excerpted from a letter to
Katharine Wright, September 18, 1892.
"Wright Brothers Historical Walking Trail" (Guide to the Huffman Prairie Flying Field).
Wright Brothers Oral History Project, University of Dayton, 1967.
Interviews by author.

Related Subjects:

Books:
Carl Becker and Patrick Nolan, *Keeping the Promise: A Pictorial History of the Miami Conservancy
District*, Landfall Press, 1988.
Paul Laurence Dunbar, *Lyrics of Lowly Life*, Citadel Press, 1991.
Allan W. Eckert, *A Time of Terror*, Little, Brown and Co., 1965.
Isaac F. Marcosson, *Colonel Deeds, Industrial Builder*, Dodd, Mead & Company, 1947.
Jay Martin & Gossie H. Hudson, eds., *The Paul Laurence Dunbar Reader*, Dodd, Mead, 1975.
Lloyd Ostendorf, *Mr. Lincoln Comes to Dayton*, Otterbein Press, 1959.
Peter Revell, *Paul Laurence Dunbar*, Twayne Publishers, 1979.
Judith Sealander, *Grand Plans*, University Press of Kentucky, 1988.
Joseph W. Sharts, *Biography of Dayton: An Economic Interpretation of Local History*,

    Miami Valley Socialist, 1922.
Damaine Vonada, *Ohio Almanac*, Orange Frazer Press, 1992.
For the Love of Dayton: Life in the Miami Valley, 1796-1996, Dayton Daily News, 1996.

Other:
John K. Barnes, "The Vindication of Squier and Deeds," *World's Work*, July 1921.
Fred Bartenstein, "A History of Dayton," notes to a guided tour of the city.
Thomas A. Boyd, "Thomas Midgley, Jr.," *Journal of the American Chemical Society*, Vol. 75, 1953
Charles F. Kettering, *Biographical Memoir of Thomas Midgley, Jr.*, National Academy of Sciences.
Olmsted Brothers, *Proposed Park System for the City of Dayton, Ohio*,
        Brookline, Massachusetts, 1911.
Linn Orear, *A Survey of the Germans of Dayton, 1830-1900*, senior project, Antioch College, 1961.
Charles H. Paul, *A Brief History of the Engineers' Club of Dayton*, Dayton Engineers' Club, 1942.
James H. Perkins, *Dayton During World War I*, masters' degree thesis, Miami University, 1959.
Alfred A. Thomas, *What Shall We Do With the Canal?* privately published, 1911.
John Thomas Walker, *Socialism in Dayton: 1912-1925*, master's degree thesis.
Dayton Centennial Board of Trade Dinner, record of remarks, 1896.
Dayton: A History of the Great Flood, Dayton Engineering Laboratories, Inc., 1913.
"The Great Flood," *Dayton Daily News*, special supplement, March 25, 1988.
Opening of the New Building, February 2, 1918, The Engineers' Club of Dayton.
The Dayton Times, March 28-April 1, 1896 (coverage of Dayton centennial observances)
The New York Times, especially March 27-30, 1913 (Dayton flood); October 28-30, 1924
        (deaths from tetraethyl lead); March 12-13, 18, 1938 (Morgan's dismissal by FDR).